FERNS
OF **ALABAMA**

Philip Henry Gosse as a young man of twenty-nine, the year of his return to England from Alabama, painted by his brother, William Gosse. (1839, watercolor on ivory, courtesy of the National Portrait Gallery—London)

Philip Henry Gosse (1810–1888) was an English naturalist and
illustrator who spent eight months of 1838 on the Alabama frontier,
teaching planters' children in Dallas County and studying the native flora
and fauna. Years after returning to England, he published the now-classic
Letters from Alabama: Chiefly Relating to Natural History, with twenty-
nine important black-and-white illustrations included. He also produced,
during his Alabama sojourn, forty-nine remarkable watercolor plates of
various plant and animal species, mainly insects, now available in *Philip
Henry Gosse: Science and Art in "Letters from Alabama" and "Entomologia
Alabamensis."*

The Gosse Nature Guides are a series of natural history
guidebooks prepared by experts on the plants and animals of Alabama
and designed for the outdoor enthusiast and ecology layman. Because
Alabama is one of the nation's most biodiverse states, its residents and
visitors require accurate, accessible field guides to interpret the wealth of
life that thrives within the state's borders. The Gosse Nature Guides are
named to honor Philip Henry Gosse's early appreciation of Alabama's
natural wealth and to highlight the valuable legacy of his recorded
observations. Look for other volumes in the Gosse Nature Guides series
at http://uapress.ua.edu.

WITH DRAWINGS BY

MARION MONTGOMERY, SUE BLACKSHEAR, AND **JOHN W. SHORT**

AND PHOTOGRAPHS BY

T. WAYNE BARGER, ALAN CRESSLER, SARAH R. JOHNSTON, L. J. DAVENPORT, AND **JOHN W. SHORT**

THE UNIVERSITY OF ALABAMA PRESS TUSCALOOSA

FERNS

OF **ALABAMA**

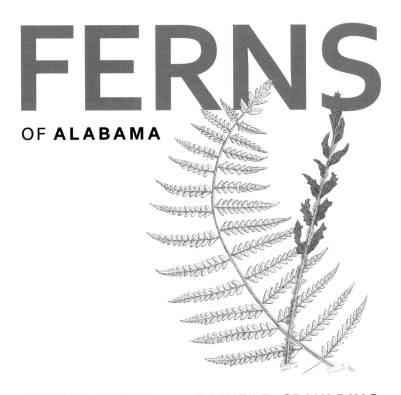

JOHN W. SHORT AND **DANIEL D. SPAULDING**

Typeface: Minion Pro and Corbel
Design: Michele Myatt Quinn

Cover photo: Widespread maiden fern *(Thelypteris kunthii),* also
known as southern shield fern, growing in a private garden in Birmingham, Alabama. Photo copyright © 2012 by Sarah R. Johnston.

Drawing on title page: Cinnamon fern (*Osmunda cinnamomea*).
Drawing by Marion Montgomery. Courtesy of the Anniston Museum of Natural History.

Appendix B reprinted by permission of *Chinquapin: The Newsletter
of the Southern Appalachian Botanical Society,* Editor Charles Horn.
The essay originally appeared in volume 17, number 1 in the spring
of 2009.

∞

The paper on which this book is printed meets the minimum
requirements of American National Standard for Information
Sciences—Permanence of Paper for Printed Library Materials,
ANSI Z39.48-1984.

Library of Congress Cataloging-in-Publication Data

Short, John W., 1952–
Ferns of Alabama / John W. Short and Daniel D. Spaulding; with
drawings by Marion Montgomery, Sue Blackshear, and John W.
Short and photographs by T. Wayne Barger . . . [et al.].
     p.   cm.—(Gosse nature guides)
Includes bibliographical references and index.
ISBN 978-0-8173-5647-7 (quality paper: alk. paper)
     1. Ferns—Alabama—Identification. 2. Ferns—Alabama—
Pictorial works I. Spaulding, Daniel D. II. Title. III. Series: Gosse
nature guides.
QK525.5.A4S56 2012
587'.309761—dc23   201200099

Publication supported in part by the Blanche Dean Publication Fund.

"I know there are *Trilliums* on the other side of that hill; I can hear them!"

To the memory of Dr. John Daniel Freeman (1941–1997), who was a professor of botany at Auburn University from 1968 to 1994. He was a naturalist of the old school, keenly interested in all of the living things he encountered, not only the plants. His enthusiasm was deeply felt by all of his many students, including me. Dr. Freeman is sorely missed by the botanical community of Alabama.

—John W. Short

To my father, Col. Harry S. Spaulding Jr., MD (1930–2006), who has been my inspiration throughout my life. As a young boy, I witnessed his deep appreciation for the outdoors and enjoyed all the times I spent with him camping, fishing, or hunting. He instilled within me a true love of nature. I am grateful for his support and encouragement in all my endeavors. He died in a hiking accident in June 2006. . . . I miss him greatly.

—Daniel D. Spaulding

In the gloom of the forest, in the silence of the wilderness, far from human abodes, my heart leaps for joy; there I am not lonely, though alone; there hundreds of objects meet my gaze, with which I have long been accustomed to hold sweet communion.

—Philip Henry Gosse, *Letters from Alabama: Chiefly Relating to Natural History*

Contents

Acknowledgments   xiii

Introduction   1

1 About Ferns and Fern Allies   7

2 Geography of Alabama Ferns   17

3 Keys to the Identification of Alabama Ferns and Fern Allies   31

4 Alabama Ferns and Fern Allies   55

Appendix A
Checklist   303

Appendix B
On Taxonomic Change by Alan Weakley   313

Appendix C
Alternative Keys to the Ferns and Fern Allies of Alabama   319

Glossary   347

References   351

Illustration Credits   355

Index to Common Names   357

Index to Scientific Names   363

Acknowledgments

We appreciate all the students and botanists who have collected ferns and fern allies in Alabama for many years and then deposited a mounted and labeled plant into a herbarium. Without their specimens, a book like this one would not have been possible. We especially acknowledge the following for being the most prolific collectors in the state: Robert Kral, Alvin R. Diamond, R. David Whetstone, Michel G. Lelong, John R. MacDonald, Robert R. Haynes, J. Mark Ballard, and Brian R. Keener.

We would also like to thank the directors, curators, and collection managers of the following institutions for allowing us access to their specimens for study:

Auburn University: Curtis Hansen and Leslie Goertzen

Botanical Research Institution of Texas (Vanderbilt Collection): Robert Kral

Jacksonville State University: David Whetstone, Jimmy Triplett, and Robert Carter

Troy University: Alvin Diamond and Michael Woods

The University of Alabama: Steve Ginzbarg, John Clark, and Robert Haynes

University of West Alabama: Brian R. Keener

Many others facilitated completion of this book project: Hope Long, librarian at the Birmingham Botanical Gardens, first conveyed that a book on Alabama ferns was much needed because folks visiting her library kept asking for one. Marion Montgomery graciously consented to the use of her exquisite drawings, and Sue Blackshear filled in the gaps with her black ink renderings from herbarium specimens. Melanie B. Johns, plant taxonomist with the Birmingham Botanical Gardens, and Greg McKee, museum specialist with the Smithsonian Institution, generously made scans from their collections to add to the book. Botanists T. Wayne Barger and L. J. Davenport and freelance photographers Alan Cressler and Sarah R. Johnston offered freely from their photographic files.

At The University of Alabama Press, student intern Daniel Hollander scanned the drawings to print specification. Natalie Jensen converted the distribution maps to Gosse Nature Guide style under the direction of Kaci Hindman, production editor. All staff members contributed in some way to the beautiful book you now hold in your hands, but Crissie Johnson, managing editor, oversaw the polishing of the text and Michele Quinn designed the entire package. The authors would especially like to thank Beth Motherwell, senior acquisitions editor, without whose firm yet gentle encouragement this book may have never been finished. We are also indebted to the Blanche Dean Publication Fund for financial contribution to this book.

Lastly, we want to thank, for their help and support through the many years of research behind this book: Mark Stevens, Larry and Mary Dalrymple, Ruth Freeman, Curt Peterson, David Lellinger, Murray Evans, Nancy Thompson, Marion Thompson Short, Steve Short, Jessie Short, Kevin White, Marydel Baines, Paul Green, Dann Kramer, Ann Sessler, Caren Gilmore, Phil Yeager, Ginny Lusk, Frank Dunnivant, Eric Batchelder, Sam Pack, and Mike Hoff. Since this project has taken over thirty years to finish, there are undoubtedly many people whose names we do not remember. To those, we apologize, but we are sincerely grateful to them.

FERNS
OF **ALABAMA**

Introduction

This book has two subjects: a group of plants known as the ferns and fern allies, and a geographic region called Alabama. The ferns and fern allies comprise four groups of plants that are not related to one another, but which are so similar in their ecology and reproductive biology that they are usually studied together. Alabama is, of course, one of the fifty states of the United States of America.

The thing that ferns and fern allies have in common is that they are vascular plants that reproduce by spores; see the following chapter of this book, "About Ferns and Fern Allies," for an explanation of what this means. Because of this, botanists of the past thought that the ferns and fern allies were more closely related to each other than to the other vascular plants, all of which reproduce by seeds. The ferns and fern allies have long been known collectively as *pteridophytes*, from the Greek words for "fern" and "plant."

We all know what ferns are, although there are some that many people would not recognize as ferns, and there are some flowering plants that look like ferns and are sometimes mistakenly thought to be ferns. The fern allies do not look like ferns. They may look like rushes, large mosses, tiny trees, or tufts of grass, and some look like nothing else. Most of them are un-familiar to most people. They include the clubmosses, spikemosses, quill-worts, and horsetails.

After the invention of the microscope and the development of the tech-niques for using it, studies of the internal structure of stems and leaves showed that the four groups of pteridophytes are not related. The ferns are actually more closely related to the seed-bearing plants than they are to the fern allies, and the three groups of fern allies are no more closely related to one another than they are to the ferns. Because of this the term *fern ally* is a misnomer, but it is understood by all, so we will use it in this book.

Alabama is in the southeastern United States on the coast of the Gulf of Mexico. It has a mild subtropical climate, usually has abundant rainfall, and has a remarkable variety of geology and landforms. This allows Alabama to have a great diversity of plant and animal life. Species that are primarily tropical are found in southern Alabama, while some northern species reach their southern limits in the mountainous regions of northern Alabama.

Alabama has long been renowned among American botanists for its ferns. Since the middle of the nineteenth century, several new species of ferns have been discovered in Alabama, and some of them were named after the state. Some of these were not found anywhere else for years, and a few have never been found elsewhere.

There have been two previous treatments of the ferns and fern allies of Alabama. Iowa resident E. W. Graves visited Alabama a number of times in the early twentieth century. While he was there, he collected and identified ferns, and he published a checklist of Alabama ferns in the *American Fern Journal* in 1920. Almost all of his fern studies were in Jackson County and Mobile County, with a few excursions into neighboring counties. These two counties lie at the extremes of the state with regard to climate and elevation, and his checklist contains a remarkable number of species for a study conducted in such a restricted area.

Educator Blanche E. Dean published the book *Ferns of Alabama and Fern Allies* in 1964 and revised it in 1969. It was the first book-length treatment of Alabama ferns, but it suffered from a number of technical inaccuracies. The passion with which she approached the study of nature was conveyed by her work to generations of enthusiasts.

Botanists and others interested in the ferns and fern allies of Alabama have long wished for a new book that is technically accurate and has verifiable distribution information. The authors hope that the current book will fulfill that need.

The senior author of this book wrote his thesis on the pteridophytes of Alabama as part of a master's degree program at Auburn University (Short 1978). That work remains unpublished, but this book is its descendant.

The purpose of this book is to document the ferns and fern allies of Alabama and their distributions, and to provide the means by which a person can identify a fern that he or she finds growing in Alabama. The plants discussed in this book are only those that can be found growing "in the wild" in Alabama; plants that grow only under cultivation, in gardens or pots, are not included. We do include plants that are mostly cultivated but have been known to "escape" from cultivation and spread to other areas. Some of these escapees were able to continue to spread far and wide by their spores and have become well established in the state; they are said to be naturalized. Some of these have become quite common.

We have made every attempt to make this book both scientifically accurate and easily accessible to the reader who is not trained in botany. Botanists are notorious for their huge number of highly technical terms, many of which have equivalents in plain English. We have attempted to avoid the use of as much of this botanical jargon as we can and to use plain English whenever possible. There are a few technical terms that do not have appropriate and simple plain-English equivalents. Some of these terms, like *rachis* and *sori*, will already be familiar to anyone who has been interested in ferns for any length of time.

The subject of *taxonomy*, the scientific names of species, genera, and so forth, is a complex subject that has long been a source of disagreement among botanists. Some will place a large number of similar species in one genus, while another might decide that the plants belong to several different genera. A particular species might be in one genus in one publication and in another genus in some other publication, even though the two works were published at about the same time. The result is that some plants, including ferns, may have several names in use at once.

This book does not attempt to resolve these naming differences. Instead, we have chosen to use names that are traditional and understood by many people. In this regard, the names of the species in this book follow those in David Lellinger's *A Field Manual of the Ferns and Fern-Allies of the United States and Canada* published in 1985 by the Smithsonian Institution. Many authors today do not agree with his nomenclature, but the names are well known to anyone who studies ferns. We have used other names only in a very few cases in which a name Lellinger used has since been found to be invalid or in which a newer name is more appropriate for other reasons. Lellinger also did not include naturally occurring hybrid ferns in his book, but we do in this one. We give a list of currently used alternate names in our treatment of each species or hybrid.

Some ferns can have several common names as well. Usually, we have used the name that is most often seen in the literature, but in some cases we have chosen an alternate name that seems more appropriate to the plant than the one more commonly seen. As with the scientific names, we have listed the other common names we have encountered.

We have included more than 120 species and hybrids of ferns and fern allies in this book. The book has five major sections. This introduction is followed by a discussion of what ferns and fern allies are and of the characteristics of the plants that are used to identify them; this includes explanations of any botanical jargon that we have used. Next is a discussion of the geology and geography of Alabama and how those factors affect the distributions of ferns and fern allies in the state. The fourth section is a set of keys that the user can employ in order to identify a plant.

The fifth section is the main body of the book. It includes a discussion of each species or hybrid, what it looks like, its usual habitat, where it may be found in Alabama, plus its range elsewhere. There are also comments on varied aspects of the plant, its distribution, its uses, if any, and so on. We have also included for each species or hybrid a small map showing the Alabama counties in which the plant has been found. With a few exceptions, we have both a line drawing and a photograph of each fern or fern ally. The exceptions are ferns and fern allies that are so rare and hard to find that we were unable to obtain photographs.

The occurrences shown on the maps are all documented by actual specimens seen by the authors. These specimens may be found in herbaria, collections of pressed and dried plant specimens. We used no anecdotal reports or literature reports without confirming specimens.

The contents of this section are arranged in the same order as are the genera and species in Lellinger's book. This arrangement puts related genera and related species within a genus near to each other, and the order is supposed to reflect the evolutionary relationships of the plant, with most "primitive" species being listed first and the most "advanced" ones last. This is a traditional way to arrange species in a book like this. As mentioned, we are not trying to show taxonomic relationships. Many people will use this book to identify something they have found by flipping through the book and comparing a specimen with the illustrations. Having similar subjects near each other facilitates this process.

The final parts of the book are a glossary of the technical terms we have used, a bibliography listing publications cited in the book, and an index to all of the scientific and common names mentioned in the book. We have also included three appendices. Appendix A is a checklist of the ferns and fern allies of Alabama. Appendix B is a reprint of an article by botanist Dr. Alan Weakley of the University of North Carolina concerning the constantly changing world of plant taxonomy. Appendix C contains a key to the ferns and fern allies of Alabama using the family classification system of *Flora of North America North of Mexico*, Volume 2 (1993), which is widely accepted today. This key contains a number of technical terms that are not defined elsewhere in this book.

1

About Ferns and Fern Allies

This book is about the ferns and fern allies that may be found growing in Alabama. As mentioned in the introduction, they are vascular plants that normally reproduce by spores rather than seeds.

This may bring up two questions with the reader who is not familiar with botanical terminology. The first is "what is a *vascular plant*?" Every vascular plant has one or more stems of some sort, and it usually has leaves and roots. The stems of vascular plants contain cells forming tiny tubes of two kinds that extend throughout the plant. Some tubes carry water and minerals from the roots to the upper portions of the plant and to the leaves. The other tubes carry nutrients produced by the green aboveground parts of the plant to the roots and other parts of the plant that need the nutrients.

The second question is this: "What exactly is a *spore*?" A spore is a single cell and is usually microscopic. Mosses, fungi, and some other living things reproduce by spores, as well as do the ferns and fern allies, but most of the plants we encounter reproduce by seeds.

A *seed,* of course, is something that one can see and touch, usually. A seed contains a "baby" plant that will directly grow into another plant like the one from which it came.

A spore, by contrast, has only the one cell. With vascular plants a spore grows into something that does not look anything like the plant from which it came. It grows into a different sort of plant called a *gametophyte*. It is called that because it produces *gametes,* like the sperm and egg of an animal, which unite to produce a cell that will grow into a new plant like the one from which the spore came, which is called the *sporophyte.* The plant that we see and think of as a fern or fern ally is the sporophyte; the gametophyte is tiny and usually short-lived and is seldom seen.

The "male" gametes of ferns and fern allies need water in order to swim from the part of the gametophyte where they are produced to the locations of the "female" gametes, which do not move. This is why most ferns are found in places that are damp for at least part of the year. The gametophytes of most ferns and fern allies produce gametes of both types, and the two gametes that unite are often from the same gametophyte. If two gametophytes are close together, they can cross-fertilize. If this happens between two different but closely related fern species, the result is a fern *hybrid*. Hybrids are not uncommon in the ferns, and several of the ferns that we regard as species actually originated as hybrids, as we will explain later.

Some species have two kinds of spores that produce "male" and "female" gametophytes that cannot fertilize themselves; both types of gametophytes must be present to produce a sporophyte. The two types of spores are of two different sizes. The "male" spores are microscopic and are called *microspores*, but the "female" *megaspores* are large enough to be seen with the naked eye.

Fern spores are usually produced by a special type of cell division called *meiosis,* or reduction division. The cells of the sporophyte plant have a certain number of *chromosomes*, which contain the DNA that is the genetic material of the plant. These chromosomes occur in matched pairs. The two in each pair carry the same genes, although the actual makeup of the genes in the two chromosomes will differ. During meiosis the pairs of chromosomes are brought together and are then pulled apart into separate daughter cells. This results in spores with only half as many chromosomes as the ordinary cells of the plant.

The sporophyte cells with the paired chromosomes are termed *diploid*; the spore and the gametophyte cells with only one set of chromosomes are called *haploid*. Groups of closely related species like genera will be characterized by a certain number of chromosomes being present in the cells. The number of chromosomes in a haploid cell is often referred to as the *"base" number* of chromosomes; diploid cells will have twice this base number. As we will see, some species can have more than twice the base number of chromosomes. A plant with three times the base number of chromosomes is called a *triploid*, four times the base number is *tetraploid*, five times the base number is *pentaploid*, and so on.

During meiosis, the chromosomes must be able to pair up, or they cannot be properly separated into the haploid spores. If the plant is a hybrid, some or all of the chromosomes may differ enough that the cellular mechanism that pairs them up cannot recognize the pairs. If this happens, meiosis fails and the end product is spores that are nothing but empty cell walls. This is why hybrids are usually sterile and cannot reproduce themselves except by vegetative means. Their spores are shriveled husks that cannot grow into gametophytes.

In the normal type of cell division, called *mitosis*, every chromosome is copied and the duplicates are paired up. The pairs are then separated into the two daughter cells, which then have exactly the same chromosomes as the original cell. However, under certain conditions of environmental stress, this process of cell division can be disrupted after the chromosomes are duplicated but before the pairs are separated and the daughter cells produced. This results in a cell with twice the diploid number of chromosomes. Such a cell is tetraploid and is also termed a *polyploid*. It will continue to divide, and its descendants may include the "mother cells" that produce spores by meiosis. Since every chromosome was duplicated in the event that produced the first tetraploid cell, every chromosome has a twin and they pair up normally in meiosis, which can proceed normally and produce fertile spores. The hybrid can now reproduce normally. It functions as an effective species that is distinct from either of its parents.

Several of the fern species in the Alabama flora arose this way. Tutwiler's spleenwort (*Asplenium tutwilerae*) is a famous example. A sterile hybrid called Scott's spleenwort (*A. × ebenoides*) occurs occasionally in the Appalachian region; it is the hybrid of the ebony spleenwort (*A. platyneuron*) and the walking fern (*A. rhizophyllum*). One of these hybrids apparently arose in a ravine in northern Hale County. Somewhere in its life, something happened to cause chromosome doubling, and viable spores were produced that in turn led to fertile polyploid plants and resulted in a self-sustaining population of the "new species." Since this fern has never been found outside of that one ravine and since fern spores are microscopic and easily spread by the wind, we must assume that the chromosome-doubling event occurred quite recently. We would expect that in time, Tutwiler's spleenwort will be found elsewhere. Two other Alabama spleenworts, the cliff spleenwort or Bradley's spleenwort (*A. bradleyi*) and the lobed spleenwort (*A. pinnatifidum*) are known to have arisen in the same way, but they are widespread in the eastern United States, and nobody knows where or when they arose.

If one of these tetraploid hybrids hybridizes with a diploid species like one of its parents, the resulting plant is triploid, with three times the base chromosome number. With three sets of chromosomes, it is not possible for the chromosomes to line up in pairs; meiosis fails and produces sterile spores. Some triploids have acquired the ability to produce spores without meiosis. These spores grow into gametophytes with the same triploid number of chromosomes as the sporophyte, and these gametophytes produce sporophytes directly, without gametes. This method of reproduction is called *apogamy* or *apogamous reproduction,* from Greek words meaning "without gametes." A few species of Alabama ferns reproduce by apogamy; they include the black-stemmed spleenwort (*Asplenium resiliens*) and the purple cliff-brake (*Pellaea atropurpurea*). These are ferns of rocky, often dry, places, so apogamy, which does not require water for gametes, is well suited to them.

In the rest of this section, we will discuss the shapes and forms, or morphology, of the fern plants and their parts. These features are used to distinguish one species from another and form the basis for much of the information in a book like this one. Ferns and fern allies, like all vascular plants, have stems, leaves, and roots.

The leaves are the most conspicuous features of ferns; their stems are generally small, growing underground, or both. Most of the process of identifying a fern involves looking at the leaves and their features. A leaf generally has a *blade,* the broad portion, which is usually connected to the stem by a *stalk* of some sort. Some plants have leaves with no stalks and a few, including one Alabama fern, have leaves that have only stalks and no blades.

The overall shape and form of the leaf blade is an important factor in the identification of ferns. The blades of fern leaves, like those of all vascular plants except the fern allies (more about them later), have numerous veins containing the cellular tubing that characterizes vascular plants. A typical leaf has a thick vein called the *midvein* that arises at the point where the leaf joins the stalk or the stem and which usually runs to the tip of the leaf. Smaller veins branch from the midvein and run to the edges or *margins* of the leaf. These branch veins can have further, smaller branches, and so on. In most fern leaves, the smallest veins simply end at the leaf margin. In some leaves, however, the smallest veins connect together to enclose small areas, called *areoles*, of the blade and forming a netlike pattern. Some ferns have leaves that have no midvein. Their veins simply fork repeatedly from the base of the leaf.

Most, but not all, fern leaves are divided into smaller segments of some sort, often in a very intricate manner. The divisions may be cut all the way to the midrib, resulting in a leaf that looks like a number of smaller leaves arranged in two rows along a thin stem. This is a *compound* leaf. The arrangement of the smaller "leaves" can resemble a feather, and a compound leaf arranged in this manner is described as being *pinnate*, from a Latin word meaning "feather." The bare, stemlike midrib of such a leaf is called the *rachis*. A leaf that is divided once in this way is said to be *1-pinnate*. The primary divisions of pinnate leaf, called *pinnae* (the singular is *pinna*) by botanists, may be divided in the same way themselves, resulting in a *2-pinnate* leaf. The secondary divisions of such a leaf are called *pinnules*. If the pinnules are also compound, the leaf is *3-pinnate*, and so on.

In this book, we use the word *leaflet* to refer to the smallest segment of a compound leaf. On a 1-pinnate leaf, we use *leaflets* to refer to the pinnae; on a 2-pinnate leaf it refers to the pinnules, and so on.

A leaf that is not compound is called a *simple leaf.* The blades of many ferns are cut into segments but are not cut all the way to the midrib. The cuts may be deep enough that the leaf looks pinnate at first glance when it actually is not. A leaf like this is not compound; it is *lobed*, and the segments are called *lobes*. Only a few Alabama ferns have leaves that are neither compound nor lobed.

A leaf can also be *palmately* compound or lobed, with the segments radiating from a center, like the fingers of a hand. No Alabama ferns have palmately compound leaves, but the American climbing fern (*Lygodium palmatum*) has palmately lobed leaflets.

Some examples of ferns with simple unlobed leaves are the Hart's tongue fern (*Phyllitis scolopendrium*) and all of the adder's-tongues (genus *Ophioglossum*). Ferns with leaves that are lobed but not quite compound include the resurrection fern (*Polypodium polypodioides*) and the net-vein chain fern (*Woodwardia areolata*). Some fern leaves are doubly lobed without actually being compound; these include the broad beech fern (*Thelypteris hexagonoptera*) and the Appalachian filmy fern (*Trichomanes boschianum*). A large number of ferns have 1-pinnate leaves. A few of them are the ebony spleenwort (*A. platyneuron*), the Christmas fern (*Polystichum acrostichoides*), and the holly ferns (*Cyrtomium*). Many ferns have 1-pinnate leaves with deeply lobed pinnae, like the widespread maiden fern (*Thelypteris kunthii*) and the cinnamon fern (*Osmunda cinnamomea*). Examples of 2-pinnate ferns include the evergreen wood fern (*Dryopteris intermedia*) and the royal fern (*Osmunda regalis*). The leaves of two Alabama ferns, the Mariana maiden fern (*Thelypteris torresiana*) and the spineless bramble fern (*Hypolepis tenuifolia*), may be 3-pinnate, or more in the case of the bramble fern, in the larger leaves of older plants.

The general outlines of leaf blades and their segments are important characteristics of ferns. These shapes fall into several broad categories, which we will describe.

The outlines of most fern leaf blades resemble the shape of a spearhead, rounded at the base, broadest a little above the base, and tapering to a pointed tip. Botanists have a large number of technical terms for this and other leaf shapes; they call this one *lanceolate*, but in our effort to avoid such terms we will call this leaf shape *spearhead-shaped* in our keys and descriptions. An *ovate* leaf blade is egg-shaped, is widest below the middle with a rounded base, and has a blunt tip; a triangular blade is just that, its base and margins form three essentially straight lines. An *oblong* blade is roughly rectangular, with little or no taper at either end; a *linear* leaf is narrow with nearly parallel sides. These shapes are also used to describe leaflets and lobes.

The margins of the leaves, leaflets, and lobes have various forms. Some are *entire*, or completely smooth. Some have teeth of various sizes and descriptions or have notches, cuts, bristles, or fringes. Some ferns have leaf margins that are rolled under and curl toward the back of the leaf.

The leaves of the fern allies are much simpler than those of the ferns; this is one of the fundamental differences between the fern allies and other vascular plants, including the ferns. The leaf of a fern ally has one and only one vein, which never branches. The leaves are usually linear in shape and very narrow, but a few fern allies have leaves that are flattened and somewhat broader. Except for the quillworts (genus *Isoëtes*), the leaves of fern allies are tiny, less than 1 cm long. The leaves of *Isoëtes* may be many centimeters long. The leaves of fern allies are never compound or lobed. A few of the species with broader leaves may have some sparse teeth at the margins, but the margins of most are entire. The whisk plant (*Psilotum nudum*) has no leaves at all; it has only tiny, veinless scales on the stem.

The spores of ferns and fern allies are borne in tiny capsules called *sporangia* (the singular is *sporangium*). In most ferns the sporangia are grouped in clusters called *sori* (one of them is a *sorus*), which are found on the back sides of the leaves; they are the familiar "fruit dots" (an inappropriate term since they are not fruits). The shapes and arrangements of sori are important to the identification of fern species. Sori may be round, kidney-shaped, spindle-shaped (straight with tapered ends), crescent-shaped, or straight with blunt ends.

The sori of many, but not all, ferns are also covered when young by a thin membrane called the *indusium* (the plural is *indusia*). Indusia also come in a variety of shapes; that and the manner in which they are attached to the sori and how they break open to expose the sporangia are also important characteristics used for identification. The indusium of a round sorus may be attached along one side and arch over the sorus like a hood, or it may be attached in the center of the sorus and cover it like an umbrella. The indusium of a round sorus may also open at the center and split into several flaps that remain attached around the sorus and form a starlike pattern when fully opened. The indusium of a kidney-shaped or crescent-shaped sorus is usually attached along the inner curve of the pattern. The indusia of straight and spindle-shaped sori usually remain attached along one side and open at the other, but some remain attached on both sides and open along the center.

The position and arrangement of the sori is another important characteristic used in the identification of ferns. They can be at the margins, near the midrib of the leaflet or lobe, or in between. They can be scattered over the leaf surface, arranged in rows, either side by side or end to end, or in strips along the leaflet margins.

Many ferns have two different-looking types of leaves that are termed *dimorphic*, from the Greek meaning "of two shapes." One type of leaf bears the sporangia, while the other type is purely *vegetative* and has no sporangia. Other ferns may have fertile, sporangia-bearing leaves on which the sporangia or sori are confined to a certain portion of the leaf, usually the upper portion. Ferns with dimorphic leaves or leaflets will often have fertile leaves or leaflets that are different in size or shape from the purely vegetative ones. With some ferns, these differences are subtle and hard to see; with others, the differences are extreme to the point that the two types of leaves or leaf segments do not resemble each other at all.

Some ferns do not have sori. The adder's-tongue ferns (genus *Ophioglossum*) and the grape ferns (genus *Botrychium*) have specialized branches of the leaves that bear the sporangia. The sporangia of the cinnamon fern (*Osmunda cinnamomea*) and the royal fern (*O. regalis*) are borne on the naked veins of modified leaves or leaf segments. The water-clovers (genus *Marsilea*), the pillwort (*Pilularia americana*), the mosquito fern (*Azolla caroliniana*), and the floating ferns (genus *Salvinia*) all bear their sporangia inside hard pill-like capsules called *sporocarps*.

Fern allies do not have sori. Usually their sporangia are borne on the top sides of the leaves at their bases where they join the stem, the leaf *axils*, and there is never more than one sporangium per leaf. The horsetails and scouring-rushes (genus *Equisetum*) bear their sporangia on the undersides of umbrella-like specialized stems called *sporangiophores*. The whisk plant (*Psilotum nudum*) bears its sporangia in the "axils" of the stem scales.

The leaves of fern allies that bear sporangia, called *sporophylls*, are usually of a different size and shape than the vegetative ones. With the majority of the fern allies the sporophylls are grouped into conelike structures called *strobili* (the singular is *strobilus*) as are the sporangiophores of *Equisetum*. Strobili are always borne at the tips of stems of some sort.

The leaf blades of ferns are usually connected to the stems by prominent leaf stalks; the leaves of fern allies are connected directly to the stem and have no stalks. These leaf stalks, and the rachises of compound leaves, have many characteristics that are used for identification. These important characteristics include length, thickness, stiffness, and color. Leaflets can also have or lack stalks where they are connected to the rachises or rachis branches.

Various types of hairs and scales may be present on the leaves of ferns. Their size, color, and location on the leaf are all important characteristics.

The stems of most ferns, including all of them that grow in Alabama, are *rhizomes*. This means that the stems do not grow up into the air; they grow either under the ground or *creeping* upon the surface of the soil, rock, or tree bark that supports them. Only the leaves can usually be seen on a living plant unless it is dug up. Some rhizomes are short and grow very little as the plant ages; others grow more rapidly and can become quite long. They may be thick or thin, hard or soft, smooth or scaly. The leaves of some ferns are clustered at the tip of the rhizome; others have leaves that are spaced apart along the rhizome. The rhizomes of many ferns can branch repeatedly to spread the plant; ferns with long horizontal rhizomes can spread over wide areas.

The roots of the plant arise from the rhizome. They may occur in tufts with portions of the rhizome lacking roots, or the rhizome may have roots all along its length. The roots themselves are rarely used for identification purposes.

Most fern allies have aerial stems. The stems of the scouring-rushes (genus *Equisetum*) can be several meters tall, but the stems of most species are only a few centimeters to less than half a meter tall. Many species have main stems that are rhizomes that produce aerial branches. The quillworts (genus *Isoëtes*) have only a bulblike rhizome that hardly grows at all during the life of the plant. This is true of all species of *Isoëtes* in Alabama, although one unusual species in the Piedmont of Georgia, the mat-forming quillwort (*I. tegetiformans* Rury), has rhizomes that grow significantly and can actually branch and form new plants, something that the stems of no other species of *Isoëtes* can do.

The aerial stems of some fern allies can have several to many branches. In some of the clubmosses (genus *Lycopodium*), these aerial stems are branched repeatedly in such a way that the plant looks like a group of tiny trees. With some other clubmosses, the only aerial stems are the stalks bearing the strobili; most of the plant grows *prostrate* on the ground. Some of the spikemosses (genus *Selaginella*) have elaborately branched aerial stems that resemble the leaves of ferns. The aerial stems of the whisk plant (*Psilotum nudum*) fork repeatedly into a brushlike pattern.

2

Geography of Alabama Ferns

Geographic factors affect the distributions of plants, including ferns and fern allies. Plants may require specific types of rocks or soils or specific conditions of moisture and light. Summer heat and winter cold are also important. The study of geographic factors and their effects on plant distributions is called *phytogeography*.

The state of Alabama extends almost 5 degrees of latitude from the Gulf of Mexico to the Tennessee state line and lies where the rocky plateaus and mountains of the Appalachians reach their southernmost limits and pass under the younger, softer sediments of the Coastal Plain. The great diversity of the Alabama landscape provides for a remarkable range of plant habitats. It is important to understand this diversity of the landscape in order to understand the distributions of many of the ferns and fern allies of Alabama.

Most of the variability in the landscape, habitats, and plant life of Alabama results from the complex geology of the state. The rocks vary from region to region in composition, age, and hardness, and the soils derived from them are as varied. Geologic forces like uplift and folding have combined with erosion to produce a great variety of landforms and topography. Some rugged terrains provide pockets of climatic conditions that are quite different from the surrounding areas.

The distributions of plants, especially those that are restricted to particular conditions, as are many ferns and fern allies, show regional patterns that follow the variations of rock types, soils, and landforms. These patterns of plant distribution suggest the division of Alabama into several major plant distribution regions, or phytogeographic provinces, some of which can be divided further into smaller regions or subprovinces.

The map below shows these regions. It is based on geological information from the digital version of the Geologic Map of Alabama (Geological
Survey of Alabama 2006) and on topographic information from the National Elevation Dataset 1 arc-second grid published online by the United
States Geological Survey (usgs.gov). The authors' knowledge of plant distributions, especially ferns, was also a factor in the creation of the map.

The map resembles physical-geographic maps drawn by geologists,
but there are some significant differences. It also resembles maps drawn
to illustrate the distribution patterns of forest types and of various groups
of animals, but again there are differences. It should be noted that it is
not possible to draw an exact border between many pairs of regions due
to the complex and often fractured nature of the geology and topography.
This is especially true in northwestern Alabama and in parts of southern
Alabama.

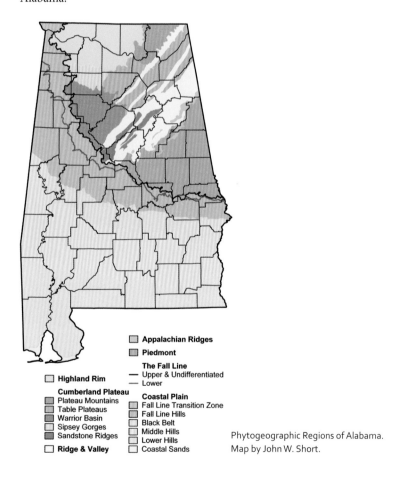

Phytogeographic Regions of Alabama.
Map by John W. Short.

There are six major phytogeographic regions or provinces in Alabama. They are, from north to south: the Highland Rim, the Cumberland Plateau, the Ridge and Valley, the Appalachian Ridges, the Piedmont, and the Coastal Plain. The first five are underlain by hard rocks that were formed before the age of the dinosaurs, 250 million years ago and earlier. The rocks of the Coastal Plain, however, are much younger and are softer; the oldest were formed at the end of the time of the dinosaurs, less than 100 million years ago. Going toward the coast, the deposits become younger and softer still until, at the coast itself, they are so young that they have not had sufficient time or geological pressure to harden into rocks. The regions of the older, harder rocks are for the most part more elevated than the Coastal Plain. These five hard-rock regions are referred to collectively as the *highland provinces* or *highland regions* in this book.

The Highland Rim is in the center and center-west part of northernmost Alabama. The rocks there are primarily limestone and similar calcium-containing, or *calcareous,* rocks that often contain inclusions of chert, flint, or quartz. A narrow band of sandstone extends across the region a bit south of its center. The northwestern part of the Alabama Highland Rim consists of rugged hills separated by steep ravines. Most of the rest of it is essentially flat with the sandstone band forming a line of hills separating this region into two broad valleys. The ferns most characteristic of the Highland Rim are those that are usually found growing on limestone, such as the purple cliff-brake (*Pellaea atropurpurea*), the bulblet bladder fern (*Cystopteris bulbifera*), the black-stemmed spleenwort *(Asplenium resiliens)*, and the walking fern (*A. rhizophyllum*).

The Highland Rim is part of a larger geologic region called the Interior Low Plateaus. The other four highland provinces, the Cumberland Plateau, the Ridge and Valley, the Appalachian Ridges, and the Piedmont, are parts of the broad region known as the Appalachians.

The Cumberland Plateau is the largest and most complex of the highland provinces in Alabama. It extends from the northeastern corner of the state to central northwestern Alabama. The region is characterized by a single rock formation, known as the Pottsville Formation, that has a base layer of hard sandstone and is underlain by the same limestone found in the Highland Rim. In most of the Alabama Cumberland Plateau, this sandstone is all there is of the Pottsville Formation, but in the southwestern Cumberland Plateau and a few places elsewhere it is covered by a mixture of this sandstone, shale, and coal beds that in places is very deep. Most of the Cumberland Plateau has been uplifted by geologic forces and is at significantly higher elevations than the surrounding areas. This uplift and the forces of erosion have produced a decidedly mountainous topography in much of the region. The varied topography and abundance of rock outcrops, both sandstone and limestone, make the Cumberland Plateau one of the most biologically diverse regions in Alabama.

The Cumberland Plateau of Alabama can be divided into five distinct subprovinces based on topography and the composition of the rocks, and on the distributions of ferns and other plants. It is important to know the characteristics of these regions to understand the distributions of many Alabama ferns and fern allies, including many that reach the southernmost limits of their distributions here and a very few that are unique to one or the other of these regions.

In the northeastern corner of the state, the streams have eroded the plateau into a series of rugged mountainous hills that we will call the Plateau Mountains. These hills are essentially flat-topped, and they all rise to about the same elevation. They are capped by the hard sandstone layer of the Pottsville Formation, which often forms precipitous cliffs at the tops of the slopes.

The lower parts of the steep slopes consist of limestone that is riddled with many caves and sinkholes. These provide particularly cool habitats for some northern fern species and a few places that never freeze that harbor a few tropical species.

The shaded lower portions of the sandstone cliffs provide habitats for rock ferns like the mountain spleenwort (*Asplenium montanum*) and the lobed spleenwort (*A. pinnatifidum*). The ground at the cliff bases supports northern species like the evergreen wood fern (*Dryopteris intermedia*) and the hay-scented fern (*Dennstaedtia punctilobula*).

Farther down the slopes, limestone boulders, ledges, and cave openings create habitats for lime-loving ferns like those mentioned above, and the cool areas in the sinks and cave mouths harbor a few rarities like the onesorus spleenwort (*Asplenium monanthes*) and the Hart's tongue fern (*Phyllitis scolopendrium*). Shaded ledges and boulders of both limestone and sandstone are home to the marginal wood fern (*Dryopteris marginalis*).

The next subprovince of the Cumberland Plateau consists of three broad unbroken pieces of the plateau known as Lookout Mountain, Sand Mountain, and Brindley Mountain. The three are similar in form and in their plant life, and we will collectively call them the Table Plateaus. The edges of these plateaus are steep escarpments similar to the slopes of the

Plateau Mountains with sandstone on top and limestone below. Caves are not nearly as abundant, so cave mouths and sinkholes are less common, but stream erosion has carved deep gorges in the escarpments in several places, including Little River Canyon and Buck's Pocket. The slopes are home to many of the same ferns found in the Plateau Mountains except for some of the cool-climate species found in the cave openings in that region. The broad surfaces of the plateaus have a few wetland areas that harbor ferns like the cinnamon fern (*Osmunda cinnamomea*) and the New York fern (*Thelypteris noveboracensis*). Sandstone flat rocks are common and provide habitats for species like the woolly lip fern (*Cheilanthes tomentosa*) and the rock spikemoss (*Selaginella rupestris*). The ground-pine (*Lycopodium obscurum*) has been found in a few places near both flat rocks and streams on Sand Mountain and nowhere else in Alabama.

The southwestern portion of the Cumberland Plateau is the Warrior Basin, so named because it is drained by the Black Warrior River and its tributaries. It is a "basin" because, instead of being uplifted, the rocks have been folded downward. The sandstone base layer of the Pottsville Formation is deep underground and is overlain by many disconnected layers of sandstone and shale. The terrain here is rolling to rugged hills with slopes that may be gentle or steep. One of the most characteristic ferns of this region is the maidenhair spleenwort (*Asplenium trichomanes*), which is often found growing on the shale. This is the main coal-producing region in Alabama, and strip mining has destroyed many once-beautiful places.

North of the Warrior Basin is a region with relatively low elevations compared to the Cumberland Plateau in the northeastern part of the state. The Pottsville rocks in this region consist almost entirely of the sandstone base layer. Geologists usually consider this region to be part of the Warrior Basin since it is drained by the Sipsey Fork, a tributary of the Black Warrior River. However, in terms of its topography and plant life it warrants recognition in its own right. Here the streams have eroded deep, narrow gorges into the sandstone and through to the underlying limestone, resulting in the name that we give it, the Sipsey Gorges. These gorges are cooler and more humid than the surrounding areas and harbor a unique assemblage of plant life.

This includes an entire forest type known as the Hemlock-Hardwood Forest Association, which occurs primarily in eastern Canada, the northeastern United States, and southward in the mountains and plateaus of the Appalachians to northern Georgia and extreme northeastern Alabama.

This forest is found in Alabama in shaded ravines at high elevations in the extreme northeastern corner of the state, in the Sipsey Gorges, and nowhere in between. An occurrence of a plant in an area that is well separated from its main range is referred to as a *disjunct* occurrence. In the Sipsey Gorges of Alabama, the Hemlock-Hardwood Forest Association and several of its members are disjunct from their main ranges to the northeast.

The evergreen wood fern (*Dryopteris intermedia*) is found here as part of the Hemlock-Hardwood Forest Association. So are Goldie's wood fern (*D. goldiana*) and the shining clubmoss (*Lycopodium lucidulum*), both of which have been found nowhere else in Alabama. One of the most characteristic ferns of the Sipsey Gorges is the Appalachian filmy fern (*Trichomanes boschianum*), which is common in this region and rare elsewhere. The Alabama streak-sorus fern (*Thelypteris pilosa* var. *alabamensis*) occurs nowhere else in the world.

The last subregion of the Cumberland Plateau consists of series of ridges that were formed by geologic folding of the Pottsville rocks. Since the highest ridges are composed of the hard sandstone of the lower Pottsville, we will call them the Sandstone Ridges. These ridges are in two groups that geologists call the Coosa Ridges and the Cahaba Ridges; they place them in the Ridge and Valley because of the folding, but the rocks and the plant life are those of the Cumberland Plateau, so we include them in that province, as do many other biologists. The characteristic ferns here are the sandstone-loving rock ferns mentioned previously. A few northern species like the hay-scented fern (*Dennstaedtia punctilobula*) are near their southernmost limits in shady ravines like the Narrows in Shelby County. The southwestern part of this region, in northeastern Bibb County, western Shelby County, and southwestern Jefferson County, has deep Pottsville deposits similar to those of the Warrior Basin. Like the Warrior Basin, it has suffered much damage from strip mining.

The Ridge and Valley in Alabama is a series of valleys formed by geologic folding. These valleys are long and fairly straight and have linear ridges in the valley floors. The rocks are mostly limestone and dolomite, but include shale and some sandstone. Many of these valleys are only a few miles wide with high escarpments on each side, but the bulk of this province is the broad Coosa Valley. The Coosa Valley is the southernmost portion of the Great Appalachian Valley, which has its northern end in Pennsylvania and is one of the longest valleys in the world.

The phytogeographic map shows several narrow arms of the Ridge and Valley extending as valleys into the Cumberland Plateau. Geologists know these valleys as the Anticlinal Valleys from the type of folding that produced them, and they place the valleys in the Cumberland Plateau. However, the rocks in the valley floors are the ones characteristic of the Ridge and Valley, and so are the plants.

The ferns characteristic of the Ridge and Valley include primarily the limestone-loving ferns mentioned earlier. Damp stream banks and floodplains in the broader valleys also support many of the ferns of upland wetlands, including the cinnamon fern (*Osmunda cinnamomea*), the royal fern (*O. regalis*), the New York fern (*Thelypteris noveboracensis*), and the broad beech fern (*T. hexagonoptera*).

Most of the southeastern border of the Ridge and Valley is marked by a series of mountainous ridges that include the highest elevations in Alabama, the highest of which is Mt. Cheaha at 634 meters (2,407 feet). The status and nomenclature of these ridges has been a subject of some controversy among geologists and biologists for many years. Geological texts usually include the main ridge system as part of the Piedmont because the rocks of these ridges are metamorphic, as are those of the Piedmont; the rocks of all of the rest of the highland provinces are sedimentary. However, there is another ridge system underlain by metamorphic rocks that the geological texts place in the Ridge and Valley because they have been folded.

The ridges that are included in the Piedmont are not separated as a subprovince from the rest of the Piedmont in the geological literature, even though the elevation of the ridges is much higher and the topography is more rugged than the rest of the Piedmont. Also, the metamorphic rocks found in the ridges are types derived from sedimentary rocks, primarily sandstone, but the metamorphic rocks in most of the Piedmont were derived from igneous rocks like granite. The plant and animal life of the ridges is also distinct from that of the Piedmont proper, and biological writers usually put these ridges in their own province.

The name chosen for the province by many who recognize it as distinct, the Blue Ridge, has been a subject of controversy. It has been rightly argued that the Blue Ridge Mountains come to an end in northern Georgia and that the high ridges in Alabama are not part of that system. We will avoid the error and call these ridges the Appalachian Ridges.

The Appalachian Ridges as construed here include the Talladega-Horseblock-Rattlesnake Mountain range, which includes Mt. Cheaha, and the Weisner Ridges, which extend into the Ridge and Valley; Choccolocco Mountain near Anniston is one of the Weisner Ridges. The characteristic rock of both of these ridge systems is quartzite, a metamorphic rock derived from sandstone. This is a very hard rock that resists weathering and is the primary reason for the existence and the elevation of the ridges. These two ridge systems are more like each other than the surrounding areas, and for this reason we group them together.

The quartzite of the Appalachian Ridges forms outcrops and boulders that support some of the ferns that are typical of the sandstone in the Cumberland Plateau, like the mountain spleenwort (*Asplenium montanum*). Some others, like the hay-scented fern (*Dennstaedtia punctilobula*), have northern ranges and reach their southern extremes in the high elevations of these ridges. The fern that seems most characteristic of the province is the cliff spleenwort or Bradley's spleenwort (*A. bradleyi*). This fern is rare through most of its range in the eastern United States and is found in Alabama only in the Appalachian Ridges and on the higher escarpments of the Cumberland Plateau. This spleenwort is known throughout most of the Appalachian Ridges. It is fairly abundant in some high places like Mt. Cheaha and has been found on the lower slopes as well.

The Piedmont is the southernmost of the highland provinces in Alabama. It is a hilly region, most of which is underlain by metamorphic rocks derived from granite and similar igneous rocks. In the northwest along the border with the Appalachian Ridges and the Ridge and Valley is a region underlain by metamorphic rocks of sedimentary origin like slate and marble. Although many biological writers have included this region in their "Blue Ridge," its topography and plant life is more similar to the rest of the Piedmont than to the Appalachian Ridges, and we have included it as part of the Piedmont. The Piedmont is often divided into an Upper Piedmont and a Lower Piedmont, often with other names than these. Although the hills of the Upper Piedmont are a bit more rugged than those of the Lower Piedmont, there is little distinction between the two regions with regard to ferns.

One very important ecological feature of the Piedmont is the presence of flat rocks, large outcroppings of rock that are for the most part approximately level and that can cover large areas. These rocks and the thin soil around their fringes harbor a unique assemblage of plant life. Some species are found nowhere else. The plants that grow in these places thrive in the winter and the spring when the potholes in the rocks are full of water and the rock margins are wet from the seasonal rains. By the summer, the rocks dry up and the plants wither and go dormant.

Most of the ferns of the Piedmont are the ones commonly found in highland woodlands like the Christmas fern (*Polystichum acrostichoides*) and the ebony spleenwort (*Asplenium platyneuron*). Stream banks are usually steep and not swampy, and shaded ones often have ferns that grow in the dry margins of damp places like the lady fern (*Athyrium filix-femina*). The naturalized Mariana maiden fern (*Thelypteris torresiana*) is becoming increasing abundant under bridges across streams and on disturbed stream banks. The running-cedar (*Lycopodium digitatum*) has become rather common in second-growth forests in the Piedmont. The flat rocks are the home of the hairy lip fern (*Cheilanthes lanosa*) and of the Piedmont quill-wort (*Isoëtes piedmontana*), which is found only on flat rocks in the Piedmont from Alabama to North Carolina.

The rocks of the highland provinces slope gradually to the south and west. They eventually become low enough that the younger sediments of the Coastal Plain cover them. The line of contact at the land surface between the old highland rocks and the younger Coastal Plain rocks is called the Fall Line. This name comes from the fact that streams that cross this line tend to form rapids or falls as they flow from the hard rocks of the highland provinces into the softer sediments of the Coastal Plain. Most of the larger streams are navigable from the coast up to this point, and the Fall Line is an important historical feature since a number of cities and towns were established at this head of navigation.

The Fall Line is well defined in the Atlantic states where the Piedmont, the only highland province there that contacts the Coastal Plain, slopes fairly abruptly and produces an easily seen line of contact with the Coastal Plain. This is generally true along the Piedmont Fall Line in Alabama, but the line of contact between the other provinces and the Coastal Plain is very complex. There, the rocks of the highland provinces slope very gradually to the south and west. As they slope downward, thicker and thicker layers of Coastal Plain sediments cover them. In many places the streams have eroded through the Coastal Plain sediments into the underlying highland rocks, producing the paradoxical effect of having "Coastal Plain" on the hilltops and highlands in the valleys. Many places have pockets of Coastal Plain deposits surrounded by highland rocks, and other places have pockets of highland rocks surrounded by Coastal Plain material. Some streams actually originate in Coastal Plain sediments, flow through highland ravines, and then back into the Coastal Plain. Both the Cumberland Plateau and the Ridge and Valley contact the Coastal Plain only in Alabama.

This situation makes it impossible to draw a single line representing the Fall Line in northwestern Alabama. For a map the size of the phytogeographic map presented here, it is necessary to draw two lines, both of which "connect the dots" and are subject to much interpretation. The inner line, called the Upper Fall Line on the map, follows the uppermost limit of the Coastal Plain deposits; many parts of the line are arbitrary and connect pockets of Coastal Plain deposits that are separated by highland rocks. An outer line, the Lower Fall Line on the map, connects the lowermost areas of the upland rocks. It too is arbitrary in many places where it connects areas of highland rocks that are separated by Coastal Plain material. We call the region between these two lines the Fall Line Transition Zone. It is neither Coastal Plain nor a highland province; it is both. Since what we are calling the Upper Fall Line corresponds fairly well with the Fall Line as it has been drawn on previous maps of Alabama, our map shows this region as part of the Coastal Plain, but it must be remembered that this region is both Coastal Plain and "highlands."

Because of its dual nature, the Fall Line Transition Zone is one of the most biologically diverse regions in Alabama. The rocky ravines of the portion of the region bordering the Cumberland Plateau contain the last outposts of the Hemlock-Hardwood Forest Association and several fern species like the Appalachian filmy fern (*Trichomanes boschianum*) that are characteristic of the Sipsey Gorges. The Dismals Gardens in southeastern Franklin County is the best-known example of these ravines.

The portion of the Fall Line Transition Zone located in central Bibb County that is associated with the Ridge and Valley is quite remarkable. Several species of plants that are known only from that area, or from there and nearby, have been discovered since the late nineteenth century. These discoveries have continued to recent times when an entirely unknown habitat type, with several species of plants that were new to science, was discovered there. This habitat is called the Ketona Dolomite Glades. It features thin alkaline soils over the rock type called the Ketona Dolomite. Dolomite is very similar to limestone but differs in that it contains a large amount of magnesium in addition to the calcium that is characteristic of limestone. Although they were discovered only recently, these places have become well known enough that some of the rental trucks that feature interesting information about various states painted on their side panels tell of the "lost world of rare plants" of the Ketona Dolomite Glades of central Bibb County, Alabama.

None of the species unique to central Bibb County are ferns, but one of them, the southwestern false cloak fern (*Notholaena integerrima*), is found in the Ketona Dolomite Glades and nowhere else east of western Texas, over 1,500 kilometers to the west of Bibb County.

The geological formations in the Coastal Plain represent a series of increasingly younger sediments going from the Fall Line to the Gulf Coast. These sediments lie in roughly parallel bands radiating to the south and west from the Fall Line. Various authors have subdivided the Coastal Plain proper in different ways, but we recognize five regions that are distinct enough for recognition based on the distributions of plants.

The oldest rocks in the Coastal Plain are in the Fall Line Hills, so named because the area's northern border is the Fall Line. These rocks consist mostly of soft conglomerates and sandstones that are generally covered by deep sandy soils; outcrops of these rocks are rare. The greatest numbers of ferns are found along stream banks and in floodplains: ferns like the cinnamon fern (*Osmunda cinnamomea*) and the royal fern (*O. regalis*), the lady fern (*Athyrium filix-femina*), and the net-vein chain fern (*Woodwardia areolata*). Some of the drier hillsides are home to ferns like the Christmas fern (*Polystichum acrostichoides*) and the ebony spleenwort (*Asplenium platyneuron*). However, most of the dry-land forests in the Fall Line Hills and throughout much of the rest of the Coastal Plain are pine forests, in which few ferns will grow. The only fern commonly found under pines is the bracken fern (*Pteridium aquilinum*).

Rock outcrops are rare in the Fall Line Hills, but there are a few areas in the region where the Coastal Plain rocks are harder and outcrops abound; this is not counting the Fall Line Transition Zone, where there are many outcrops of the older rocks of the highland provinces. One of the most prominent of these areas is in northern Hale County, where the pebbly conglomerate rock is particularly hard, and cliffs and ledges are common. This small area includes the ravine near Havana that is the only known place where Tutwiler's spleenwort (*Asplenium tutwilerae*) and its hybrid descendant Boydston's spleenwort (*A. × boydstoniae*) may be found. This conglomerate rock is apparently similar chemically to the Pottsville sandstone of the Cumberland Plateau, with which it has been confused by some writers. In addition to the endemic spleenworts, the Havana ravine has several fern species that are characteristic of the Cumberland Plateau, including the marginal wood fern (*Dryopteris marginalis*) and the Appalachian filmy fern (*Trichomanes boschianum*). The maidenhair spleenwort (*A. trichomanes*) is abundant in the ravine and on rock outcrops in nearby areas. This is the only place in the Coastal Plain where these ferns may be found.

The next region of the Coastal Plain to the south of the Fall Line Hills is the Black Belt. This region is underlain by a different type of rock: chalk.

This is a soft type of limestone that is almost snow white in color. The region was given the name Black Belt because the Native Americans once burned off large areas in order to maintain a grassland habitat for bison. This burning caused the soil to be black. The chalk of the Black Belt is similar in age and composition to that which forms the famous White Cliffs of Dover in England. There are several places along the rivers of the Black Belt where erosion has carved similar high white cliffs into the hillsides. One of these places can be seen from Interstate 20/59 where it crosses the Tombigbee River near the town of Epes. Here we have Alabama's own White Cliffs of Epes.

The soils of the Black Belt contain an unusual type of heavy clay that makes them unsuitable for most ferns. However, in some places where the soils are thin over the chalk, the limestone adder's-tongue (*Ophioglossum engelmannii*) may be found in great abundance. Most of the ferns of the Black Belt are found near streams where sandy banks and chalk bluffs provide habitats for them. One of the most commonly seen ferns is the sensitive fern (*Onoclea sensibilis*), which is often found growing on some of the lower, shaded chalk bluffs. The ferns are rooted near the top of the bluff at the line of contact of the chalk with the soil layer above it, and their leaves hang downward, giving the bluff a distinctive ferny fringe.

The next two regions of the Coastal Plain, the Middle Hills and the Lower Hills, are simplifications of the usual representations of the subprovinces of the Coastal Plain. Many names have been given to parts of this area, including Red Hills, Lime Hills, and Southern Pine Hills. Many of these have validity based on geology or the distributions of some plants or animals, but there seems to be little distinction among them with regard to the distributions of ferns. With the ferns, it seems most appropriate to divide all of the Coastal Plain south of the Black Belt, except for a narrow coastal strip, into these two regions. In general, the landscape of the Middle Hills is higher and more rugged than that of the Lower Hills. Limestone is more common in the Lower Hills than in the Middle Hills, and limestone ravines and sinkholes are found in a number of places in the Lower Hills. Swamps and other wetlands are common in both regions, particularly in the Lower Hills.

Most of the ferns of these two regions are the wetland species found along stream banks and the margins of swamps. These include the cinnamon fern (*Osmunda cinnamomea*), the royal fern (*O. regalis*), the net-vein chain fern (*Woodwardia areolata*), and the lady fern (*Athyrium filix-femina*). The lady fern tends to be much larger here than in the highland provinces, with broad leaves that are often almost 3-pinnate. The widespread maiden fern (*Thelypteris kunthii*) is another wetland fern that is common in the Coastal Plain. It grows in a variety of habitats, but it is most abundant near limestone. The ebony spleenwort (*Asplenium platyneuron*) is common in drier woodlands here, as it is in the rest of Alabama. It too grows to a much larger size in the Coastal Plain than it does elsewhere. In both regions, in places where the dominant rock type is limestone, the streams have often carved narrow ravines with steep walls where the southern maidenhair fern (*Adiantum capillus-veneris*) may often be found. The Florida wood fern (*Dryopteris ludoviciana*), though not common, is found in the Lower Hills, usually in the vicinity of limestone.

Two of the most common ferns in the Coastal Plain are rarely seen because they are tiny and they grow most commonly in places where one does not expect to find ferns, grassy lawns. These are the bulbous adder's-tongue (*Ophioglossum crotalophoroides*) and the winter grape fern (*Botrychium lunarioides*). Both of these were once thought to be quite rare, but they were just overlooked. They are most commonly collected in cemeteries of rural churches, but they have also been found in residential lawns and at the margins of pastures. These plants are so tiny that mowing does not usually cut them, but this makes them very hard to see.

Many of the hills in the Middle Hills consist of steep, north-facing escarpments. These include the Red Hills, the Lime Hills, and others, with the Red Hills in western Alabama being the best known and most rugged of them. These lines of hills provide, where the forests have not been cut and replaced with pine plantations, habitats for many fern species. These very occasionally include ferns of more northern affinities like the American maidenhair fern (*Adiantum pedatum*).

The bog clubmosses—the foxtail clubmoss (*Lycopodium alopecuroides*), the tight-leaf clubmoss (*L. appressum*), the feather-stem clubmoss (*L. prostratum*), and their hybrids—are commonly found in the Lower Hills growing in open, often disturbed wet areas and in roadside ditches. As the land of the Coastal Plain becomes lower and lower to the south, these wetland habitats become more frequent, and so do the bog clubmosses. Their distant relative, the staghorn clubmoss (*Lycopodium cernuum*), is found in the same types of habitats, but it is much less common and is mostly confined to the southern portions of the Lower Hills.

The last part of the Coastal Plain consists of a narrow strip of land along the coast of the Gulf of Mexico, plus Dauphin Island and several smaller Gulf islands. These areas are underlain by sand that has not yet begun to harden into rocks, so we call the region the Coastal Sands. The bog club-mosses are common in ditches and other wet areas away from the influence of salt spray. The nearly horizontal limbs of the live oak trees that are common here are often covered profusely by the resurrection fern (*Polypodium polypodioides*), which is probably the most common fern in the region.

Counties of Alabama

3

Keys to the Identification of Alabama Ferns and Fern Allies

KEY TO GENERA

1a Plant without stems, leaves, or roots; plant filamentous, ribbonlike, or like an irregularly shaped leaf; mostly growing in crevices of acidic rocks. Go to **2**.
1b Plant having stems or stemlike parts and usually having leaves and roots; plant not filamentous, ribbonlike, or resembling a liverwort; habitats various. Go to **4**.

2a Plant leaflike with many lobes and an irregular outline. *Vittaria*
2b Plant filamentous or ribbonlike, branched but not lobed. Go to **3**.

3a Plant filamentous, profusely branched into a tangled mass. *Trichomanes*
3b Plant ribbonlike, growing flat on the ground. *Hymenophyllum*

4a Leaves absent, stems naked except for veinless scales; sporangia 3-lobed. *Psilotum*
4b Leaves present, having at least one vein each; sporangia not lobed. Go to **5**.

5a Plant floating on water with roots dangling or plants stranded at edge of water, but not rooted in soil. Go to **6**.
5b Plant rooting in soil, even if growing in water, or plants growing on trees or rocks. Go to **7**.

6a Leaves minute, much less than 5 mm broad, overlapping, dark green to red-brown in color. *Azolla*

6b Leaves distinct, 5 mm or more broad, rounded, or oval, usually not overlapping, bright green or occasionally reddish olive in color. *Salvinia*

7a Leaves stalkless, blades with only a single vein, usually less than 2 cm long, or, if longer, narrow and grasslike. Go to **6.**

7b Leaves with stalks, usually with blades that have several to many veins but occasionally consisting of bladeless stalks, usually more than 2 cm long and generally broad. Go to **11.**

8a Stems hollow and ridged; nodes conspicuous and jointlike; leaves tiny, toothlike, with many leaves encircling each node; sporangia borne beneath umbrella-like appendages arranged in conelike strobili terminating the erect stems. *Equisetum*

8b Stems solid or spongy, not hollow, lacking ridges; nodes neither conspicuous nor jointlike; leaves conspicuous, one or two at each node; sporangia borne at the bases of leaves that may or may not be arranged in strobili. Go to **9.**

9a Stems short and thick, entirely underground; leaves greater than 2 cm long, crowded at the stem tip; plants resembling tufts of grass. *Isoëtes*

9b Stems thin and elongated, at least some appearing above or on the surface of the ground; leaves less than 2 cm long, occurring along the lengths of the visible stems; plants resembling large mosses or tiny trees. Go to **10.**

10a Sporangia borne in conelike strobili that are 4-sided in cross section or flattened; spores of two distinct sizes. *Selaginella*

10b Sporangia borne either in strobili that are round in cross section or borne singly at the bases of stem leaves; spores all of one size. *Lycopodium*

11a Leaves completely lacking blades, consisting of slender green leaf stalks only. *Pilularia*

11b Leaf blades present. Go to **12.**

12a Leaves compound with 4 leaflets, all of which appear to be attached to the tip of the thin leaf stalk, resembling 4-leaved clovers; sporangia, when present, borne inside hard pill-like enclosures. *Marsilea*

12b Leaves either simple or compound, if compound then with leaflets attached in two rows along a rachis and never more than two leaflets appearing to be attached at the same point of the rachis; sporangia borne on the surfaces of leaves or on branches of leaves. Go to **13**.

13a Leaves compound with highly elongated rachises and widely separated pinnae, vinelike and twining, usually climbing on shrubs, trees, and fences. *Lygodium*
13b Leaves simple or compound, if compound, usually with short rachises and closely spaced pinnae, not vinelike, not climbing on other plants or objects. Go to **14**.

14a Sporangia 1 mm or more in diameter, borne on specialized branches arising from the leaf stalk beneath the blade; plant usually producing only 1 or 2, sometimes 3, leaves per growing season. Go to **15**.
14b Sporangia less than 1 mm in diameter, borne on the leaf blade or segments of the blade, not on a branch of the leaf stalk; plant usually producing many leaves per growing season. Go to **16**.

15a Blades compound or deeply lobed, blades triangular, fernlike; spore-bearing segment branched, resembling a tiny bunch of grapes. *Botrychium*
15b Blades simple, blades ovate to spearhead-shaped, spoonlike; spore-bearing segment not branched, resembling the tail of a rattlesnake. *Ophioglossum*

16a Leaf blades only one cell thick between veins, nearly transparent. Go to **17**.
16b Leaf blades several to many cells thick between veins, translucent to opaque. Go to **18**.

17a Stems short, bearing only 4 tiny leaves; leaves less than 1 cm long, bearing hairs with starlike branches. *Hymenophyllum*
17b Stems long-creeping, bearing many leaves; leaves usually more than 1 cm long, hairless or with unbranched hairs. *Trichomanes*

18a Leaves repeatedly forking into approximately equal segments, forks often with hairy dormant buds. *Dicranopteris*
18b Leaf blades simple, lobed, or pinnately compound, not forking, without buds. Go to **19**.

19a Vegetative and spore-bearing leaves or segments of leaves differing strongly, the spore-bearing leaflets lacking blade tissue and the sporangia borne on naked veins; roots black, tough, and wiry, forming a dense, tangled mass surrounding the rhizome. *Osmunda*

19b Vegetative and spore-bearing leaves or segments of leaves dissimilar or alike, the spore-bearing leaflets with at least some blade tissue, although this may be reduced or rolled up and not immediately obvious; roots brown to white, firm but not particularly tough, not forming a dense mass around the rhizome. Go to **20**.

20a Sori elongate, arranged in chainlike rows close to and parallel to midveins. *Woodwardia*

20b Sori of various shapes, if linear or elongate then borne along margins or side by side and not parallel to midveins. Go to **21**.

21a Leaves simple and unlobed except for basal ears. Go to **22**.

21b Leaves either compound or deeply lobed or both. Go to **23**.

22a Leaf tip long, tapering, and very narrow, tip often rooting; veins connected into a netlike pattern throughout the blade; sori curved, less than 5 mm long, scattered over the leaf surface. *Asplenium* (in part)

22b Leaf tip abruptly pointed, not rooting; veins not connected or only a very few connected, not forming a netlike pattern; sori straight, up to several cm long, borne singly or in pairs along veins and parallel to each other. *Phyllitis*

23a Vegetative and spore-bearing leaves strongly dissimilar, the vegetative blades deeply lobed, occasionally compound at the very base, spore-bearing blades 2-pinnate with rolled up beadlike leaflets; sori hidden inside the rolled up leaflets. *Onoclea*

23b Vegetative and spore-bearing leaves similar in appearance or only slightly dissimilar, variously cut or lobed; spore-bearing leaves or leaflets flat or essentially so with margins that are at most recurved or rolled under; sori visible, borne on the back surfaces or margins of leaves or leaflets. Go to **24**.

24a Sori located along margins of leaf segments and at least partially covered by recurved or rolled under leaf margins. Go to **25**.

24b Sori positioned variously, if at the margins, the leaf margins essentially flat and not covering any part of the sori. Go to **31**.

25a Leaves broadly triangular; rhizome deeply buried, widely creeping. Go to **26**.
25b Leaves of various shapes, but not broadly triangular; rhizome growing on ground surface, erect or short-creeping. Go to **27**.

26a Rachis and leaf stalk covered with stiff prickly hairs; sori, if present, distinct and not continuous along margin of leaflets. *Hypolepis*
26b Rachis hairless, leaf stalk hairless or at most with a few fine hairs at base when young; sori, if present, continuous along margins of leaflets. *Pteridium*

27a Leaflets diamond or fan-shaped, without midveins; sori discrete, obviously separated, on reflexed marginal lobes of leaflets that almost fully cover the sporangia. *Adiantum*
27b Leaflets round, oblong, or linear, with well-developed midveins; sori crowded into continuous bands along leaflet margins that curve under only partially and that only partially cover the sporangia. Go to **28**.

28a Largest leaflets about 1 cm long or less. Go to **29**.
28b Largest leaflets much greater than 1 cm long. Go to **30**.

29a Blades 1-pinnate with leaflets unlobed to deeply lobed; underside of leaf covered with fringed or star-shaped scales; leaf surface waxy, especially underneath. *Notholaena*
29b Blades 2- to 5-pinnate, at least toward the base; underside of leaf without fringed or star-shaped scales; leaf surface not waxy. *Cheilanthes*

30a Rachis and leaf stalk dark brown to black; leaflets usually less than 4 cm long. *Pellaea*
30b Rachis and leaf stalk green to yellowish; leaflets often over 4 cm long. *Pteris*

31a Sori located along margins of leaflets within cuplike indusia, less than 0.5 mm in diameter, black; leaf blades and rachises bearing gland-tipped whitish hairs; leaves mostly 2-pinnate with lobed segments and pale green, with a noticeable haylike fragrance when crushed; rhizome hairy. *Dennstaedtia*

31b Sori located elsewhere on the leaf blade than the margins, or if at the margins then lacking indusia or with kidney-shaped indusia, more than 0.5 mm (usually 1 mm or more) in diameter, usually brown; leaf blades hairless or with various types of hairs; leaves lobed to compound to various degrees, pale green to dark green, usually with little or no odor when crushed; rhizome often scaly. Go to **32**.

32a Sori round, lacking indusia, 2 or more mm in diameter. Go to **33**.
32b Sori of various shapes, if round then either with indusia or 1.5 mm or less in diameter. Go to **34**.

33a Blade veins connected into a netlike pattern; rhizome with gold-colored scales. *Phlebodium*
33b Blade veins not connected, not netlike; rhizome with brown or tan scales. *Polypodium*

34a Sori round or nearly so. Go to **35**.
34b Sori straight to crescent-shaped. Go to **42**.

35a Indusia not present. *Thelypteris* (in part)
35b Indusia present, at least in young sori. Go to **36**.

36a Indusium attached around the entire perimeter of the sorus, at maturity splitting into a number of flaps surrounding the sorus, creating a star-like pattern. *Woodsia*
36b Indusium attached on one side or in the center of the sorus, umbrella-like, kidney-shaped, or hoodlike. Go to **37**.

37a Indusium umbrella-like, attached at the center of the sorus. Go to **38**.
37b Indusium kidney-shaped or hoodlike, attached at or near one side of the sorus. Go to **40**.

38a Veins connected in a netlike pattern; sori scattered on surfaces of leaflets. *Cyrtomium*
38b Veins free, not netlike; sori in rows on leaflet surfaces. Go to **39**.

39a Leaves thick, leathery; leaflet margins with small stiff bristles; rhizome-lacking stolons. *Polystichum*
39b Leaves thin, papery; leaflet margins lacking bristles; rhizome-bearing stolons. *Nephrolepis*

40a Indusium hoodlike, attached along one side of the sorus and arching over it. *Cystopteris*
40b Indusium kidney-shaped, attached at a point on one side of the sorus and spreading over it. Go to **41**.

41a Leaf blades thin-textured, with transparent, needlelike hairs; leaf stalks with a few small scales or none; rhizome long, creeping, often with well-spaced leaves, slender, often less than 1 cm in diameter. *Thelypteris*
41b Leaf blades thick-textured, hairless; leaf stalks distinctly scaly, especially at base; rhizome short, creeping or ascending, thick, with leaves clustered at the tip. *Dryopteris*

42a Sori curved, bordering veins only along one side; leaf blades narrow, usually less than 10 cm wide and evergreen; leaf stalks wiry and usually dark brown or black, at least near base. *Asplenium* (in part)
42b Sori straight or curved, usually partially covering veins; leaf blades usually more than 10 cm wide, dying back in winter; leaf stalks stout, pale green or straw-colored throughout, occasionally red. Go to **43**.

43a Leaves 1-pinnate with unlobed leaflets, or 2- or more pinnate. *Athyrium* (in part)
43b Leaves 1-pinnate with lobed leaflets. Go to **44**.

44a Leaves narrowed at base, blade mostly oblong; base of leaf stalk distinctly swollen and toothed. *Athyrium* (in part)
44b Leaves widest at base, blade mostly ovate; base of leaf stalk not distinctly swollen or toothed. *Deparia*

KEY TO SPECIES

Adiantum (Maidenhair Ferns)

1a Leaf stalk forked near top, producing twin main rachises curving away

from each other; branches of each main rachis all arising from the same side of main rachis. *A. pedatum* (**American maidenhair fern**)
1b Leaf stalk not forked, leaf with a single main rachis; branches of main rachis arising from both sides of main rachis. Go to **2**.

2a Leaf stalk and rachis hairless; leaflets fan-shaped, deeply notched. *A. capillus-veneris* (**southern maidenhair fern**)
2b Leaf stalk and rachis with short, stiff hairs; leaflets diamond-shaped, without notches. *A. hispidulum* (**rough maidenhair fern**)

Asplenium (Spleenworts)
1a Leaves simple and unlobed except for basal ears; leaf often rooting at tip. *A. rhizophyllum* (**walking fern**)
1b Leaves lobed or compound; leaf usually not rooting at tip. Go to **2**.

2a Blade lobed but not compound, even at base. *A. pinnatifidum* (**lobed spleenwort**)
2b Blade compound, at least at base. Go to **3**.

3a Leaf blades 2- to 4-pinnate or leaflets deeply lobed, at least lower ones. Go to **4**.
3b Leaf blades 1-pinnate at most and leaflets not lobed except for basal ears. Go to **6**.

4a Blades with 2–5 pairs of leaflets; leaf stalks entirely green; plants on calcareous rock, usually limestone. *A. ruta-muraria* (**wall-rue spleenwort**)
4b Blades usually with more than 5 pairs of leaflets; leaf stalks brown, at least at base; plants growing in soil or on acidic rock, usually sandstone. Go to **5**.

5a Leaf stalk dark brown only at base, rachis green; leaves 2-pinnate throughout most of blade. *A. montanum* (**mountain spleenwort**)
5b Leaf stalk and lower portion of rachis dark brown; leaves 2-pinnate only at base, upper leaflets merely lobed. *A. bradleyi* (**cliff spleenwort**)

6a Blade compound for all or nearly all of its length. Go to **7**.
6b Blade compound only at base, the upper third or more only lobed. Go to **12**.

7a Leaflets strongly asymmetrical, with main veins running along lower edges of leaflets; sori few, usually only 1 per leaflet, located on only one side of main vein. *A. monanthes* (one-sorus spleenwort)

7b Leaflets symmetrical or nearly so, main veins running along or near the middle of leaflet; sori numerous, more than 4 per leaflet, located on both sides of the main vein. Go to **8**.

8a Leaflets oval to bluntly oblong, almost as wide as long, usually less than 9 mm long, unlobed or with very low, indistinct ears at base. *A. trichomanes* (maidenhair spleenwort)

8b Leaflets oblong or spearhead-shaped, much longer than wide, usually more than 9 mm long, usually lobed or with distinct ears at base, tapering to a narrow point if unlobed and earless. Go to **9**.

9a Lower leaflets tapering to a narrow point, broadest near the base; blades broad, spearhead-shaped to nearly triangular; leaf stalks green to light gray-brown. *A. abscissum* (cut spleenwort)

9b Lower leaflets with blunt tips, broadest near the middle; blades narrow, oblong to linear in shape; leaf stalks dark brown. Go to **10**.

10a Leaflets mostly opposite, arranged in pairs along the rachis. *A. resiliens* (black-stemmed spleenwort)

10b Leaflets mostly alternate, arranged singly along the rachis. Go to **11**.

11a Most leaflets with short stalks; leaflets notched or lobed, not overlapping rachis. *A. bradleyi* (cliff spleenwort)

11b All leaflets completely stalkless; most leaflets with basal ears that often overlap rachis. *A. platyneuron* (ebony spleenwort)

12a Lowermost leaflets deeply lobed. *A.* × *trudellii* (Trudell's spleenwort)

12b Lowermost leaflets not lobed, toothed at most. Go to **13**.

13a Rachis green throughout or brown only to the first or second pair of leaflets; leaflets rounded. *A.* × *gravesii* (Graves's spleenwort)

13b Rachis brown for a third or more of its length; leaflets oblong to narrowly triangular. Go to **14**.

14a Blade compound only at its base, with only one or two pairs of true leaflets; blade tip very narrow, long-tapering. *A. tutwilerae* (Tutwiler's spleenwort)

14b Blade compound for about half of its length or more, with many pairs of true leaflets; blade tip narrow, but ending abruptly. *A.* × *boydstoniae* (Boydston's spleenwort)

Athyrium (Lady Ferns)

1a Leaves 2- to 3-pinnate; sori crescent-shaped, usually 1 mm or less long. *A. filix-femina* (lady fern)

1b Leaves 1-pinnate with simple or lobed leaflets; sori curved but almost straight, usually 1.5 mm or more long. Go to **2**.

2a Leaflets not lobed; rachis hairless. *A. pycnocarpon* (glade fern)

2b Leaflets deeply lobed; rachis with hairs. *A. thelypterioides* (silvery glade fern)

Azolla (Mosquito Ferns)

A single species *A. caroliniana* (eastern mosquito fern)

Botrychium (Grape Ferns)

1a Leaf blades thin, almost filmy, translucent; sporangia-bearing branch arising from top of long leaf stalk, well above the ground; leaf sheaths open; leaves dying back in winter. *B. virginianum* (rattlesnake fern)

1b Leaf blades thick, papery or leathery, opaque or nearly so; sporangia-bearing branch arising from base of leaf stalk, at or below the ground; leaf sheaths closed; leaves persisting through the winter. Go to **2**.

2a Leaves short-stalked, blades often prostrate on ground; plants usually with 2 or more leaves; leaflets fan-shaped and lacking central veins; spore-bearing branch maturing in late winter or early spring; new leaves appear in late fall and die before summer; roots yellowish and smooth. *B. lunarioides* (winter grape fern)

2b Leaves long-stalked, blades held well above ground; plants usually with 1 or 2 leaves; leaflets usually longer than wide, with a weak to strong central vein; spore-bearing branch maturing in summer or fall; new leaves appear in spring or summer and persist until the following spring; roots brownish and ribbed. Go to **3**.

3a Leaflets only slightly longer than broad, tips rounded, central veins weak and obscure; plants often producing 2 leaves per year. *B. jenmanii* (**Alabama grape fern**)

3b Leaflets much longer than broad, tips angular, central veins distinct; plants normally producing 1 leaf per year. Go to **4**.

4a Leaves 2-pinnate at most, texture thin and papery; leaflets sparse, oblong with blunt tips; leaf margins finely toothed. *B. biternatum* (**sparse-lobed grape fern**)

4b Leaves usually 3-pinnate or more, texture somewhat thick, often leathery; leaflets numerous and diamond-shaped or irregularly angular with sharp tips; leaf margins smooth to deeply cut. *B. dissectum* (**cutleaf grape fern**)

Cheilanthes (Lip Ferns)

1a Leaves hairless or essentially so, 2-pinnate with leaflets that are undivided or lobed only at base. *C. alabamensis* (**Alabama lip fern**)

1b Leaves hairy, 2-pinnate with deeply lobed leaflets or 3-pinnate. Go to **2**.

2a Lobes of leaflets oblong, broad at base; leaflets and rachis moderately hairy, undersurfaces of leaflets and rachis clearly visible; hairs of rachis with several noticeable dark bands along their lengths. *C. lanosa* (**hairy lip fern**)

2b Lobes of leaflets rounded, narrowed at base, or blade 3-pinnate; leaflets and rachis densely woolly, undersurfaces of leaflets and rachis sometimes obscured by hairs; hairs of rachis without noticeable dark bands along their length. *C. tomentosa* (**woolly lip fern**)

Cyrtomium (Net-Veined Holly Ferns)

1a Leaflets leathery, with shiny, dark-green lower surfaces; leaves usually with 4–10 pairs of leaflets; margins wavy or coarsely toothed. *C. falcatum* (**Japanese holly fern**)

1b Leaflets papery, with dull, light-green lower surfaces; leaves usually with 10–25 pairs of leaflets; margins with small rounded teeth. *C. fortunei* (**Fortune's holly fern**)

Cystopteris (Bladder Ferns)

1a Rhizome elongated with leaves spaced apart, tip protruding past leaves, usually by more than 1 cm; leaf blades widest near the middle, 2-pinnate with deeply lobed leaflets to 3-pinnate near middle of blade. *C. protrusa* (**lowland brittle fern**)

1b Rhizome short with leaves clustered at tip; leaf blades widest at or near base, 2-pinnate with deeply lobed leaflets at most. Go to **2**.

2a Leaf blades narrowly triangular with elongated tips, 3 or more times as long as broad, 2–3 times longer than leaf stalks; smallest veins all ending in minute notches at leaflet margins. *C. bulbifera* (**bulblet bladder fern**)
2b Leaf blades spearhead-shaped, tips not elongated, about 2 times longer than broad, about the same length as leaf stalks; smallest veins ending in either minute notches or short teeth at leaflet margins. *C. tennesseensis* (**Tennessee bladder fern**)

Dennstaedtia (Cuplet Ferns)
A single species *D. punctilobula* (hay-scented fern)

Deparia (False Spleenworts)
A single species *D. petersenii* (Japanese false spleenwort)

Dicranopteris (Forking Ferns)
A single species *D. flexuosa* (drooping forked fern)

Dryopteris (Wood Ferns)
1a Leaf blades 2-pinnate to 3-pinnate. Go to **2**.
1b Leaf blades 1-pinnate with deeply lobed leaflets. Go to **3**.

2a Teeth on blade margins with long bristlelike tips; spores full, fertile. *D. intermedia* (**evergreen wood fern**)
2b Teeth on blade margins with short blunt tips; spores shrunken, infertile. *D. intermedia* × *marginalis* (**hybrid wood fern**)

3a Sori borne at the margins of the leaflets, no blade tissue visible on underside of blade between sori and margins; indusia thick and swollen; leaves gray-green and leathery; plants growing on dry rocks, cliffs, and ledges. *D. marginalis* (**marginal wood fern**)
3b Sori borne between margins and midribs of leaflet lobes, at least some blade tissue visible between sori and margins; indusia thin and flat; leaves green and papery; plants growing in moist to swampy soil. Go to **4**.

4a Leaves bearing sori only on upper half of blade; spore-bearing leaflets with narrower lobes than vegetative ones. Go to **5**.

4b Leaves bearing sori over most or all of blade; spore-bearing and vegetative leaflets similar. Go to **6**.

5a Spore-bearing leaflets much narrower than vegetative leaflets and obviously more widely spaced; spores full, fertile. *D. ludoviciana* (**Florida wood fern**)
5b Spore-bearing leaflets only slightly narrower than vegetative leaflets and spaced about the same; spores shrunken, infertile. *D.* × *australis* (**southern wood fern**)

6a Blade spearhead-shaped, tapering gradually at the tip and bluntly at base; sori borne about halfway between midribs and margins of leaflet lobes; scales at the base of leaf stalk medium to dark brown, with a narrow black central band. *D. celsa* (**log fern**)
6b Blade oblong to ovate, tapering sharply at tip and slightly or not at all at base; sori closer to midribs than to margins of leaflet lobes; scales at the base of leaf stalk dark brown, nearly black, with a narrow pale margin. *D. goldiana* (**Goldie's wood fern**)

Equisetum (Horsetails and Scouring-Rushes)

1a Vegetative and spore-bearing stems dissimilar, less than 50 cm tall; vegetative stems green and bushy with many thin branches circling each node; spore-bearing stems brownish and unbranched; strobili with rounded tips, maturing early spring before vegetative stems appear; aerial stems flexible, all deciduous, spore-bearing stems disappearing soon after spores are shed, vegetative stems persisting until the end of the growing season. *E. arvense* (**field horsetail**)
1b Stems all alike, 100 cm or more tall; green and not branched, occasionally with a very few thin branches at injury sites; strobili with pointed tips, maturing late spring through summer; aerial stems rigid, mostly evergreen. Go to **2**.

2a Stems entirely evergreen, persisting for two years, surfaces rough and gritty like fine sandpaper; spores green and spherical. *E. hyemale* (**tall scouring-rush**)
2b Stems partially deciduous, the upper portions dying back in winter, the lower portions persistent until spring, surface roughness very fine and barely detectable; spores white and shrunken. *E.* × *ferrissii* (**Ferriss's scouring-rush**)

Hymenophyllum (Filmy Ferns)

A single species *H. tayloriae* (Taylor's filmy fern)

Hypolepis (Bramble Ferns)

A single species *H. tenuifolia* (spineless bramble fern)

Isoëtes (Quillworts)

1a Plants aquatic, submerged or emergent, growing in persistently wet soils in or near streams, ponds, and swamps, typically not associated with rock outcrops. Go to **2**.

1b Plants growing in thin clay soils of short-lived seasonal pools and seeps of rock outcrops or away from water in prairielike habitats. Go to **5**.

2a Less than one-half of sporangium covered by a velum, a thin membranous flap of tissue. Go to **3**.

2b More than one-half of sporangium covered by a velum. Go to **4**.

3a Surfaces of megaspores mostly with networks of unbroken, honeycomblike ridges; sporangium walls whitish, uniform in color; plants mostly of the highland provinces. *I. engelmannii* (**Engelmann's quillwort**)

3b Surfaces of megaspores with irregular, broken ridges; sporangium walls often with brown streaks; plants mostly of the Coastal Plain. *I. louisianensis* (**Louisiana quillwort**)

4a Leaves dark green, limp and drooping, 25–60 cm long; velum covering more than three-fourths of the sporangium; sporangium walls white, often with sparse brown streaks; surfaces of megaspores with low, broad bumps and ridges. *I. flaccida* (**Florida quillwort**)

4b Leaves yellow-green and more or less erect, 15–40 cm long; velum covering less than three-fourths of the sporangium; sporangium walls uniform white, without streaks; surfaces of megaspores with high ridges in a ragged netlike pattern. *I. valida* (**strong quillwort**)

5a Plants growing on granite, rarely sandstone, outcrops; sporangium wall with a uniform brown color, less than 6 mm long. *I. piedmontana* (**Piedmont quillwort**)

5b Plants growing on limestone outcrops or in prairielike habitats; sporangium wall mottled with brown, usually more than 6 mm long. Go to **6**.

6a Leaves usually less than 1 mm wide at the middle, with pale to brown bases; surfaces of megaspores with tiny wartlike bumps; plants of limestone outcrops. *I. butleri* (limestone quillwort)

6b Leaves usually more than 1 mm wide at the middle, with dark brown to shiny black bases; plants of prairielike habitats. *I. melanopoda* (**black-foot quillwort**)

Lycopodium (Clubmosses)

1a Sporangia borne at the bases of leaves that are similar to vegetative leaves and borne in zones along the length of the stems. Go to **2**.

1b Sporangia borne in conelike strobili that appear at the tips of branches or on stalks. Go to **4**.

2a Vegetative leaves widest above middle, margins toothed toward the tips; sporangia-bearing leaves distinctly shorter than vegetative leaves; plants usually growing in soil in rich rocky woods or under damp rock ledges; stomata, tiny pores, present on lower leaf surfaces and absent on the upper surfaces. *L. lucidulum* (**shining clubmoss**)

2b Vegetative leaves widest at or below middle, margins toothless or nearly so; sporangia-bearing leaves the same size as vegetative leaves or only slightly shorter; plants growing on dry acidic rocks; stomata present on both leaf surfaces. Go to **3**.

3a Vegetative leaves widest near the middle, stomata distinctly less abundant on the upper surfaces than the lower; spore-bearing leaves slightly shorter than vegetative leaves, fertile zones easily seen. *L. × bartleyi* (**Bartley's clubmoss**)

3b Vegetative leaves widest below middle, stomata about as abundant on the upper surface as the lower; all leaves nearly the same length, fertile zones obscure. *L. porophilum* (**rock clubmoss**)

4a Main stems with no erect branches except unbranched strobili-bearing stalks, which are present only in late summer and autumn; plants appearing like large mosses. Go to **5**.

4b Main stems bearing erect vegetative branches that are profusely further branched and are present throughout the growing season; plants appearing like tiny trees. Go to **11**.

5a Vegetative stems prostrate, growing flat on the ground and rooted throughout. Go to **6**.
5b Vegetative stems arching, at least weakly so, with zones that lack roots. Go to **9**.

6a Vegetative leaves of two distinct lengths, 1.3–2.1 mm wide, toothless; strobili compact and firm; tips of sporangia-bearing leaves barely extending beyond the sporangia. *L. carolinianum* (**slender clubmoss**)
6b Vegetative leaves all about the same length, 0.5–1.2 mm wide, often with fine hairlike teeth; strobili more or less diffuse and soft; tips of sporangia-bearing leaves extending far beyond the sporangia. Go to **7**.

7a Spore-bearing leaves ascending vertically, flattened against the stem or each other; vegetative leaves of main stem spreading in all directions except toward the ground. *L. appressum* (**tight-leaf clubmoss**)
7b Spore-bearing leaves spreading away from the stem; vegetative leaves of the main stem tending to spread to the sides of the stem, creating a two-rowed, featherlike appearance. Go to **8**.

8a Strobili bushy, spore-bearing leaves spreading nearly horizontally from the stem; two-rowed appearance of leaves on main stems readily apparent. *L. prostratum* (**feather-stem clubmoss**)
8b Strobili slim, spore-bearing leaves spreading upward at a sharp angle to the stem; two-rowed appearance of the leaves on the main stem obscure and may be evident only by a tendency for the leaves to lean one way or the other. *L.* × *brucei* (**Bruce's clubmoss**)

9a Strobili slim, spore-bearing leaves spreading at an acute angle to the stem. *L.* × *copelandii* (**Copeland's clubmoss**)
9b Strobili bushy, spore-bearing leaves spreading nearly horizontally from the stem. Go to **10**.

10a Main stems arching strongly, rising several cm above the ground; vegetative leaves of main stem spreading in all directions from the stem. *L. alopecuroides* (**foxtail clubmoss**)
10b Main stems arching weakly, rising barely above the ground; vegetative leaves of main stems weakly spreading into 2 rows, a trait that may be evident only by a tendency for the leaves to lean one way or the other. *L. alopecuroides* × *prostratum* (**hybrid clubmoss**)

11a Main stems slightly arching, with rootless zones; lateral branches of erect stems drooping at the tips; strobili borne at the tips of drooping lateral branches. *L. cernuum* (**staghorn clubmoss**)
11b Main stems buried or prostrate on the ground and rooted throughout; lateral branches of erect stems ascending or held nearly horizontally; strobili borne erect in clusters at the tops of erect stems or on long stalks. Go to **12**.

12a Leaves dark green, narrow and needlelike, completely separated, borne in 6 rows on the stem; branches bushy; strobili stalkless, borne in clusters at the tops of erect stems. *L. obscurum* (**ground-pine**)
12b Leaves pale green or bluish, broad at base, overlapping, borne in 4 distinct rows; branches flattened; strobili borne on long stalks. Go to **13**.

13a Main stems growing on or very near the surface of the ground, usually covered only by leaf litter; lateral branches of erect stems all fan-shaped and held nearly horizontally; leaves on bottoms of branches much smaller than those on top. *L. digitatum* (**running-cedar**)
13b Main stems buried several cm deep; some lateral branches of erect stems brushlike and ascending, at least toward the upper part of the erect stem; leaves on bottoms of branches the same size as those on top. *L. tristachyum* (**ground-cedar**)

Lygodium (Climbing Ferns)
1a Leaflets palmately lobed, fanlike or like a hand with many fingers; blade tissue absent or nearly so on spore-bearing lobes. *L. palmatum* (**American climbing fern**)
1b Leaflets pinnately compound, fernlike; blade tissue present on spore-bearing lobes. *L. japonicum* (**Japanese climbing fern**)

Marsilea (Water-Clovers)
1a Leaflets two-toned green, lighter at base; spore-bearing capsules, when present, at base of plant, without teeth. *M. mutica* (**Australian water-clover**)
1b Leaflets evenly green; spore-bearing capsules, when present, with teeth on top. Go to **2**.

2a Leaflets hairless or with a few scattered hairs; margins with shallow lobes; roots present throughout the lengths of rhizomes. *M. minuta* (**dwarf water-clover**)

2b Leaflets with conspicuous white hairs; margins with rounded teeth or smooth; roots present on rhizomes only at nodes. *M. macropoda* (**big-foot water-clover**)

Nephrolepis (Sword Ferns)
A single species *N. cordifolia* (**tuber sword fern**)

Notholaena (Cloak Ferns)
A single species *N. integerrima* (**southwestern cloak fern**)

Onoclea (Sensitive Ferns)
A single species *O. sensibilis* (**sensitive fern**)

Ophioglossum (Adder's-Tongues)
1a Underground stems globular and bulblike; leaf blades triangular to heart-shaped. *O. crotalophoroides* (**bulbous adder's-tongue**)
1b Underground stems cylindrical or tuberlike; leaf blades oval to elliptical. Go to **2**.

2a Leaf stalks short, blades and spore-bearing spikes appearing to rise from the ground, spore-bearing spikes more than 2 times as long as leaf stalks; underground stems thick and tuberlike, distinctly thicker than leaf stalks; roots thin, 1 mm or less wide. *O. nudicaule* (**least adder's-tongue**)
2b Leaf stalks long and well developed, blades and spore-bearing spikes held well above the ground, spore-bearing spikes less than 2 times as long as leaf stalks; underground stems thin, only slightly thicker than leaf stalks; roots thick, more than 2 mm wide. Go to **3**.

3a Tips of leaf blades ending abruptly in a slender point; veins netted and of two distinct sizes with large heavy veins enclosing more numerous light veins. *O. engelmannii* (**limestone adder's-tongue**)
3b Tips of leaf blades rounded or angular; veins netted, all more or less alike. Go to **4**.

4a Leaf blades oval to elliptical, broadest near the middle, tapering abruptly at base, rounded or bluntly angular at tip; roots tan to pale brown; plants occurring singly or rarely in pairs, not spreading. *O. pycnostichum* (**southeastern adder's-tongue**)

4b Leaf blades arrowhead-shaped, broadest near the base, blunt at the base, tapering toward angular tips; roots dark brown; plants spreading by root buds, forming thick tufts. *O. petiolatum* (**stalked adder's-tongue**)

Osmunda (Royal Ferns)

1a Vegetative leaves 2-pinnate; leaflets unlobed. *O. regalis* (**royal fern**)
1b Vegetative leaves 1-pinnate; leaflets deeply lobed. Go to 2.

2a Spore-bearing leaves usually completely lacking blade tissue, covered with long brown hairs; leaflets of vegetative leaves with well-separated lobes that have angular tips, with persistent tufts of brown hairs on the undersurfaces near the rachis. *O. cinnamomea* (**cinnamon fern**)
2b Spore-bearing leaves hairless or nearly so with vegetative leaflets having blade tissue above and below the bladeless spore-bearing leaflets, the spore-bearing leaflets near the middle of the leaf; vegetative leaflets with lobes that are close together, touching neighbors or nearly so, with rounded tips, mature leaflets hairless or nearly so. *O. claytoniana* (**interrupted fern**)

Pellaea (Cliff-Brake Ferns)

A single species *P. atropurpurea* (**purple cliff-brake**)

Phlebodium (Serpent Ferns)

A single species *P. aureum* (**gold-foot fern**)

Phyllitis (Hart's Tongue Ferns)

A single species *P. scolopendrium* (**American Hart's tongue fern**)

Pilularia (Pillworts)

A single species *P. americana* (**American pillwort**)

Polypodium (Polypody Ferns)

1a Lower leaf surfaces gray-green, with numerous dark scales; lobes of leaf blade with smooth margins. *P. polypodioides* (**resurrection fern**)
1b Lower leaf surfaces green, lacking scales; lobes of leaf blade with minutely toothed margins. *P. virginianum* (**rock cap fern**)

Polystichum (Sword Ferns)

1a Leaves 1-pinnate; spore-bearing leaflets occurring only at the leaf tip. *P. acrostichoides* (**Christmas fern**)

1b Leaves 2-pinnate; spore-bearing leaflets occurring throughout the blade. *P. polyblepharum* (**Japanese tassel fern**)

Psilotum (Whisk Plants)
A single species *P. nudum* (**whisk plant**)

Pteridium (Bracken Ferns)
A single species *P. aquilinum* (**bracken fern**)

Pteris (Brake Ferns)
1a Leaf stalk scaly; leaflets not lobed or compound. *P. vittata* (**ladder brake**)
1b Leaf stalk smooth; basal leaflets deeply lobed, occasionally compound. Go to **2**.

2a Rachis winged almost throughout; leaf stalk much shorter than blade. *P. multifida* (**spider brake**)
2b Rachis winged just below terminal leaflet only; leaf stalk longer than blade. *P. cretica* (**Cretan brake**)

Salvinia (Floating Ferns)
1a Floating leaves 1.5–3.0 cm long and often folded along midrib; hairs on upper surface of leaf with four spreading branches that are joined together at their tips, forming an eggbeater-like structure. *S. molesta* (**kariba-weed**)
1b Floating leaves 0.5–1.5 cm long and flat or concave; hairs on upper surface of leaf with four spreading branches that are not connected. *S. minima* (**water-spangles**)

Selaginella (Spikemoss)
1a Vegetative leaves needlelike, nearly round in cross section, all about the same size; leaves spirally arranged on all sides of the stem. Go to **2**.
1b Vegetative leaves broad, flat in cross section, of two distinct sizes, arranged in 4 rows on stem; leaves in 2 rows on top of the stem smaller than leaves in the 2 bottom rows and pressed flat against the stem, leaves in the 2 bottom rows spreading. Go to **3**.

2a Stems erect or ascending, rooted only at or near the base; plants forming tufts; megaspores with honeycombed surfaces. *S. arenicola* ssp. *riddellii* (**Riddell's spikemoss**)

2b Stems mostly creeping, often with ascending tips, rooted all along except at tips; plants forming mats; megaspores nearly smooth. *S. rupestris* (**rock spikemoss**)

3a Leaves bluish green; margins of lateral leaves smooth. *S. uncinata* (**blue spikemoss**)
3b Leaves yellowish green; margins of lateral leaves with fine teeth. Go to **4**.

4a Main stems buried with erect aerial stems that are repeatedly branched in a single plane; plant appearing fernlike. *S. braunii* (**Braun's spikemoss**)
4b Main stems creeping or weakly arching, on or above the ground surface, erect branches absent or very sparse; plant appearing mosslike. Go to **5**.

5a Stems all prostrate with only the tips turned upward; leaf margins without fringes. *S. apoda* (**meadow spikemoss**)
5b Stems weakly arching, usually with stiffly erect lateral branches; leaf margins with translucent fringes. *S. ludoviciana* (**gulf spikemoss**)

Thelypteris (**Maiden Ferns**)
1a Blades broadly triangular in outline, 1-pinnate with lobed leaflets or 2-pinnate with deeply lobed leaflets to 3-pinnate. Go to **2**.
1b Blades narrowly to broadly spearhead-shaped, lobed to 1-pinnate with lobed leaflets or 2-pinnate with unlobed leaflets. Go to **3**.

2a Blades 1-pinnate with lobed leaflets; most "leaflets" actually lobes, connected to others by wings along rachis. *T. hexagonoptera* (**broad beech fern**)
2b Blades 2-pinnate with lobed leaflets, occasionally 3-pinnate; rachis without wings. *T. torresiana* (**Mariana maiden fern**)

3a Sori elongate; indusia absent; sporangia minutely hairy; leaves 15 cm or less long. *T. pilosa* (**Alabama streak-sorus fern**)
3b Sori round or slightly oblong; indusia present, at least on young leaves; sporangia hairless; leaves of mature plants mostly greater than 15 cm long. Go to **4**.

4a Base of blade gradually long-tapering, lowest leaflets very much smaller than longest leaflets near the middle of the blade. *T. noveboracensis* (**New York fern**)

4b Base of blade blunt, lowest leaflets only slightly shorter than those above, if at all. Go to **5**.

5a Vegetative and spore-bearing leaves dissimilar, spore-bearing leaflets with strongly rolled-under margins; smallest veins of sterile leaflets mostly forking; leaves 1-pinnate with very deeply lobed leaflets to fully 2-pinnate. *T. palustris* (**marsh fern**)
5b Vegetative and spore-bearing leaves essentially alike or leaves all spore-bearing, margins of leaflets flat or only slightly curved under; smallest veins of leaflets rarely or never forked; leaves 1-pinnate with lobed leaflets. Go to **6**.

6a Basal veins of at least some adjacent leaflet lobes united into a single vein running to the leaf margin at the bottom of the notch between the two lobes. Go to **7**.
6b Basal veins of adjacent lobes unconnected, or converging only at the margin in the bottom of the notch but not united into a single vein. Go to **8**.

7a Veins united beneath all or nearly all notches of leaflets; leaf stalks usually purplish; lower surfaces of leaves with short hairs of uniform length. *T. dentata* (**downy maiden fern**)
7b Veins united only sporadically, many notches without joined veins; leaf stalks usually straw-colored to brown; lower surface of leaves with hairs of various lengths. *T. hispidula* (**variable maiden fern**)

8a Upper surfaces of leaflet veins with stout hairs; leaflets often with yellowish stalked glands; leaf blade spearhead-shaped to narrowly triangular; leaflets notched one-half to two-thirds of the way to the midrib. *T. kunthii* (**widespread maiden fern**)
8b Upper surfaces of leaflet veins hairless, or rarely with a few scattered hairs; leaflets lacking glands; leaf blade ovate to broadly spearhead-shaped; leaflets notched three-fourths or more of the way to the midrib. *T. ovata* (**ovate maiden fern**)

Trichomanes (Bristle Ferns)

1a Plant filamentous, lacking leaves, stems, and roots. *T. intricatum* (**weft fern**)
1b Plant with leaves, stems, and roots. Go to **2**.

2a Leaf blades undivided to very slightly lobed, usually less than 3 cm long; leaf margins with dark hairs. *T. petersii* (**Peters's filmy fern**)

2b Leaf blades deeply lobed to 2-pinnate, usually greater than 4 cm long; leaf margins hairless. *T. boschianum* (**Appalachian filmy fern**)

Vittaria (**Shoestring Ferns**)

A single species *V. appalachiana* (**Appalachian shoestring fern**)

Woodsia (**Cliff Ferns**)

A single species *W. obtusa* (**blunt-lobed cliff fern**)

Woodwardia (**Chain Ferns**)

1a Vegetative and spore-bearing leaves dissimilar, spore-bearing leaves 1-pinnate with narrow leaflets, vegetative leaves deeply lobed with broad lobes; veins joined and netlike throughout vegetative leaves. *W. areolata* (**net-vein chain fern**)

1b Vegetative and spore-bearing leaves alike, all 1-pinnate with deeply lobed leaflets; veins not joined except along midribs of leaflets. *W. virginica* (**Virginia chain fern**)

4

Alabama Ferns and Fern Allies

The following pages contain information about and illustrations of the ferns and fern allies known to grow outside of cultivation in Alabama.

The treatment of each plant begins with the common name and scientific name as accepted by the authors of this book. As mentioned earlier, a single species may have more than one scientific name validly associated with it. Which name is "correct" depends upon one's viewpoint with regard to which characteristics of plants should be used to separate one genus from another or one species from another. This book takes a traditional approach that may seem outdated to some readers, but it is one that will be familiar to the most readers.

Following the names is a short description of the plant. The description is sufficient to distinguish the plant from other Alabama ferns and fern allies and those that occur nearby, but it may not be detailed enough to make comparisons with plants from other regions.

Following the description of the plant is an account of the habitat type or habitat types in which the plant is known to occur in Alabama. In some cases in which the plant reaches an extreme limit of a broad range in Alabama, this may be different from the usual habitat in the main part of its range, and it will be mentioned.

The next section of the treatment of the plant is a detailed description of the range of the plant in Alabama. This is followed by a more general description of the range of the plant in the United States and then by a brief account of its occurrences elsewhere in the world, if any.

Next is a "Comments" section containing general information about the plant, such as unusual occurrences, history of knowledge of the plant in

Alabama, human uses, taxonomic notes, hybrid parents, and so forth. It also gives the meaning of the scientific name and tells how the common name came to be.

If there is more than one common name for the plant, the ones not given already are mentioned following the "Comments."

If the plant is known or has been recently known by more than one scientific name, the ones other than the one accepted by the authors are given here under the heading "Synonyms."

In most cases, the treatment of each plant includes three illustrations: a line drawing showing diagnostic features of the plant, a photograph of the plant in life, and a small map showing the county-by-county distribution of the plant in Alabama. Some plants that are especially rare and difficult to find may lack the photograph or the drawing.

Whisk Plant

Psilotum nudum (Linnaeus) Beauvois

DESCRIPTION Rhizome short-creeping; roots lacking, rhizome bearing only short rhizoids, absorptive functions performed by fungal hyphae. Stems erect, green, repeatedly forking equally. Leaves absent, stems bearing only minute veinless scales. Sporangia 3-lobed, borne in the angle between the stem and the scales.

HABITAT Found primarily on trees, stumps, and humus in swamps; rarely growing on the ground in mixed pine-hardwood forests or on shaded, protected masonry.

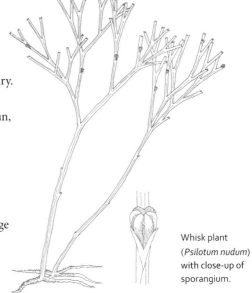

RANGE Known from Baldwin, Calhoun, and Lee Counties in Alabama. In the United States: frequent in peninsular Florida, rare northward to South Carolina and west to eastern Texas, in the Coastal Plain except for known occurrences in the Piedmont and Ridge and Valley regions of Alabama; also in southern Arizona. Occurs in the tropics throughout the world.

Whisk plant
(*Psilotum nudum*)
with close-up of
sporangium.

COMMENTS This distinctive plant was unknown from Alabama until 1986, when John D. Freeman found it in the Piedmont of Lee County, a few kilometers above the Fall Line (Freeman 1987). This is the first discovery of *Psilotum* from above the Fall Line anywhere in the United States.

While *Psilotum* is known to grow mostly on trees, stumps, rotting logs, and other organic substrates, in Lee County it grows on the ground with the rhizome in the soil beneath the leaf litter of a mixed pine and hardwood forest that was only a few decades old at the time of the discovery. As Freeman pointed out, this type of forest is extremely common throughout the Piedmont of Alabama, and *Psilotum* may be present in more places in the Piedmont.

Hayes Jackson discovered the Calhoun County population in 2008 growing along the north-facing wall of an old building in Anniston.

Wayne Barger found this plant growing on a palm tree in Baldwin County in early 2011.

For several decades there has been some disagreement among botanists about the nature of this plant. Some have maintained that *Psilotum* and its relatives are actually ferns and not fern allies and that the aerial stems of the plant are actually rachises and rachis branches of leaves. They make this argument based on the details of the anatomy of the stems. Not all botanists accept this view, and it is not accepted here.

The genus name *Psilotum* is derived from the fossil genus *Psilophyton*, which means "shining plant." The fossil was so named because it appeared as lustrous markings on the surface of the shale in which it was first found. The specific epithet *nudum* refers to the essentially naked stems.

The common name comes from the broomlike appearance of large plants of this species. Most references give the common name as whisk fern, but at least one gives it as whisk plant. Since this plant does not look at all like a fern, and since we do not accept the view that this plant really is a fern, the latter seems more appropriate.

OTHER COMMON NAMES Whisk fern

Above Left: Close-up showing three-lobed sporangia.

Above Right: Whisk plant growing directly from leaf litter of mixed pine-hardwood forest near Auburn, Lee County.

Shining Clubmoss
Lycopodium lucidulum Michaux

DESCRIPTION Stems short-creeping on soil surface with erect tips rising to 25 cm tall, forking as many as 3 times in the erect portion. Strobili absent, vegetative and fertile leaves grouped in zones along the stem; spore-bearing leaves distinctly shorter than vegetative leaves, giving the plant a decidedly knobby appearance. Leaves dark shiny green, to 1.5 cm long, vegetative leaves broadest above the middle, with a few conspicuous teeth near the tip. Stomata, tiny pores, present on the lower leaf surface only. Spores fertile.

HABITAT In Alabama, restricted to wet rocky soil at bases of sandstone cliffs, always in deep shade. Elsewhere known from shaded, often rocky stream banks, swamp margins, and moist hillsides and ledges.

RANGE Very rare in Alabama, known only from a few localities in the Sipsey Gorges region of the Cumberland Plateau. Common in the northeastern United States and southeastern Canada west to the upper Mississippi Valley and south to the mountains of Tennessee, North Carolina, and Georgia; disjunct in northwestern Arkansas and northwestern Alabama.

Shining clubmoss (*Lycopodium lucidulum*) with close-up of single blade.

COMMENTS This species may also be present in far northeastern Alabama. The known southwestern limit of its primary range is in the Cumberland Plateau of Marion County, Tennessee, which is adjacent to Alabama. Dean (1969) reported it from Jackson County, but there are no specimens to document the report. Since *Lycopodium lucidulum* is easily confused with *L. porophilum*, and since the two species are known to produce a hybrid that furthers the confusion, it should be excluded from the list of Jackson County plants until definite evidence of its presence there is produced.

The genus name *Lycopodium* means "wolf's foot" and is derived from the name the ancient Greeks gave to a European member of this genus. The specific epithet *lucidulum* means "somewhat shiny"; it and the common name are derived from the shiny appearance of the leaves.

OTHER COMMON NAMES Shining firmoss

SYNONYMS *Huperzia lucidula* (Michaux) Trevisan

Shining clubmoss growing out of leaf mold along a mountain stream bank.

Rock Clubmoss
Lycopodium porophilum Lloyd & Underwood

DESCRIPTION Stems short-creeping on soil surface with erect tips rising to 18 cm tall, forking as many as 3 times in the erect portion. Strobili absent, vegetative and fertile leaves grouped in zones along the stem; spore-bearing leaves nearly the same size as vegetative leaves, knobby appearance of plant obscure. Leaves somewhat shiny, medium green, to 9 mm long, vegetative leaves broadest at or below the middle, teeth few and obscure. Stomata, tiny pores, abundant on both leaf surfaces. Spores fertile.

HABITAT Grows in hollows and on ledges of shaded sandstone cliffs.

RANGE Rare in Alabama, known only from the Sipsey Gorges region of the Cumberland Plateau. Occurs rarely from Maryland west to the upper Mississippi Valley and south to the Cumberland Plateau of Tennessee and Alabama and the mountains of North Carolina.

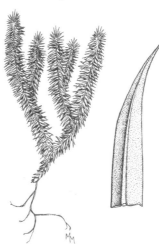

Rock clubmoss (*Lycopodium porophilum*) with close-up of single blade.

COMMENTS Like *Lycopodium lucidulum*, this species appears to be disjunct in northwestern Alabama with the main range of *L. porophilum* approaching northeastern Alabama in Tennessee. This species tolerates somewhat drier habitats than does *L. lucidulum* and may be present in suitable habitats along the escarpments of the Cumberland Plateau in northeastern Alabama.

This species is often difficult to distinguish from *Lycopodium lucidulum*. The surest way is to examine the upper surfaces of the leaves with a microscope: *L. porophilum* has abundant microscopic pores, technically known as stomata, on the upper surface, but *L. lucidulum* has none. *Lycopodium porophilum* also tends to be shorter and more stiffly erect than *L. lucidulum*. The leaves are shorter and a lighter shade of green and are a bit more densely crowded on the stem. The difference in length between the sterile and fertile leaves is also less pronounced. The fact that these two species hybridize complicates the task of identification.

The specific epithet *porophilum* means "cavity loving" and refers to the tendency of this species to occur in pockets and crevices in rock cliffs.

OTHER COMMON NAMES Rock firmoss

SYNONYMS *Huperzia porophila* (Lloyd & Underwood) Holub

Right: Close-up of rock clubmoss showing sporangia.

Below: Rock clubmoss growing just inside the drip line of a sandstone overhang in Winston County.

Bartley's Clubmoss
Lycopodium × bartleyi Cusick

DESCRIPTION Stems short-creeping on soil surface with erect tips rising to 20 cm tall, forking as many as 3 times in the erect portion. Strobili absent, vegetative and fertile leaves grouped in zones along the stem; spore-bearing leaves shorter than vegetative leaves, giving the plant a knobby appearance. Leaves shiny, medium to dark green, to 10 mm long or more, vegetative leaves broadest near the middle, teeth few and obscure. Stomata, tiny pores, sparsely present on the upper leaf surface and abundant on the lower. Spores shrunken, abortive.

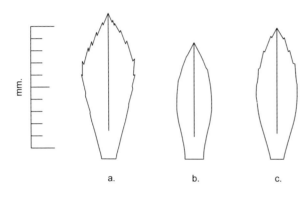

mm.

a.   b.   c.

Leaves of three clubmosses (*Lycopodium*), enlarged for comparison.
a. Shining clubmoss (*L. lucidulum*).
b. Rock clubmoss (*L. porophilum*).
c. Bartley's clubmoss (*L. × bartleyi*).

HABITAT Grows in crevices and on ledges of shaded sandstone cliffs.

RANGE Known in Alabama from a single collection in a sandstone gorge in southern Franklin County. Range is from northern Alabama to southern Ohio and southern Wisconsin, most frequent in the northern part of its range.

COMMENTS This is the hybrid between *Lycopodium lucidulum* and *L. porophilum* and is very difficult to distinguish from its parents, just as they are difficult to distinguish from each other. While *L. lucidulum* and *L. porophilum* can be distinguished by the size, shape, and color of the vegetative leaves, these characters are subtle at best and are intermediate in the hybrid. Identification of the hybrid is certain only by microscopic examination of the upper leaf surfaces for pores, or stomata, or by finding sporangia with aborted, shrunken spores. The upper surfaces of the leaves have pores, but much fewer than do the lower surfaces. The upper leaf surfaces of *L. lucidulum* have no pores at all, while they are almost as abundant on the upper leaf surfaces of *L. porophilum* as they are on the lower leaf surfaces. They are abundant on the lower leaf surfaces of all three of these plants.

This hybrid was named in honor Floyd Bartley, a noted collector of plants in southeastern Ohio in the early and mid-twentieth century.

OTHER COMMON NAMES Bartley's firmoss

SYNONYMS *Huperzia* × *bartleyi* (Cusick) Kartesz & Gandhi

Ground-Pine
Lycopodium obscurum Linnaeus

DESCRIPTION Rhizomes long-creeping, deeply buried. Erect stems profusely branched, treelike, to 30 cm tall. Leaves dark green, linear, spreading from the stem, in six rows on the branchlets. Strobili erect, tipping short ordinary branches at the crown of the erect stem.

HABITAT Grows in rich, moist hardwood or coniferous forests in acid soil.

RANGE Very rare in Alabama, known only from a few localities in the Cumberland Plateau in the far northeast. Common in the northeastern United States and southeastern Canada west to the upper Mississippi Valley and south to the Cumberland Plateau of Tennessee and Alabama and the mountains of the Carolinas and Georgia; also known from a single seemingly disjunct locality in the Piedmont of western Georgia.

Ground-pine (*Lycopodium obscurum*).

COMMENTS This strikingly beautiful plant looks like a miniature forest of dark green pine trees.

This plant has traditionally been harvested in large quantities for use in Christmas decorations, a practice that has significantly reduced its abundance in many places. Since it is very rare in Alabama, it should not be collected in the state.

This species has been found in Heard County in the Piedmont of western Georgia (Snyder and Bruce 1986). That county lies on the Alabama state line, and there is a chance that this clubmoss may also be present in the Piedmont of Alabama.

The specific epithet *obscurum* refers to the deep, hidden rhizome. The common name comes from the way the plant looks like a forest of tiny pine trees.

OTHER COMMON NAMES Tree clubmoss, princess-pine

SYNONYMS *Dendrolycopodium obscurum* (Linnaeus) A. Haines

Ground-pine growing in a seepy, sandy floodplain in Jackson County.

Running-Cedar
Lycopodium digitatum Dillenius *ex* A. Braun

DESCRIPTION Rhizomes creeping on soil surface, covered only by leaf litter and humus. Erect stems profusely branched, treelike; lateral branches flattened into a regular, fanlike pattern held horizontally; annual constrictions absent. Leaves in four rows on the branchlets, broad and fused to stem at base; leaves on bottom side of stem tiny, much smaller than the lateral leaves or those on top of stem, which are only a little smaller than lateral leaves. Strobili borne in fours on naked stalks arising from the crown of the erect stem, often with sterile tips.

HABITAT Grows in dry to moist woods, often young mixed hardwood and coniferous trees.

RANGE Scattered over most of the highland provinces of Alabama, seemingly common in the Piedmont. Rare in the Coastal Plain. Common from southeastern Canada and the northeastern United States south to Alabama, Mississippi, and Georgia.

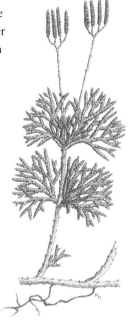

Running-cedar (*Lycopodium digitatum*) with close-up of stem.

COMMENTS Hunters often report seeing this distinctive plant in the Piedmont of Alabama, typically in second-growth mixed forests of the type that abound in the region. It was probably rare in the Piedmont in the early twentieth century when the region was mostly cleared and under cultivation. Since soil erosion resulting from the poor farming practices of the past has reduced the agricultural value of the land, much of the Piedmont has been allowed to return to forest. As a result, *Lycopodium digitatum* seems to be increasing in abundance in the Alabama Piedmont, a situation that has been reported to be occurring in Georgia as well (Duncan and Blake 1965).

The rhizomes of this plant branch and spread to create a ground cover. The plant can grow to cover large areas of ground in just a few years. A colony in Chambers County that is easily accessible to the senior author has come to cover several hundred square feet in the decade or so since its first appearance.

This species was for many years known as *Lycopodium flabelliforme* (Fernald) Blanchard. However, Dillenius's earlier name *digitatum* had been overlooked because it was published in an obscure manner. This name was discovered in 1975 (Hickey and Beitel 1979) and is now accepted due to precedence.

The specific epithet *digitatum* means "like fingers" and refers to the pattern of the branches. The plant resembles a forest of tiny cedars and the rhizome "runs" along the surface of the ground, hence the common name.

OTHER COMMON NAMES Running ground-pine, fan ground-pine, fan clubmoss

SYNONYMS *Diphasiastrum digitatum* (Dillenius *ex* A. Braun) Holub, *Lycopodium flabelliforme* (Fernald) Blanchard

Running-cedar growing in a mixed pine and hardwood forest near Waverly, Chambers County.

Ground-Cedar
Lycopodium tristachyum Pursh

DESCRIPTION Rhizome long-creeping, deeply buried in the soil. Erect stems profusely branched, treelike; lower lateral branches weakly flattened into a horizontal fanlike pattern, upper branches ascending, not flattened, brushlike; annual constrictions conspicuous on branchlets. Leaves in four rows on the branchlets, fused to stem at base; leaves on top and bottom of stem similar, both only a little smaller than lateral leaves. Strobili borne in fours on naked stalks arising from the crown of the erect stem, tips of strobili fertile.

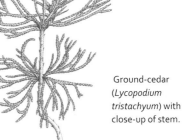

HABITAT Grows in acidic, usually sandy, soil in dry open, mostly coniferous, woods.

RANGE Known from Alabama from two collections in northern Jackson County. Frequent in the northeastern United States and eastern Canada west to the upper Mississippi Valley and south to extreme northern Alabama and Georgia. Also occurs in Europe.

Ground-cedar (*Lycopodium tristachyum*) with close-up of stem.

COMMENTS E. W. Graves collected this clubmoss in 1917 in a sandy pine forest on Sand Mountain near Higdon, Jackson County. It was also collected from a creek bank near Swaim in north-central Jackson County in 1983. Apparently no other records of its occurrence in Alabama exist, and its status here is uncertain, as recent attempts to find both localities have failed.

Lycopodium tristachyum may be present at other localities in northeastern Alabama. It should be looked for in older pine woods on Sand and Lookout Mountains and the mountaintops of the Plateau Mountains. The latter is probably more likely since many of the mountains there are still lacking roads and accessibility is difficult.

The specific epithet *tristachyum* means "three-spiked" and refers to the strobili-bearing stalks, which often appear three per erect shoot. The plant resembles a forest of tiny cedars, resulting in the common name.

OTHER COMMON NAMES Slender ground-pine, deep-root clubmoss, blue running-cedar

SYNONYMS *Diphasiastrum tristachyum* (Pursh) Holub

Staghorn Clubmoss
Lycopodium cernuum Linnaeus

DESCRIPTION Main stems arching, rooting at intervals, sparsely leafy, 5 mm or less in diameter, including the spread of the leaves, with frequent upright branches. Upright stems repeatedly branched, often treelike, leafy, to 9 mm broad, including the leaf spread. Leaves narrow, less than 0.5 mm broad at base. Spore-bearing leaves in strobili that are nodding at the tips of lateral branches.

HABITAT Grows in damp sandy meadows, ditches, and road cuts, usually in partial sun.

RANGE Occasional throughout the lower Coastal Plain of Alabama. Occurs in the United States from peninsular Florida north to southeastern Georgia and west to Louisiana. Known from the tropics worldwide.

COMMENTS This is a tropical plant that reaches the northernmost limits of its distribution in southern Alabama and nearby. Collections indicate that it has become more frequent in Alabama in recent years. Although the treelike aerial branches of *Lycopodium cernuum* may reach as much as 80 cm in height in the tropics, they are typically less than 25 cm tall in the United States north of Florida.

The specific epithet *cernuum* means "nodding" and refers to the drooping strobili. The common name comes from the resemblance of a large upright shoot to the antlers of a deer.

OTHER COMMON NAMES Nodding clubmoss

SYNONYMS *Lycopodiella cernua* (Linnaeus) Pichi Sermolli, *Palhinhaea cernua* (Linnaeus) Vasconcellos & Franco

Staghorn clubmoss.

Slender Clubmoss
Lycopodium carolinianum Linnaeus

DESCRIPTION Main stems growing on soil surface, rooted all along, short and leafy, often branched several times. Leaves on the top side of the stem conspicuously shorter than the lateral leaves; cross section of stem with leaves semicircular to flat, total leaf spread 5 to 10 mm. Erect stems unbranched strobili-bearing stalks only; stalks with sparse leaves that ascend vertically and are pressed against the stem, to 30 cm tall. Strobili tight and hard, less than 5 mm broad; spore-bearing leaves visible only as tiny tips extending beyond the sporangia.

HABITAT Grows in damp sandy acid soil in meadows, ditches, and embankments, usually in partial or full sun.

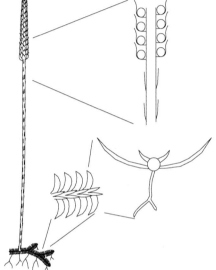

Slender clubmoss (*Lycopodium carolinianum*): upper side of the stem showing the leaves of two sizes in four rows; cross section of the stem showing the arrangement of the leaves; longitudinal section of the strobilus and its stalk showing the arrangement of the leaves and sporangia.

RANGE Occurs throughout the Coastal Plain of Alabama up to the Fall Line, seemingly infrequent. Range in the United States is from Florida to eastern Texas and increasingly rare northward along the Atlantic Coast to New England. Found in the tropics and subtropics throughout the world.

COMMENTS This clubmoss grows close to the ground and is typically surrounded by grasses and other plants that are often at least as tall as the slender stalks of the strobili. Since this plant is inconspicuous in its natural habitat, it may have been overlooked by collectors and may be more common than is currently known. It is winter-hardy, evident by the fact that it grows as far north as New England, and should be present in most or all counties of the Alabama Coastal Plain.

Linnaeus named this species from material presumably collected in the Carolinas. The common name comes from the thin strobili and their stalks.

OTHER COMMON NAMES Carolina clubmoss, Carolina bog clubmoss

SYNONYMS *Lycopodiella caroliniana* (Linnaeus) Pichi Sermolli, *Pseudolycopodiella caroliniana* (Linnaeus) Holub

Slender clubmoss growing in sandy soil of an embankment.

Tight-Leaf Clubmoss
Lycopodium appressum (Chapman) Lloyd & Underwood

DESCRIPTION Main stems creeping on soil surface, rooting all along, to 5 mm thick, occasionally branching. Leaves spreading from all sides of the stem except underneath; stem with leaves semicircular to elliptical in cross section, total leaf spread 1 cm or more. Erect stems unbranched strobili-bearing stalks only; stalks to 40 cm tall with leaves ascending vertically and pressed against the stem. Strobili narrow and tight, to 6 mm wide; spore-bearing leaves ascending vertically, not spreading, much longer than sporangia.

HABITAT Grows in acid sandy soil in meadows, ditches, and open pinelands, usually in full or partial sun.

RANGE Occurs throughout the Alabama Coastal Plain, infrequent near the Fall Line; rare in bogs in the Cumberland Plateau and Ridge and Valley. Known only from eastern North America, occurring mainly from central Florida north to Newfoundland and west to eastern Texas along the coasts, and inland from the Gulf Coast to southeastern Oklahoma, southern Arkansas, and western Kentucky; rare and widely scattered in the mountains of North Carolina and Tennessee and north to the Great Lakes.

COMMENTS Another of the inconspicuous bog clubmosses, this one is probably present in most or all counties of the Alabama Coastal Plain. This species frequently hybridizes with *Lycopodium alopecuroides* and *L. prostratum*.

The common name and the species epithet *appressum* refer to the way the leaves of the upright stem and spore-bearing leaves are tightly pressed against the stem.

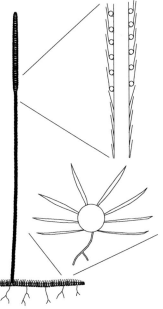

Tight-leaf clubmoss (*Lycopodium appressum*): cross section of the stem showing the arrangement of the leaves; longitudinal section of the strobilus and its stalk showing the arrangement of the leaves and sporangia.

OTHER COMMON NAMES Southern clubmoss, appressed bog clubmoss

SYNONYMS *Lycopodiella appressa* (Chapman) Cranfill

Tight-leaf clubmoss growing on a roadside near Sandfield, Pike County.

Foxtail Clubmoss
Lycopodium alopecuroides Linnaeus

DESCRIPTION Main stems conspicuously arching, rooting at intervals, branching rarely except for erect strobili-bearing stalks, to 5 mm or more thick with total leaf spread of 1 cm or more. Leaves all about the same size and spreading from all sides of the stem except near rooting points; stem with leaves circular in cross section. Erect stems unbranched strobili-bearing stalks; stalks densely leafy, to 25 cm or taller with leaves spreading, making them appear similar to the main stems. Strobili bushy, to 2 cm or more broad; spore-bearing leaves several times longer than sporangia, spreading widely and nearly horizontal.

HABITAT Grows in damp acid sandy meadows, ditches, and open pinelands, usually in full or partial sun.

Foxtail clubmoss (*Lycopodium alopecuroides*): cross section of an arching portion of the stem showing the arrangement of leaves; longitudinal section of the strobilus and its stalk showing the arrangement of the leaves and sporangia.

RANGE Frequent in the lower Coastal Plain of Alabama, increasingly rare toward the Fall Line; also found in bogs in the Cumberland Plateau and Ridge and Valley. Range in the United States is from Florida north along the East Coast to New England and west to eastern Texas along the Gulf Coast; rare in the highland provinces of Alabama, Georgia, and North Carolina and disjunct in the Cumberland Mountain region of Tennessee, Kentucky, and Virginia. Widespread in tropical America.

COMMENTS This is the largest of the bog clubmosses in Alabama, but it is often associated with thickly growing grasses and tends to be somewhat inconspicuous. It is probably present in all counties of the Alabama Coastal Plain. The fact that it occurs rarely in the highland provinces and mountains of the Southeast indicates that it may be present more widely in the Alabama highland provinces as well, although it has not yet been found far from the Fall Line here.

This species is believed to be one of the first American members of the bog clubmosses to be examined by Linnaeus (Thieret 1980).

This species frequently hybridizes with *Lycopodium prostratum* and *L. appressum*.

The specific epithet *alopecuroides* means "like *Alopecurus*," a genus of grasses known as "foxtails" because of their bushy flowering spikes. This and the common name refer to the bushy strobilus, which resembles the tail of a fox to some.

OTHER COMMON NAMES Foxtail bog clubmoss

SYNONYMS *Lycopodiella alopecuroides* (Linnaeus) Cranfill

Foxtail clubmoss growing in a roadside ditch in Baldwin County.

Feather-Stem Clubmoss
Lycopodium prostratum Harper

DESCRIPTION Main stems creeping on the surface of the soil, rooted all along, 3 mm or less thick, branching infrequently. Leaves spreading to the sides of the stem; stem with leaves with a featherlike appearance, nearly flat in cross section, total leaf spread 1 cm or more. Erect stems unbranched strobili-bearing stalks only, to 30 cm or more tall; leaves on stalks ascending, spreading only slightly. Strobili bushy, to 2 cm broad; sporophylls several times longer than sporangia, spreading widely and nearly horizontal.

HABITAT Grows in damp acid sandy meadows, ditches, and open pinelands, usually in full or partial sun.

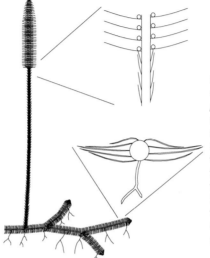

Feather-stem clubmoss (*Lycopodium prostratum*): cross section of the stem showing the arrangement of the leaves; longitudinal section of the strobilus and its stalk showing the arrangement of the leaves and sporangia.

RANGE Found throughout the Coastal Plain of Alabama; frequent in the south and increasingly rare toward the Fall Line, which it barely crosses. Occurs from Florida north to North Carolina and west to Texas in the Coastal Plain, rare in the highland regions of Georgia, Tennessee, and North Carolina. Not known outside of the southeastern United States.

COMMENTS As with the other bog clubmosses, this one can probably be found in almost every county of the Alabama Coastal Plain. It may also be found in the highland provinces, especially the Cumberland Plateau. It is very inconspicuous in the spring and summer before the strobili appear.

Roland M. Harper, who was the Alabama state botanist in the early twentieth century, named this species in 1906. The name being used at the time, *Lycopodium pinnatum* (Chapman) Lloyd & Underwood, was found to be invalid since it had been previously used for an entirely different species.

Curiously, Graves (1920) reported both *Lycopodium prostratum* and "*L. pinnatum*" from Alabama, noting that the former was plentiful in southern Alabama and the latter was rare. Since true *L. pinnatum* does not occur in North America, his "*L. pinnatum*" probably represents one of the hybrids involving *L. prostratum*.

This species frequently hybridizes with *Lycopodium alopecuroides* and *L. appressum*.

The specific epithet *prostratum* refers to the main stems, which grow flat on the ground. The common name refers to the feathery appearance of the stems and leaves.

OTHER COMMON NAMES Creeping clubmoss, prostrate bog clubmoss

SYNONYMS *Lycopodiella prostrata* (Harper) Cranfill

Feather-stem clubmoss growing in damp, acidic soil in south Alabama.

Copeland's Clubmoss
Lycopodium × *copelandii* Eiger

DESCRIPTION Main stems mostly creeping on soil surface, occasionally arching above the ground slightly and having rootless zones, to 5 mm thick, rarely branching. Leaves spreading from all sides of the stem, but not from the lower side of creeping portions; stem with leaves round in cross section in arches, semicircular to elliptical on creeping portions, total leaf spread 1 cm or more. Erect stems unbranched strobili-bearing stalks, to 30 cm tall; stalk leaves ascending and weakly spreading, but not pressed to the stem. Strobili loose but compact, to 1 cm wide or slightly more; spore-bearing leaves ascending but not pressed to the stem, extending far beyond the sporangia.

HABITAT Grows in acid sandy soil in meadows, ditches, and open pinelands, usually in full or partial sun.

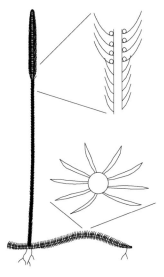

Copeland's club-moss (*Lycopodium* × *copelandii*): cross section of an arching portion of the stem showing the arrangement of the leaves; longitudinal section of the strobilus and its stalk showing the arrangement of the leaves and sporangia.

RANGE Scattered throughout the Coastal Plain of Alabama. Occurs in the United States throughout the overlapping portions of the ranges of its parents, *Lycopodium alopecuroides* and *L. appressum*, from Florida west to eastern Texas and north to Long Island, mostly in the Coastal Plain. Not known from elsewhere in the world.

COMMENTS This is the hybrid between *Lycopodium alopecuroides* and *L. appressum*. Hybrids are frequent among the bog clubmosses since several species are often found growing together in the same place, and this is one of the best known of those hybrids.

This hybrid is distinguished from *L. alopecuroides* by the weak arching of the stems and the ascending sporophylls; *L. alopecuroides* has prominently arching stems and widely spreading spore-bearing leaves. The other parent, *L. appressum*, does not arch at all, and its sporophylls are pressed tightly to the stem.

This hybrid was named for Edwin B. Copeland, who studied ferns and fern allies in the early and middle twentieth century.

OTHER COMMON NAMES Intermediate clubmoss, Chapman's clubmoss

SYNONYMS *Lycopodiella × copelandii* (Eiger) Cranfill, *Lycopodium chapmanii* Underwood *ex* Maxon *sensu* Wherry (1964)

Hybrid Clubmoss
Lycopodium alopecuroides × prostratum

DESCRIPTION Main stems mostly creeping on soil surface, occasionally arching slightly above the ground and with rootless zones, less than 5 mm thick, occasionally branching. Leaves tending to spread horizontally from the stem; the stem with leaves somewhat featherlike in appearance, nearly flat to elliptical in cross section, total leaf spread to 1 cm or more. Erect stems unbranched strobili-bearing stalks, to 30 cm tall; stalk leaves ascending, weakly spreading. Strobili bushy, to 2 cm broad; sporophylls much longer than sporangia, spreading widely and nearly horizontal.

HABITAT Grows in sandy acid ditches, meadows, and pinelands, usually in full or partial sun.

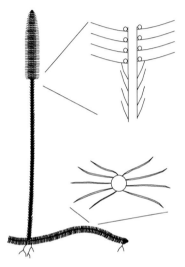

Hybrid clubmoss (*Lycopodium alope-curoides × prostra-tum*): cross section of the stem showing the arrangement of the leaves; longitudinal section of the strobilus and its stalk showing the arrangement of the leaves and sporangia.

RANGE Infrequent in the Coastal Plain of Alabama. Occurs throughout the overlapping portions of the ranges of its parents from Florida west to Texas and north to North Carolina, mostly in the Coastal Plain. Not known outside of the southeastern United States.

COMMENTS This hybrid bog clubmoss is difficult to distinguish from its parents, especially *Lycopodium prostratum*. The main stems of the hybrid often arch for short distances, while those of *L. prostratum* are rooted throughout. The feathery appearance of the leafy stems is less pronounced in the hybrid.

Like the other bog clubmosses, this one is inconspicuous and may be present in more Alabama counties than is presently known.

This little-known hybrid has not been given a common name.

SYNONYMS *Lycopodiella alopecuroides × prostrata*

Hybrid clubmoss growing in a roadside ditch near Sandfield, Pike County.

Bruce's Clubmoss
Lycopodium × brucei (Cranfill) Lellinger

DESCRIPTION Main stems creeping on soil surface, rooted all along, never arching, less than 5 mm thick, seldom branching. Leaves tending to spread to the sides of the stem; stem with leaves somewhat featherlike, nearly flat to elliptical in cross section, total leaf spread to 1 cm or more. Erect stems unbranched strobili-bearing stalks only, to 30 cm tall; stalk leaves strongly ascending, spreading only slightly, but not pressed against the stem. Strobili loose but compact, to 1 cm or so broad; sporophylls ascending but not pressed to the stem, much longer than sporangia.

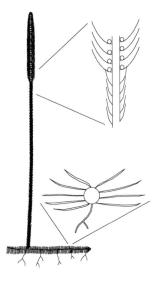

Bruce's clubmoss (*Lycopodium × brucei*): cross section of the stem showing the arrangement of the leaves; longitudinal section of the strobilus and its stalk showing the arrangement of the leaves and sporangia.

HABITAT Grows in sandy acid ditches, meadows, and pinelands, usually in full or partial sun.

RANGE Occurs throughout the Alabama Coastal Plain, seemingly infrequent. Known throughout the overlapping portions of the ranges of its parents, *Lycopodium appressum* and *L. prostratum*, from Florida west to Texas and north to North Carolina, mostly in the Coastal Plain. Not known outside of the southeastern United States.

COMMENTS This is the hybrid between *Lycopodium appressum* and *L. prostratum*. It is little known and may be more common than is presently indicated.

This plant is inconspicuous and is often difficult to distinguish from its parents. The ascending sporophylls of the hybrid produce strobili that are narrower and tighter than the bushy strobili of *L. prostratum* and are broader and looser than those of *L. appressum*. The leafy stems have a feathery appearance that is less pronounced than with the stems of *Lycopodium prostratum*; *L. appressum* does not exhibit this feature.

This hybrid is named for James G. Bruce, who worked out the relationships among this group of clubmosses in the early 1970s as a graduate student at the University of Georgia.

SYNONYMS *Lycopodiella* × *brucei* Cranfill

Riddell's Spikemoss
Selaginella arenicola Underwood ssp. *riddellii* (Van Eseltine) Tryon

DESCRIPTION Stems mostly erect, to 10 cm or more tall, growing in tufts or clumps, sparsely branched. Vegetative leaves all alike, spirally arranged on the stem. Sporangia borne in 4-sided strobili at the tips of erect stems.

HABITAT Known in Alabama only from dry, essentially flat sandstone or granitic rocks. Other subspecies that grow in sand are known from nearby states, but they have not been found in Alabama.

RANGE Rare in Alabama in the western Cumberland Plateau with one locality in the Piedmont. Occurs primarily in western Arkansas, northwestern Louisiana, northeastern Texas, and eastern Oklahoma; seemingly disjunct in northern Alabama and central Georgia. Other subspecies are found primarily in the Coastal Plain from Florida north to North Carolina.

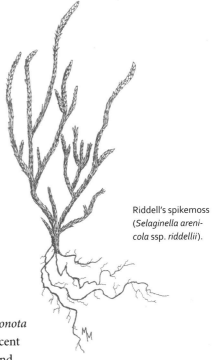

Riddell's spikemoss (*Selaginella arenicola* ssp. *riddellii*).

COMMENTS This species has been subdivided into three subspecies: ssp. *arenicola*, ssp. *acanthonota* (Underwood) Tryon, and ssp. *riddellii*. Some recent authors feel that the differences are too minor and intermediates too common for recognition of these subspecies (Lellinger 1985); others have gone to the other extreme and recognized the subspecies as independent species (Snyder and Bruce 1986).

All material known from Alabama belongs to subspecies *riddellii*, although some specimens have been reported to be intermediate with ssp. *arenicola*, which is very similar (Tryon 1955).

In Alabama and Georgia subspecies *riddellii* is usually found growing on rocks, but in the western part of its range and in a few localities in the Coastal Plain of Georgia it grows in sand. *Selaginella arenicola* ssp. *arenicola*, sand spikemoss, and *S. arenicola* ssp. *acanthonota*, spiny spikemoss, are found only in sand.

The genus name *Selaginella* means "little selago," an ancient name for a firlike plant. The species epithet *arenicola* means "living in sand." The subspecific epithet *riddellii* honors John Leonard Riddell, inventor of the binocular microscope and author of an early flora of Louisiana.

The one known Piedmont population, in Lee County, appears to have fallen victim to plant succession. The formerly bare rock upon which it grew has accumulated soil on its surface and is now overgrown by shrubs and small trees. The authors of this book visited the site in 2009 and could find no sign of the spikemoss.

SYNONYMS *Selaginella corallina* (Riddell) Wilbur & Whitson, *Selaginella riddellii* Van Eseltine

Riddell's spikemoss in early morning light.

Rock Spikemoss
Selaginella rupestris (Linnaeus) Spring

DESCRIPTION Stems creeping and profusely branched, often forming dense mats, with slightly ascending branch tips that are only sparsely branched. Sterile leaves all alike, spirally arranged. Sporangia borne in 4-sided strobili at the tips of nearly erect stems.

HABITAT Grows in thin soil on dry sandstone and granitic flat rocks, usually at or near the margins of the rock.

RANGE Infrequent and scattered in Alabama in the Cumberland Plateau and Piedmont. Frequent in the eastern United States and southeastern Canada south to the Fall Line of Alabama and Georgia and west to the upper Mississippi Valley and southwest to Oklahoma; known from a few places in the Coastal Plain of Georgia.

Rock spikemoss (*Selaginella rupestris*).

COMMENTS This spikemoss forms dense carpetlike mats on the surfaces of the dry flat rocks on which it grows.

Like other plants that grow on flat rocks, this one grows actively in the winter and spring when the weather is cool and rain is plentiful. The thin soil dries out with the summer heat and the plant appears dead, only to be revived when the winter rains come.

The specific epithet *rupestris* means "of rocks"; it and the common name refer to the habitat of this plant.

OTHER COMMON NAMES Ledge spikemoss, dwarf spikemoss

Rock spikemoss growing over loose pebble substrate in Jackson County, 2001.

Blue Spikemoss
Selaginella uncinata Spring

DESCRIPTION Stems long-creeping at the soil surface, with frequent side branches. Branches partially erect, to 5 cm long, further branched several times and flattened into a single plane, appearing somewhat fernlike. Leaves distinctly bluish green, of two types in four rows, with larger ones spreading laterally from each side of the stem and smaller ones appressed to the top of the stem. Sporangia borne in 4-sided strobili at the tips of branchlets.

HABITAT Grows on stream and lake banks and in moist woods, usually around old homesites.

RANGE Known in Alabama from a single collection in Monroe County. Rare and widely scattered from Florida to southwestern Georgia and west to southern Louisiana. Naturalized from China.

Blue spikemoss (*Selaginella uncinata*) with close-up of leaf arrangement along the stem.

COMMENTS This is a commonly cultivated plant that is usually found near present or former homesites. The one known Alabama locality for this species does not appear to have occurred in this manner. It was found in 1954 growing in limey clay near the mouth of a cave next to a rock quarry, nowhere near any homesite. Whether the spikemoss is still present at the site or nearby is unknown at this time; habitats near quarries tend to be destroyed eventually by quarry operations. It may be present at other places in the Coastal Plain of Alabama.

The specific epithet *uncinata* means "hooked" and was applied by its author for reasons that are not presently known. The common name refers to the bluish color of the leaves.

OTHER COMMON NAMES Peacock-moss, hooked spikemoss

Blue spikemoss growing at the base of a stump in the Fern Glade at the Birmingham Botanical Gardens.

Braun's Spikemoss
Selaginella braunii Baker

DESCRIPTION Rhizomes long-creeping, subterranean. Erect stems to 50 cm long, branching many times and flattened in a single plane, appearing fernlike. Leaves of two sizes in four rows with two rows spreading laterally from the stem and the other two rows of smaller leaves pressed flat against the top of the stem. Sporangia borne in 4-sided strobili at the tips of branchlets.

HABITAT Found at old homesites, in churchyards, and in wet woods.

RANGE Known in Alabama from three localities, two in Blount County in the central Cumberland Plateau, the other in Mobile County in the lower Coastal Plain. Rare and widely scattered in the southeastern United States from southeastern North Carolina west to southeastern Louisiana, chiefly in the Coastal Plain. A native of China that escapes from cultivation and is possibly naturalized in the southeastern United States.

Braun's spikemoss (*Selaginella braunii*) with close-up of leaf arrangement along the stem.

COMMENTS This plant has been found at two abandoned homesites in Alabama. Except for these two localities in the Cumberland Plateau, *Selaginella braunii* has been found in the southeastern United States only in the Coastal Plain. It is commonly cultivated in Alabama, especially in the southern part of the state, and the deeply buried rhizomes are winter hardy even in the far northern counties. According to Lellinger (1985), it is naturalized in the southeastern United States, but Snyder and Bruce (1986) list it as an escape. The two finds in northern Alabama are decidedly escapes.

Species is named in honor of Emma Lucy Braun, an American ecologist of the early and middle twentieth century.

OTHER COMMON NAMES Treelet spikemoss, arbor vitae fern

Braun's spikemoss growing by a stream in the Fern Glade at the Birmingham Botanical Gardens.

Gulf Spikemoss
Selaginella ludoviciana A. Braun

DESCRIPTION Stems long-creeping on the surface of the ground, with semierect tips and lateral branches. Branches and tips to 20 cm long, lax, usually not rising more than 5 cm above the ground. Leaves in four rows, of two sizes, spreading laterally from the stem or appressed to the top of the stem; leaf margins with distinct thin, whitish fringes. Sporangia borne in 4-sided strobili at the tips of ascending branches.

HABITAT Grows at swamp margins and in wet pinelands.

RANGE Rare in Alabama, known only from a few counties in the lower Coastal Plain. Rare in the southeastern United States from northern Florida and southern Georgia west to eastern Louisiana. Occurs nowhere else in the world.

COMMENTS Although this species is somewhat taller and looser than the much more common *Selaginella apoda*, the two species are very similar looking and are difficult to tell apart. They are best distinguished by examining the margins of the larger vegetative leaves with a hand lens or a low-power microscope. The leaves of *S. ludoviciana* will have a distinct pale fringe around the whole margin, while *S. apoda* will have no fringe or only indistinct tatters at irregular intervals along the margin.

Gulf spikemoss (*Selaginella ludoviciana*) with close-up showing distinctive fringe around the leaf.

Since this is an inconspicuous plant and since it is easily confused with the common *Selaginella apoda*, it is likely to be more common than is presently known.

This species hybridizes with *S. apoda*. The hybrid has not been found in Alabama, but it may be present.

The specific epithet *ludoviciana* means "of Louisiana," where it was first found. The common name refers to the range of this species along the coast of the Gulf of Mexico.

OTHER COMMON NAMES Louisiana spikemoss

SYNONYMS *Diplostachyum ludovicianum* (A. Braun) Small

Gulf spikemoss growing at the edge of a pitcher plant bog near Weeks Bay, Baldwin County.

Meadow Spikemoss
Selaginella apoda (Linnaeus) Spring

DESCRIPTION Stems creeping on the ground surface, frequently branched, rooting all along except at the tips; tips prostrate or very slightly upturned. Leaves in four rows, of two sizes, spreading laterally from the stem or appressed to the top of the stem; pale fringes at leaf margins absent or indistinct. Sporangia borne in 4-sided strobili, slightly upturned at the tips of branches.

HABITAT Grows in wet meadows, on stream and lake banks, and on damp rocks, ledges, and cliff bases.

RANGE Occurs throughout Alabama. Frequent throughout the eastern United States from New England west to the Mississippi Valley and south to Texas and Florida, most frequent in the highland regions.

Meadow spikemoss (*Selaginella apoda*) with close-up of leaf arrangement along the stem.

COMMENTS This is the most common *Selaginella* in Alabama. It is probably present in every county.

This species is known to hybridize with *S. ludoviciana* in Florida and Louisiana and may do so in Alabama as well. The hybrid is particularly difficult to distinguish from its parents; its identification is usually based on finding shrunken spores.

The specific epithet *apoda* is Latin for "footless" and refers to the lack of a well-developed root system.

OTHER COMMON NAMES Field spikemoss

SYNONYMS *Lycopodioides apodum* (Linnaeus) Kuntze, *Diplostachyum apodum* (Linnaeus) Beauvois

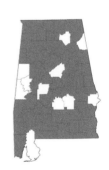

A lush growth of meadow spikemoss.

Florida Quillwort
Isoëtes flaccida Shuttleworth *ex* A. Braun

DESCRIPTION Stems short, erect, underground, and cormlike. Leaves linear, 10–60 cm long, slender, white at base. Sporangia recessed into leaf bases, 3–5 mm long, white, entirely covered by the velum, a thin flap of tissue. Megaspores cream-colored, 0.3–0.5 mm in diameter; surfaces ornamented with low bumps or short ridges.

HABITAT Grows in wet low woodlands, clear ponds, streams, ditches, and in fresh or brackish marshes; often rooted in sand.

RANGE Known in Alabama from a few localities in the Coastal Plain. Occurs in Florida and in southern Georgia and Alabama.

COMMENTS Some authors recognize two varieties of *Isoëtes flaccida*. Lellinger (1985) states that neither variety is worthy of recognition. Boom (1982) also states that these varieties are largely products of environmental influences. Plants stunted by brackish water have been called var. *rigida* Engelmann, and specimens more robust than typical *I. flaccida* have been called var. *alata* N. E. Pfeiffer.

The genus name *Isoëtes* is an ancient word that apparently means "equal points"; Linnaeus applied it to these plants for reasons that are not known today. The specific epithet *flaccida* means "limp" and refers to the thin leaves that often droop. It was discovered in Florida and is most abundant there, giving it the common name.

OTHER COMMON NAMES Southern quillwort

Florida quillwort
(*Isoëtes flaccida*).
with close-up of
spore.

Engelmann's Quillwort
Isoëtes engelmannii A. Braun

DESCRIPTION Stems short, erect, underground, and cormlike. Leaves linear, 6–35 or more cm long, white at base. Sporangia recessed into leaf bases, 6–13 mm long, white, each one covered from less than one-fifth to one-half or more of their length by a velum or thin flap of tissue. Megaspores white, 0.4–0.5 mm in diameter; surface ornamented with sharp ridges or crests that are connected into a netlike or honeycomb-like pattern.

HABITAT Grows in mud at the margins of streams, swamps, and ponds, and in ditches.

RANGE Widely scattered and seemingly uncommon in Alabama, mostly in the highland provinces. Occurs throughout the eastern United States from northern Florida to southern New England and west to the Mississippi Valley; frequent in the Appalachian highlands, infrequent and widely scattered elsewhere.

COMMENTS This is the largest quillwort found in Alabama, but like all members of the genus it is inconspicuous because of its grasslike appearance and is easily overlooked. It is probably more common in Alabama than is presently known. This is the most widely distributed quillwort in North America.

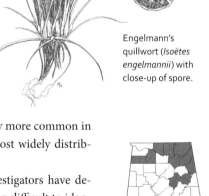

Engelmann's quillwort (*Isoëtes engelmannii*) with close-up of spore.

This species is quite variable, and recent investigators have described several species within it, but these are often difficult to identify in the field. They are differentiated by detailed comparisons of megaspore size and ornamentation, and by degree of coverage of the sporangium by the velum, a thin flap of tissue. Not all authors recognize these segregates. We take a "middle-ground" approach here and recognize some of these while grouping others together.

Several members of this species complex have been identified in

Alabama. True *Isoëtes engelmannii* is found primarily in the highland provinces with the others being found mostly in the Coastal Plain. These are discussed with the two segregate species that we do recognize: *I. louisianensis*, the Louisiana quillwort, and *I. valida*, the strong quillwort.

George Engelmann discovered this species in 1842 near St. Louis; Alexander Braun named it in Engelmann's honor.

Engelmann's quillwort growing in a small swamp between Evergreen and Owassa, Conecuh County.

Louisiana Quillwort
Isoëtes louisianensis Thieret

DESCRIPTION Stems short, erect, underground, and cormlike. Leaves linear, 6–35 or more cm long, white at base. Sporangia recessed into leaf bases, 6–13 mm long, white with brown streaks, covered less than one-fifth of their length by a velum or thin flap of tissue. Megaspores white, 0.5–0.6 mm in diameter; surface ornamented with thick broken ridges in a netlike pattern.

HABITAT Grows in sand, gravel, or mud bars in small streams or on stream banks, the stream water usually stained brown with tannins released from leaf decomposition.

RANGE Known from Alabama from a few collections in the Coastal Plain. Rare in the lower Coastal Plain of Louisiana, Mississippi, and Alabama.

COMMENTS During higher water, plants of this species may be partially submersed and leaves may be seen trailing in the current. Coarse, stable soil is apparently preferred, and *Isoëtes louisianensis* is not usually rooted in soft fine mucky soil.

The megaspores of this species are a little larger than *Isoëtes engelmannii*. It is believed by some to be a fertile hybrid between *I. engelmannii* and *I. melanopoda* (Boom 1982).

Lellinger (1985) assumed this to be a sterile hybrid and did not treat it separately from *I. engelmannii*. It is a fertile species in its own right and we include it here.

This species is part of the *Isoëtes engelmannii* complex. Three of the other members of the complex found in Alabama are *I. appalachiana* D. F. Brunton & D. M. Britton, Appalachian quillwort, which has megaspores with short ridges or spines that form a netlike pattern; *I. boomii* N. Luebke, Boom's quillwort, which has ridges on

Louisiana quillwort (*Isoëtes louisianensis*) with close-up of spore.

the megaspores similar to those of typical *I. louisianensis* but with thin ridges instead of thick; and *I. hyemalis* D. F. Brunton, evergreen quillwort, which has megaspores with a network of interconnecting ridges in a honeycomb pattern. We have treated these three as parts of *I. louisianensis*.

This quillwort was first discovered in Louisiana, and Louisiana botanist John W. Thieret named it in 1973.

The federal government lists this species as endangered.

Louisiana quillwort growing in a muddy floodplain of a seasonal creek in Butler County.

Strong Quillwort
Isoëtes valida (Engelmann) Clute

DESCRIPTION Stems short, erect, underground, and cormlike. Leaves linear, to 60 cm long, pale toward the base. Sporangia recessed into leaf bases, 6–13 mm long, uniform white in color, covered between one-half to three-fourths of their length by a velum or thin flap of tissue. Megaspores white, 0.4–0.55 mm in diameter; surface with irregular high broken ridges in a netlike pattern.

HABITAT Grows along margins of swamps, streams, ponds, and bogs.

RANGE Poorly known and widely scattered in Alabama, found both in the Coastal Plain and the highland provinces. Occurs in the Appalachian Mountains and Piedmont from Pennsylvania to northern Alabama, disjunct in the Coastal Plain of Delaware, Georgia, and Alabama.

COMMENTS This species is sometimes placed in the *Isoëtes engelmannii* complex. It differs from other members of the group by its velum that covers more than one-half of the white, unmarked sporangium wall and its raggedly netlike megaspore ornamentation.

This quillwort has been called *Isoëtes caroliniana*, but *I. valida* is an earlier name for it and has priority.

The epithet *valida* means "strong" or "well developed" and may refer to the large velum.

OTHER COMMON NAMES Carolina quillwort, true quillwort, mountain quillwort

SYNONYMS *Isoëtes caroliniana* (A. A. Eaton) N. Luebke, *Isoëtes engelmannii* A. Braun var. *caroliniana* A. A. Eaton

Strong quillwort growing in a small swamp between Evergreen and Owassa, Conecuh County.

Limestone Quillwort
Isoëtes butleri Engelmann

DESCRIPTION Stems short, erect, underground, and cormlike. Leaves linear, 6–20 cm long, white to pale reddish brown at base. Sporangia recessed into leaf bases, 6–10 or more mm long, mottled with brown or marked with brown lines, covered one-tenth to one-half of their length by a velum, a thin flap of tissue. Megaspores white to pale brown, 0.48–0.65 mm in diameter; surface ornamented with unconnected low bumps.

HABITAT Grows in thin, seasonally wet soil underlain by limestone.

RANGE Known in Alabama from a few localities in the Highland Rim and in the Ridge and Valley. Occurs in the southeastern United States from northern Alabama and Georgia north to Kentucky and west to central Texas and southeastern Kansas.

COMMENTS This species grows in thin soil that is wet only during the winter and spring. The rest of the year, the soil is dry and the plants die back and persist only as dormant underground stems. This is also true of *Isoëtes piedmontana* and generally of *I. melanopoda* as well.

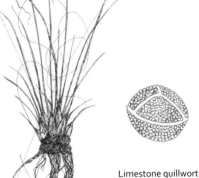

Limestone quillwort (*Isoëtes butleri*) with close-up of spore.

Like all *Isoëtes*, this one is inconspicuous and may have been overlooked by collectors in many places. It is evident only in the winter and spring.

Isoëtes butleri, along with *I. melanopoda*, *I. piedmontana*, and a few quillworts not known from Alabama, are closely related and have been considered to be the same species by some authors. They place them all under the earliest name, *I. melanopoda*. Studies by Taylor et al. (1975) and Boom (1979) have indicated that all of these species are distinct.

George Engelmann named this species in 1878 in honor of its discoverer, George D. Butler, a lawyer, teacher, and botanist who

corresponded with Engelmann. The common name refers to lime-stone habitats preferred by the quillwort.

OTHER COMMON NAMES Glade quillwort, Butler's quillwort

Limestone quillwort growing in the Kathy Stiles Freeland Glades Preserve, Bibb County.

Black-Foot Quillwort
Isoëtes melanopoda Gay & Durieu

DESCRIPTION Stems short, erect, underground, and cormlike. Leaves linear, 7–40 cm long, dark brown to black at base. Sporangia recessed into leaf bases, 5–30 mm long, with brown spots, covered one-fifth to two-thirds of their length by a velum or thin flap of tissue. Megaspores white, 0.25–0.45 mm in diameter; surface ornamented with unconnected low bumps and ridges.

HABITAT Grows in mud at the margins of ponds and streams and in seasonal pools on sandstone outcrops.

RANGE Rare in Alabama with a few localities in the Highland Rim and in the Coastal Plain. Occasional from Minnesota and South Dakota south to Louisiana and Texas and east to Tennessee and northern Alabama and Georgia, rare in the Coastal Plain from Louisiana to eastern Alabama.

Black-foot quillwort
(*Isoëtes melanopoda*)
with close-up of
spore.

COMMENTS This midwestern species reaches the southeastern limits of its main range in Alabama and Georgia, and is consequently rare here. It has also been found in several locations in southern Alabama and Mississippi and in most of Louisiana.

The specific epithet *melanopoda* means "black-foot" and refers to the darkened leaf bases, from which the common name is also derived.

OTHER COMMON NAMES Midland quillwort

Black-foot quillwort growing in open canopy, wet/sandy soils in Dallas County.

Piedmont Quillwort

Isoëtes piedmontana (Pfeiffer) Reed

DESCRIPTION Stems short, erect, underground, and cormlike. Leaves linear, 7–15 cm long, usually brown at base. Sporangia recessed into leaf bases, 3–5 mm long, brown, covered up to one-third of their length by a velum, a thin flap of tissue. Megaspores off-white, 0.40–0.48 mm in diameter; surface ornamented with unconnected low bumps and ridges.

HABITAT Grows in thin seasonally wet soil at the margins of and in depressions in granitic rock outcrops.

RANGE Known in Alabama from a number of localities from the Piedmont in the east-central part of the state. Occurs only in the Piedmont of the southeastern United States from eastern Alabama to central North Carolina.

COMMENTS Although some authors consider it rare, this species seems to be quite frequent throughout its range. It is the most common quillwort in Georgia (Snyder and Bruce 1986). This species may be found in the Alabama Piedmont on most granitic flat rocks that are wet in the spring.

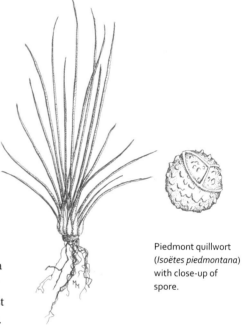

Piedmont quillwort (*Isoëtes piedmontana*) with close-up of spore.

The granitic flat rocks of the southern Piedmont are renowned to botanists for their large number of plant species that are found nowhere else. Unfortunately, the popularity of off-road vehicles is posing a serious threat to the flat rocks and their plant life. Some unthinking, uncaring drivers of these vehicles seem to take delight in causing the most destruction possible by driving directly through the mud and potholes where these unusual plants grow. Flat rocks have also been perceived as useless "waste" ground, resulting in many of them being used as dumps for trash and other refuse. Many rocks are littered with rusted cans and shards of broken glass.

Another granite outcrop species, *Isoëtes melanospora* Engelmann, the black-spored quillwort, has been erroneously reported from Alabama. It can be distinguished from *I. piedmontana* by its blackish spores, leaves that are usually less than 8 cm long, and an unpigmented sporangium wall.

This quillwort was originally named as a variety of *Isoëtes virginica*, and some recent authors treat it as such. It has also been considered to be the same as *I. melanopoda*, but studies by Taylor et al. (1975) and Boom (1979) have indicated that it is distinct.

The specific epithet *piedmontana* and the common name refer to the region in which this species occurs.

OTHER COMMON NAMES Black-base quillwort

SYNONYMS *Isoëtes virginica* Pfeiffer var. *piedmontana* Pfeiffer

Piedmont quillwort growing on a granite flat rock near Auburn, Lee County.

Field Horsetail
Equisetum arvense Linnaeus

DESCRIPTION Rhizomes creeping, subterranean. Aerial stems annual, with conspicuous joints or nodes, of two types; vegetative stems green with many thin branches in whorls at the nodes, 25 to 50 cm tall, persisting throughout the growing season; fertile stems unbranched, pink to tan in color, 15 to 30 cm tall, appearing in the early spring and withering as soon as the spores are shed. Leaves tiny, in whorls at nodes and fused into toothed sheaths. Sporangia borne on the undersides of umbrella-like sporangiophores that are grouped into strobili at the ends of the fertile shoots.

HABITAT In Alabama, seemingly restricted to wet sand on stream banks at the bases of limestone or chalk bluffs and cliffs; elsewhere known from damp woods and meadows and along railroad tracks and roadsides.

Field horsetail
(*Equisetum arvense*).

RANGE Rare in Alabama; known from only four localities, one each in the Cumberland Plateau and Ridge and Valley, and two from the Black Belt in the Coastal Plain. Common throughout almost all of North America, but rare in the southeastern United States and absent from Florida and most of the Gulf Coast. Also occurs in Europe and Asia.

COMMENTS This distinctive plant is abundant and weedy in the northern United States, but it is quite rare in Alabama and the surrounding states. It reaches the southeastern limit of its primary range in the highland regions of northern Alabama and Georgia. It is seemingly disjunct in the Black Belt of Alabama.

R. M. Harper first found this species in Alabama on a bank of the Tombigbee River in Marengo County near Demopolis in 1908. This population was still present in 1983 growing on the sandy river bank beneath a low chalk bluff. At that time the colony was small and appeared to have been damaged by recent floods.

The horsetail was not found elsewhere in Alabama until 1974, when the Morgan County locality in the Cumberland Plateau was found near Hughes Spring in the northeastern corner of the county. There it grows in sand next to a spring at the base of a shaded limestone bluff. The Greene County colony was discovered in 1978. It grows at the base of a high chalk bluff on the bank of the Black Warrior River, covering an extensive area of sand on the river bank. The Ridge and Valley population was discovered in 1992 near Willett Spring in Calhoun County.

In Europe the juice of this plant has been mixed with vinegar and used as a remedy for ulcers and dropsy (Abbe 1981).

The genus name *Equisetum* means "horse bristle"; it and the common name refer to the resemblance of the bushy vegetative shoots to the tail of a horse. The specific epithet *arvense* means "of fields."

Above left: Vegetative stem of field horsetail.

Above right: Early vegetative and fertile stems growing in sandy soil next to a large limestone spring near Union Hill, Morgan County.

Tall Scouring-Rush
Equisetum hyemale Linnaeus

DESCRIPTION Rhizomes creeping, subterranean. Aerial stems with conspicuous joints or nodes, unbranched and all alike, green, to 100 or more cm tall, evergreen; stems ridged, decidedly rough and gritty on the surface. Leaves tiny, in whorls at nodes and fused into toothed sheaths, the teeth deciduous. Sporangia borne on the undersides of umbrella-like sporangiophores that are grouped into strobili at the ends of upright stems; spores dark, round, and fertile.

HABITAT Grows on damp shaded stream banks, pond shores, and roadsides. Most Alabama localities seem to be in the proximity of limestone and other calcareous rocks.

RANGE Scattered throughout Alabama, particularly in the limestone regions of both the highland provinces and the Coastal Plain. Occurs essentially throughout North America with other varieties in Europe and Asia.

Tall scouring-rush
(*Equisetum hyemale*).

COMMENTS The cells of this and many other *Equisetum* species contain minute crystals of silica, a hard, sandlike substance, giving the stems a rough, scratchy feel to the touch. Because of this property, they have been used for scouring pots and pans, giving rise to the common name scouring-rush.

Although seldom used any more for this purpose in developed countries, scouring-rush stems are sometimes used as very fine "sandpaper" for certain delicate tasks. One of these uses is in the making of the double reeds for oboes, bassoons, and other double-reed musical instruments. Pieces of scouring-rush stem, known as Dutch rush to musicians, are used for the final smoothing and tuning of the reeds.

This and other *Equisetum* species are considered poisonous to horses and other livestock when consumed with hay (Pohl 1955).

This species occurs throughout the nontropical Northern Hemisphere,

and several regional varieties have been described. All North American material belongs to var. *affine* (Engelmann) A. A. Eaton.

The specific epithet *hyemale* means "winter" and refers to the fact that this species persists throughout winter. The varietal epithet *affine* means "related to," but what Engelmann was referring to is unknown to us.

OTHER COMMON NAMES Common scouring-rush, Dutch rush

SYNONYMS *Equisetum hyemale* Linnaeus ssp. *affine* (Engelmann) Calder & R. L. Taylor, *Equisetum praealtum* Rafinesque, *Hippochaete hyemalis* (Linnaeus) Bruhin ssp. *affinis* (Engelmann) W. A. Weber

Clockwise from top left:

Close-up of aerial stem.

Close-up of strobilus.

Tall scouring-rush growing in the Fern Glade of the Huntsville Botanical Gardens, 2011.

Ferriss's Scouring-Rush
Equisetum × ferrissii Clute

DESCRIPTION Rhizomes creeping, subterranean. Aerial stems with conspicuous joints or nodes, unbranched, all alike, green, to 100 cm tall; lower portions evergreen, upper parts dying back in winter; stems ridged, slightly rough and sandy on the surface. Leaves tiny, in whorls at nodes and fused into toothed sheaths, the teeth deciduous. Sporangia borne on the undersides of umbrella-like sporangiophores that are grouped into strobili at the ends of upright stems; spores pale, shrunken, and aborted.

Ferriss's scouring-rush (*Equisetum × ferrissii*).

HABITAT Grows in damp, often disturbed soil along stream banks, lake shores, and roadsides.

RANGE Known in Alabama from two collections, one from near the Fall Line in Bibb County, the other from the Coastal Plain of Sumter County; neither collection is recent. Occurs rarely throughout the northern United States and southern Canada, southwest to Arizona and California and southeast to Louisiana, North Carolina, and central Alabama.

COMMENTS This is a sterile hybrid between *Equisetum hyemale*, which is found in Alabama, and *E. laevigatum* A. Braun, the smooth scouring-rush, which is not. It is difficult to distinguish *E. × ferrissii* from *E. hyemale*, as both are quite similar in appearance. The easiest character to use is the fact that the upper portions of the stems of *E. × ferrissii* die back in winter, leaving only short stubble, but the stems of *E. hyemale* are fully evergreen. Also, the stem surfaces of *E. × ferrissii* are decidedly less rough and gritty than surfaces of *E. hyemale*. If spores are available, those of *E. × ferrissii* will be pale and shrunken, but the spores of *E. hyemale* will be dark and round.

The range of this sterile hybrid is remarkable. One parent, *Equisetum laevigatum*, occurs primarily in western North America and is found east of the Mississippi River only in the Great Lakes region; the other parent, *E. hyemale*, occurs essentially throughout North America. The hybrid *E.* × *ferrissii* is found throughout the overlapping areas of the two ranges, but it is also found in a number of places in the eastern and southeastern United States that are far from the range of *E. laevigatum*.

The specific epithet *ferrissii* honors James H. Ferriss, an avid collector of ferns in the late nineteenth and early twentieth centuries.

OTHER COMMON NAMES Intermediate scouring-rush

SYNONYMS *Hippochaete* × *ferrissii* (Clute) Škoda & Holub

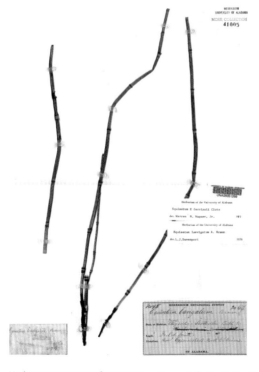

Herbarium specimen of Ferriss's scouring-rush first collected in Bibb County in 1879 and identified as *Equisetum laevigatum* Braun; verified by Dr. E. A. Smith in 1885 and Dr. L. J. Davenport in 1976, then reidentified as *Equisetum* × *ferrissii* Clute by Warren H. Wagner Jr. in 1977.

Rattlesnake Fern
Botrychium virginianum (Linnaeus) Swartz

DESCRIPTION Vegetative blade stalkless, arising directly from the junction with the fertile branch, held high above the ground, triangular, 3 or more pinnate at base, to 25 cm long and 40 cm broad at base; blade tissue thin, membranous; blade segments deeply lobed, with sharp tips; midribs distinct; margins jaggedly toothed. Fertile branch to 40 cm long, profusely branched. New growth appearing in the spring.

HABITAT Grows in moist forests in well-drained soil.

RANGE Common in the Alabama highland provinces, scattered in the Coastal Plain. Common throughout most of North America except northern Canada and the southwestern deserts; also occurs in Europe and Asia.

COMMENTS This is the most common *Botrychium* in Alabama and is the most widespread *Botrychium* of North America (Wagner and Wagner 1993). It may be found in almost any well-drained hardwood forest in the highland provinces. It is found in similar habitats in the Coastal Plain and may also be found near streams in pinewoods there.

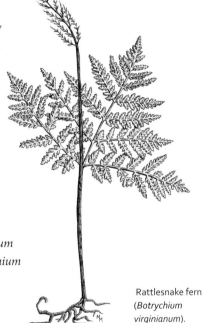

Rattlesnake fern (*Botrychium virginianum*).

This species is quite distinct from the other *Botrychium* species found in Alabama because of the thin texture of the sterile blade. It is also different in that the plant appears in the spring and dies back in the fall. The other species of *Botrychium* have thicker blades that in some species are almost leathery; their new growth appears in the fall or winter, and the plants are essentially evergreen.

Native Americans once used the rhizome of this plant to make a poultice for snakebites, bruises, cuts, and sores (Foster and Duke 1990).

The genus name *Botrychium* is from the Greek and means a "bunch of grapes," referring to the appearance of the sporangia and

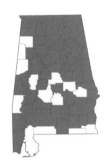

the fertile branch. Because of this, many of the species in this genus are known as grape ferns. The specific epithet *virginianum* means "of Virginia," where this species was originally discovered. The origin of the common name "rattlesnake fern" is obscure but has been said by some to refer to the fertile stalk that someone apparently thought resembled the tail of this snake, although it actually does not.

OTHER COMMON NAMES Virginia grape fern

SYNONYMS *Botrypus virginianus* (Linnaeus) Holub, *Osmundopteris virginiana* (Linnaeus) Small

Rattlesnake fern growing in the Kaul Wildflower Garden at the Birmingham Botanical Gardens.

Winter Grape Fern
Botrychium lunarioides (Michaux) Swartz

DESCRIPTION Vegetative blade stalkless, arising directly from the junction with the fertile branch, held low to the ground, triangular, 3 or more pinnate at base, to 5 cm long and 8 cm broad at base; blade tissue thick, somewhat leathery; blade segments round to fan-shaped, with rounded, indistinct tips; midribs absent, veins forking from leaflet base; margins finely toothed. Fertile branch to 15 cm long, sparsely branched. New growth appearing in the winter.

HABITAT Grows in sandy soil in lawns, pastures, churchyards, cemeteries, and other grassy areas, often ones that are regularly mowed, usually in full sun; occurs less commonly in dry open woods.

Winter grape fern (*Botrychium lunarioides*) with close-up of leaf.

RANGE Frequent in the Coastal Plain of Alabama, extending at least as far north as Tuscaloosa County. Rare in the Piedmont and Cumberland Plateau. Frequent along the Gulf Coast, except the Mississippi River delta, from eastern Texas to northern Florida and southern Georgia; increasingly rare along the Atlantic Coast northward to North Carolina.

COMMENTS This fern was considered to be very rare for many years. However, collections made by a number of southern botanists in the last several decades have shown that *Botrychium lunarioides* is indeed quite common in the Coastal Plain from Louisiana to southern Georgia. It is most often collected in rural cemeteries, which not only provide a habitat for the fern, but which also are semipublic places accessible to botanists.

That this fern was so thoroughly overlooked for so long is not surprising. It is quite small, and the leaf blade usually grows flat on the ground, giving the fern one of its common names. Its favored habitat seems to be among thick grasses that are regularly mowed.

Not only do the grasses obscure the fern, but also collectors of ferns traditionally overlooked such locations since larger, more obvious species are not present. The bulbous adder's-tongue, *Ophioglossum crotalophoroides*, is frequently found growing with *Botrychium lunarioides*, but it is even smaller and more inconspicuous.

The specific epithet *lunarioides* means "like a *Lunaria*," another plant. The common name refers to the fact that it grows during the winter.

This species was known for more than half of the twentieth century as *Botrychium biternatum* (Savigny) Underwood, due to a misunderstanding of Savigny's original name.

OTHER COMMON NAMES Prostrate grape fern

SYNONYMS *Botrypus lunarioides* Michaux, *Sceptridium lunarioides* (Michaux) Holub

Winter grape fern growing in well-drained sandy soils near Ft. Morgan, Baldwin County.

Sparse-Lobed Grape Fern
Botrychium biternatum (Savigny) Underwood

DESCRIPTION Vegetative blade with a long stalk to the junction with the fertile branch, held high above the ground, triangular, 2-pinnate at base, to 12 cm long and 15 cm broad at base; blade tissue thin, papery; larger segments sparsely lobed, the indentations becoming increasingly shallow and indistinct toward the tip, the outlines of the lobes rounded; margins of lobes and segments finely toothed to smooth; midribs distinct; tips of lobes and segments forming acute angles. Fertile branch to 40 or more cm long, sparsely 2-pinnately branched. New growth appearing in the fall.

HABITAT Grows in overgrown fields, in young mixed woods, and along wooded creek bottoms and swamp margins.

RANGE Scattered to frequent throughout Alabama, seemingly most frequent in the Coastal Plain and along the Fall Line. Frequent in the southeastern United States from Florida west to eastern Texas and north to Maryland and southern Illinois.

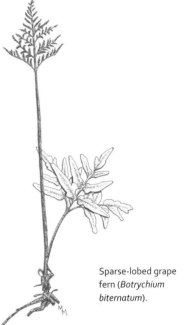

Sparse-lobed grape fern (*Botrychium biternatum*).

COMMENTS This species and *Botrychium dissectum* forma *obliquum* are at times among the most difficult of Alabama ferns to distinguish from each other. The characters used to distinguish the two are subtle at best, and the two species seem to intergrade with each other in the southeast. In general, *B. biternatum* will have a more blunt appearance than *B. dissectum*; it will be more sparsely lobed and the leaflets will not be lobed near their tips. The outer margins of the lobes are decidedly rounded in *B. biternatum*, but in *B. dissectum*, they tend to be rather straight and angular. The blade tissue of *B. dissectum* is usually somewhat thicker than that of *B. biternatum*.

When Underwood published the name combination *B. biternatum* in 1896, he was under the mistaken impression that Savigny's

original name, *Osmunda biternata*, referred to the species we now know as *B. lunarioides*, as were other authors at the time. He later published the name *B. tenuifolium* to refer to the present species, and it was known by this name for decades. In the early 1960s it was found that Savigny was actually referring to the present species. Since *biternatum* is the earlier of the two epithets, it is the valid one for this species.

The specific epithet *biternatum* means "divided into threes twice" and refers to the vegetative blades that are divided into three major parts, each of which is again divided into three parts. The common name comes from the fact that the divisions of the blade are few and well separated.

OTHER COMMON NAMES Southern grape fern

SYNONYMS *Botrychium tenuifolium* Underwood, *Botrychium dissectum* Sprengel var. *tenuifolium* (Underwood) Farwell

Sparse-lobed grape fern growing at the base of a pine tree.

Alabama Grape Fern
Botrychium jenmanii Underwood

DESCRIPTION Sterile blade with a long stalk to the junction with the fertile branch, held high above the ground, triangular, 3 or more pinnate at base, to 15 cm long and 20 cm broad at base; blade tissue thick, somewhat leathery; blade segments rounded or forming obtuse angles; midribs indistinct but present; margins finely toothed. Fertile branch to 30 cm long, sparsely 2-pinnately branched. New growth appearing in late summer.

HABITAT Grows on dry to moist forested slopes, often in young second-growth forests; occasional in lawns and cemeteries.

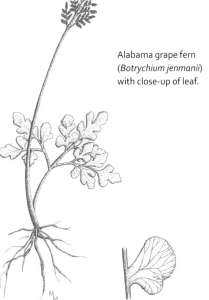

Alabama grape fern
(*Botrychium jenmanii*)
with close-up of leaf.

RANGE Very rare in Alabama; definitely known at this writing from only three localities, one in the Coastal Plain, one in the Piedmont near the Fall Line, and one in the Ridge and Valley. Scattered in the southeastern United States from Florida north to Virginia and west to Louisiana, seemingly most abundant in the Piedmont and Blue Ridge of northeastern Georgia and western North Carolina. Also in the Caribbean islands.

COMMENTS This species was traditionally known as *Botrychium alabamense* Maxon. William Maxon named it from material collected on the campus of Spring Hill College in Mobile, Alabama, in 1906, although the first US collection was actually made in the Piedmont of Georgia in 1900 (Dean 1969).

Recent studies have shown that *B. alabamense* is the same as *B. jenmanii* of the Caribbean region. Since *B. jenmanii* is the earlier name, it prevails.

This species is believed to have arisen as a hybrid between *Botrychium biternatum* and *B. lunarioides*.

The specific epithet *jenmanii* honors George Jenman, a British gardener who studied the plants of Jamaica and British Guiana. Although this species is no longer known by the name *alabamense*, the common name Alabama grape fern is still the most frequently used one in the United States.

OTHER COMMON NAMES Dixie grape fern, Jenman's grape fern

SYNONYMS *Botrychium alabamense* Maxon, *Sceptridium jenmanii* (Underwood) Lyon

Alabama grape fern growing in mixed woods near Auburn, Lee County.

Cutleaf Grape Fern
Botrychium dissectum Sprengel

DESCRIPTION Vegetative blade with a long stalk to the junction with the fertile branch, held well above the ground, triangular, 3 or more pinnate at base, to 40 cm long and 50 cm broad at base; blade tissue somewhat thick, almost leathery; larger leaflets profusely and deeply lobed nearly to the tip; outlines of the lobes nearly straight; margins of lobes and segments finely toothed to deeply fringed; midribs distinct; tips of lobes and segments forming acute angles. Fertile branch to 40 or more cm long, profusely 2-pinnately branched. New growth appearing in the fall.

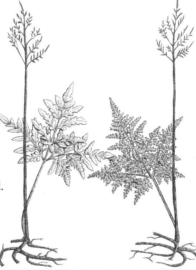

HABITAT Grows in a variety of open woodlands, often young second-growth mixed forests; generally in moist but not wet soil.

Cutleaf grape fern (*Botrychium dissectum*).

RANGE Scattered to frequent throughout Alabama, most frequent in the east and the highland provinces, especially the Piedmont. Frequent throughout eastern North America from southern Canada to the Gulf Coast and west to the eastern margin of the Great Plains.

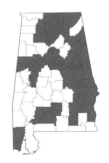

COMMENTS This species is highly variable. Two forms are known based on the dissection of the margins of the lobes and segments; forma *obliquum* has finely toothed margins that are otherwise uncut, but the margins of forma *dissectum* are deeply cut into many fine projections, giving the blade a lacy appearance. The former is much more frequent in Alabama than the latter.

These two forms intergrade with each other, producing a variety of intermediate plants. These are usually similar to forma *obliquum* but have margins that are cut as much as a quarter of the way to the midrib.

Leaves persist throughout the winter, darkening to bronze or copper in color.

The specific epithet *dissectum* and the common name both refer to the finely cut leaflet margins of many examples of this fern.

OTHER COMMON NAMES Dissected grape fern, lace-leaf grape fern

SYNONYMS *Botrychium obliquum* Muhlenberg *ex* Willdenow, *Sceptridium dissectum* (Sprengel) Lyon

Cutleaf grape fern growing in mixed woodlands of Tuscaloosa County, 2010.

Bulbous Adder's-Tongue
Ophioglossum crotalophoroides Walter

DESCRIPTION Rhizome globular, bulblike, one to three leaves per rhizome. Vegetative blades elliptic to ovate, sometimes nearly heart-shaped, 1.5–3 cm long, 1–2 cm broad, borne horizontally, nearly prostrate; veins all alike. Fertile branch arising from the base of the vegetative blade, to 7 or more cm long, with a conspicuous sterile tip.

HABITAT Grows in sandy soil in lawns, pastures, churchyards, and other grassy areas, often ones that are regularly mowed, usually in full sun.

RANGE Common in the Alabama Coastal Plain to the Fall Line as far north as Tuscaloosa County with a few collections in the Highland Rim, Ridge and Valley, and Piedmont. Common in the southeastern United States along the Gulf Coast from eastern Texas to Florida and northward to South Carolina and southeastern Oklahoma; also occurs in Central and South America.

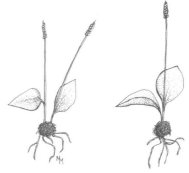

Bulbous adder's-tongue (*Ophioglossum crotalophoroides*) with close-up of leaf.

COMMENTS This tiny fern was once thought to be very rare. A number of collectors have shown that this species and the winter grape fern (*Botrychium lunarioides*), also once thought to be rare, are actually quite common in the Gulf Coastal Plain, where they are frequently found growing together. Both are diminutive and hard to see and grow in mowed grassy areas that past fern collectors had rarely considered investigating. Both species are most often collected in rural cemeteries. This miniscule plant is easily overlooked, so it is best to get down on your knees with your head close to the ground in order to find it.

The first collection in the Alabama highland provinces was in Morgan County in the southernmost part of the county at the foot of the Cumberland Plateau escarpment.

Thomas Walter first discovered this species in the late eighteenth century; he included it in *Flora Caroliniana* in 1788 (Dean 1969).

The genus name *Ophioglossum* means "snake tongue" and was applied to these plants in ancient times; although it is inapt, it was taken up by Linnaeus and also persists in the common name adder's-tongue. The specific epithet *crotalophoroides* comes from Greek words that mean "like a rattle bearer" and refers to the resemblance of the fertile branch to the tail of a rattlesnake.

OTHER COMMON NAMES Tuber adder's-tongue

Bulbous adder's-tongue fern growing in rich, mesic limestone woods in Jackson County.

Limestone Adder's-Tongue
Ophioglossum engelmannii Prantl

DESCRIPTION Rhizome cylindrical with one or two leaves per rhizome. Sterile blades elliptic to nearly spearhead-shaped, to 10 cm long and 3 cm broad, borne vertically or nearly so; veins of two distinct sizes, the thicker ones forming a coarse network that contains finer networks of thinner veins. Fertile branch arising from the base of the vegetative blade, to 12 cm long, not conspicuously sterile at the tip.

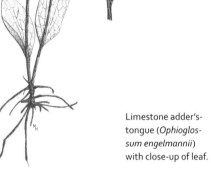

HABITAT Grows in thin soil over limey rocks in pastures and cedar glades and on roadsides.

RANGE Seemingly infrequent in Alabama, occurring in the limestone regions of the highland provinces and in the Black Belt region of the Coastal Plain. Occurs across the southern United States from Florida north to Virginia and the Ohio Valley and west to eastern Arizona and northern Mexico.

Limestone adder's-tongue (*Ophioglossum engelmannii*) with close-up of leaf.

COMMENTS The dual pattern of the veins in this species is highly distinctive. It is best seen by holding a leaf up with a strong light behind. This species forms extensive colonies by vegetative reproduction. Fresh plants have an unpleasant odor and the blades are commonly folded when alive.

Since this species is quite small, it may be hidden by other vegetation. It may be more common than is presently indicated, both in the highland provinces and the Black Belt; it may also be present in other regions of the Coastal Plain where limestone is present.

The specific epithet *engelmannii* honors George Engelmann, an American plant taxonomist.

OTHER COMMON NAMES Engelmann's adder's-tongue

Limestone adder's-tongue after rain.

Least Adder's-Tongue
Ophioglossum nudicaule Linnaeus f.

DESCRIPTION Rhizome thickened and irregularly shaped with one or two leaves per rhizome. Vegetative blades elliptic to ovate, to 1.5 cm long and 0.6 cm broad, borne horizontally or nearly so; veins all alike. Fertile branch arising at the base of the vegetative blade, to 10 cm long, not conspicuously sterile at the tip.

HABITAT Grows in damp sandy, often peaty, soil in lawns and other grassy areas; also on lake shores and in seepages, usually in shade.

RANGE Seemingly rare in Alabama, occurring in the lower Coastal Plain. Occurs in the Coastal Plain of the southeastern United States from Texas to Florida and South Carolina; also occurs in the tropics throughout the world.

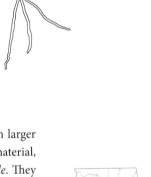

Least adder's-tongue (*Ophioglossum nudicaule*).

COMMENTS This is the smallest Alabama member of a most inconspicuous group of ferns. *Ophioglossum nudicaule* has likely been overlooked and is probably much more common than is presently known throughout its range. It should be expected throughout the Alabama Coastal Plain south of the Black Belt.

This species is quite variable in Florida and can be much larger there. Several species have been described from Florida material, but some authors recognize these as varieties of *O. nudicaule*. They are not generally accepted as distinct today and are considered to be merely variations resulting from habitat differences. All Alabama material would belong to *O. tenerum* Mettenius, also known as *O. nudicaule* var. *tenerum* Clausen.

The specific epithet *nudicaule* means "bare-stemmed" and refers to the stalk of the fertile branch. The common name refers to the tiny size of the plant.

OTHER COMMON NAMES Slender adder's-tongue, dwarf adder's-tongue

Synonyms *Ophioglossum tenerum* Mettenius, *Ophioglossum dendroneu-ron* E. St. John, *Ophioglossum mononeuron* E. St. John

Least adder's-tongue fern growing in open field with sandy soils in Baldwin County.

Stalked Adder's-Tongue

Ophioglossum petiolatum Hooker

DESCRIPTION Rhizome cylindrical, roots often budding to form new plants, one to two leaves per rhizome. Sterile blades spearhead-shaped, to 7 cm long and 3 cm broad, borne vertically or nearly so; veins all alike. Fertile branch to 15 cm long, not conspicuously sterile at the tip. Vegetative blade with a short stalk between the base and the junction with the fertile branch.

HABITAT Grows in damp sandy soil in grassy areas and ditches and on lake shores and swamp margins, usually in shade. Plants sometimes weedy in lawns and around buildings.

RANGE Infrequent on the Coastal Plain of Alabama. Naturalized in the southeastern Coastal Plain from eastern Texas to Florida and north to North Carolina. A native of the world tropics.

Stalked adder's-tongue (*Ophioglossum petiolatum*).

COMMENTS As with other members of *Ophioglossum*, this one has probably been overlooked and should be expected throughout the lower Coastal Plain of Alabama.

The roots of this species bear buds that can form new plants, often resulting in dense colonies.

Unlike most members of the genus, *Ophioglossum petiolatum* grows readily in pots, making it suitable for botany instruction. Earliest records in North America date from 1900 to 1930, suggesting that it was introduced through nurseries and horticulture (Wagner and Wagner 1993). It probably came in as a weed with cultivated plants.

The specific epithet *petiolatum* means "stalked"; it and the common name refer to the stalk between the vegetative blade and the fertile branch.

OTHER COMMON NAMES Long-stem adder's-tongue

SYNONYMS *Ophioglossum floridanum* E. St. John

Stalked adder's-tongue growing on a swamp margin.

Southeastern Adder's-Tongue
Ophioglossum pycnostichum (Fernald) A. & D. Löve

DESCRIPTION Rhizome cylindrical, one or rarely two leaves per rhizome. Sterile blades ovate, to 8 cm long and 4 cm broad, borne vertically or nearly so; veins all alike. Fertile branch to 18 cm long, not conspicuously sterile at the tip. Fertile branch arising at the base of the vegetative blade.

HABITAT Grows in damp soil in floodplains of creeks and rivers and along swamp margins, also in damp meadows and grassy areas, usually in shade.

RANGE Occasional in the highland provinces of Alabama, rare in the Coastal Plain. Occurs throughout the eastern United States south of the Great Lakes.

COMMENTS Some authors believe that this North American species is not distinct from *Ophioglossum vulgatum* of Eurasia and have treated *O. pycnostichum* as a synonym of that species (Wagner and Wagner 1993). Other authors list it as a variety of the Eurasian species.

The specific epithet *pycnostichum* means "crowded rows" and refers to the sporangia.

OTHER COMMON NAMES Southern adder's-tongue, common adder's-tongue

SYNONYMS *Ophioglossum vulgatum* Linnaeus var. *pycnostichum* Fernald

Southeastern adder's-tongue (*Ophioglossum pycnostichum*) with close-up of leaf.

Southeastern adder's-tongue fern growing in rich, mesic limestone woods in Jackson County.

Royal Fern
Osmunda regalis Linnaeus

DESCRIPTION Rhizome stout, erect, growing at ground surface or a little above, with tangled wiry black roots. Leaves ovate, 2-pinnate, to 1 m or more tall, hairless or nearly so; leaves of two similar-looking kinds: sterile leaves with leaflets held horizontally, fertile leaves with ascending vegetative leaflets and bearing sporangia at the tip only; vegetative leaflets widely spaced, oblong, with nearly smooth margins; fertile segments lacking blade tissue and bearing naked sporangia.

HABITAT Grows in wet soil in floodplains, swamps, and ditches, and on the banks of streams and lakes.

RANGE Frequent throughout Alabama. Occurs throughout eastern North America from Newfoundland west to Saskatchewan and south to Texas and Florida. Varieties occur throughout much of the world.

Royal fern
(*Osmunda regalis*).

COMMENTS This fern is large, handsome, and easily cultivated. As with other species of *Osmunda*, the rhizomes and roots form a tangled mass that orchid growers use as a growth substrate. Fiber from the rhizome and roots is also used to make twine, rope, netting, and mats (Dunbar 1989). A portion of the rhizome is white and edible; because of its pungent taste it has been called bog onion (Abbe 1981).

The spores contain chlorophyll, giving them a green color and causing the young sporangia to be green as well. As the spores mature and are shed, the sporangia change color to a distinctive, rusty brown.

Several varieties are known for this worldwide species. All North American material belongs to var. *spectabilis* (Willdenow) A. Gray; the type variety of this fern, *Osmunda regalis* var. *regalis*, occurs in Eurasia.

Osmunda ferns are host plants for the Osmunda borer moth (*Papaipema speciosissima*).

The generic name *Osmunda* is derived from Osmunder, the Saxon name for Thor, the Norse god of war. In northern Europe these ferns grew in bogs where bog iron was found, a native form of the metal that was used to make weapons and other items.

The specific epithet *regalis* refers to the stately "regal" appearance of this large fern, as does the common name.

Royal fern growing in floodplain of Chewacla Creek, Lee County.

Cinnamon Fern
Osmunda cinnamomea Linnaeus

DESCRIPTION Rhizome stout, erect, growing at ground surface or a little above, with tangled wiry black roots. Leaves of two completely dissimilar kinds: vegetative leaves spearhead-shaped, 1-pinnate with deeply lobed leaflets, to 1.5 m tall; fertile leaves 2-pinnate, lacking blade tissue, "leaflets" consisting only of midribs that are covered with naked sporangia; leaves of both types with long, tufted orange to brown hairs at the bases of leaflets and leaf stalks; fertile leaves appearing in early spring and withering as soon as the spores are shed. Lobes of vegetative leaflets separated by broad gaps, the sides of adjacent lobes well apart from each other; lobe tips somewhat angular.

Cinnamon fern
(*Osmunda cinna-
momea*).

HABITAT Grows in wet soil in floodplains, swamps, and ditches, and on the banks of streams and lakes.

RANGE Frequent throughout Alabama. Occurs throughout eastern North America from Labrador west to Minnesota and south to Mexico and Florida; also in the West Indies.

COMMENTS Occasionally, variant leaves of this species may be found that have both sterile and fertile leaflets; sometimes the fertile leaflets will even have small amounts of blade tissue. Although such material has been named *Osmunda cinnamomea* forma *frondosa* Britton, it appears that this phenomenon results from injuries and other environmental stresses and does not warrant taxonomic recognition.

Usually the lower portion of these variant leaves will lack sporangia, with the sporangia only on the upper portions. Rarely, a leaf will be found that is vegetative at the base, fertile in the middle, and

vegetative at the tip and resembling the fertile leaf of the interrupted fern, *Osmunda claytoniana* Linnaeus.

Cherokee Indians ate young fiddleheads of this fern as a vegetable (Dunbar 1989). The rhizome is also edible and is reported to taste like raw cabbage (Clute 1938).

This species is widely cultivated as an ornamental.

The species epithet *cinnamomea* and the common name both refer to the cinnamon-like color of the orange-brown hairs on the leaves.

SYNONYMS *Osmundastrum cinnamomeum* (Linnaeus) C. Presl

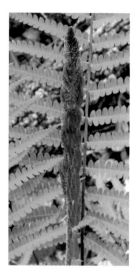

Above: Close-up of fertile and sterile leaves.

Right: Cinnamon fern growing in moist open flat woods of Cherokee County.

Interrupted Fern
Osmunda claytoniana Linnaeus

DESCRIPTION Rhizome stout, erect, growing at ground surface or a little above, with tangled wiry black roots. Leaves elliptical, 1-pinnate with deeply lobed leaflets, to 1.5 m tall, of two dissimilar kinds: fertile leaves with spore-bearing leaflets in the middle of the blade, the spore-bearing leaflets bearing only sporangia and lacking blade tissue; leaves of both kinds hairless or nearly so except for nonpersistent brown hairs at the base of the leaf stalk. Lobes of vegetative leaflets separated by very narrow gaps, the sides of adjacent lobes touching each other or nearly so; lobe tips rounded.

HABITAT Grows in well-drained soil in woods and on hummocks in swamps.

RANGE Recently found in Jackson County in northeastern Alabama. Common in eastern North America from Manitoba to Newfoundland and to the south from Missouri to western North Carolina and barely into northern Georgia and Alabama.

COMMENTS Alabama has long been listed as a state in which this species occurs in floras of the region and of nearby states, but it was not actually found here until the spring of 2011. Earlier reports are considered erroneous and were probably based on the misidentification of variant leaves of the cinnamon fern, *Osmunda cinnamomea*.

For example, there is a specimen in the herbarium of Auburn University with fertile leaflets in the middle of a leaf having vegetative leaflets at the tip and at the base, exactly the pattern of *O. claytoniana*, and the specimen was identified as that species. A close examination of the specimen is required to see the tufts of brown hairs at the bases of the leaflets.

This species is known to hybridize with *Osmunda regalis* to form *O.* × *ruggii* in the northeastern United States, but it does not hybridize with *O. cinnamomea*. This would imply that *O. claytoniana* is more closely related to *O. regalis* than the similar-looking *O. cinnamomea*.

Like all members of this genus, the interrupted fern is generally easy to grow in a garden. However, since this is a northern species that barely reaches the northeastern corner of Alabama, it may prove difficult to keep alive in much of the state.

Linnaeus gave this species the name *claytoniana* in honor of English-born colonial botanist John Clayton, who found this fern in Virginia in the early 1700s; the common name comes from the way the centrally located spore-bearing leaflets interrupt the outline of the leaf blade.

Clockwise from top left:

Vegetative leaves of interrupted fern collected by T. Wayne Barger in Jackson County, 2011.

Close-up of fertile pinnae between vegetative pinnae.

Mature plant in a private garden in Shelby County.

Drooping Forked Fern
Dicranopteris flexuosa (Schrader) Underwood

DESCRIPTION Rachis repeatedly forking; terminal branches each with a pair of deeply lobed leaflets to 25 cm long; pairs of smaller leaflets present at each fork; hairy dormant buds often present in the forks. Sori round, without indusia.

HABITAT Found in the southeastern United States in open pine forests.

RANGE Known in Alabama from a single locality, discovered in 1913 and destroyed by railroad construction in 1917 (Graves 1920). Also known from several localities along the Gulf Coast of Florida, none of which has persisted for very long. Native to the West Indies, Central America, and South America.

Drooping forked fern (*Dicranopteris flexuosa*) with close-up of leaf underside showing sori arrangement.

COMMENTS This fern is common in the West Indies and tropical America. Spores are apparently carried to the Gulf Coast of the United States by hurricanes and tropical storms, causing this species to appear and persist for a few years only to be killed during the next winter that is severe enough to cause hard freezes all the way to the coast.

The genus name *Dicranopteris* is from the Greek and means "twice-forked fern"; it refers to the branching of the rachis. The specific epithet *flexuosa* means "flexible" and refers to the long rachis branches.

OTHER COMMON NAMES Net fern

Herbarium specimen of drooping forked fern collected by A. H. Howell in Mobile County, December 3, 1916.

American Climbing Fern
Lygodium palmatum (Bernhardi) Swartz

DESCRIPTION Leaves vinelike with elongated rachises, climbing over other plants, to 3 m long; leaflets palmately lobed, of two dissimilar types: completely vegetative leaflets each with two segments to 6 cm broad, each having 2–7 long, fingerlike lobes; fertile leaflets with numerous segments less than 2 cm broad with sori on the numerous short lobes; completely vegetative leaflets occur on lower portion of leaf, fertile ones on upper portion.

HABITAT Grows in wet strongly acid soil rich in humus in bogs and swamps and on damp rocky slopes.

RANGE Very rare in Alabama, currently documented only from Lookout Mountain in DeKalb and Cherokee Counties. Rare in the eastern United States from New England west to Ontario and south to northern Georgia and Alabama.

American climbing fern (*Lygodium palmatum*) with close-up of leaf underside showing sori arrangement.

COMMENTS Blanche Dean (1969) reported having personally found both *Lygodium palmatum* and *L. japonicum* growing in the same woods south of the city of Mobile, but there are no known specimens to verify it.

The "leaves" of this genus are actually leaflets; the actual leaf is the whole "vine," several of which are produced by each plant. These leaves continue to grow at the tip as long as they are alive; this is unlike the leaves of most other plants, which grow to a certain size and then stop.

Lygodium palmatum was once common around Hartford, Connecticut, but because of overcollecting, the state legislature passed a law to protect this fern from being taken from another person's property. One of the common names for this plant became "Hartford fern," after the town.

The generic name *Lygodium* is from the Greek *lygodes*, meaning flexible, in reference to its twining habit. The specific epithet *palmatum* means "like the palm of a hand" and refers to the shape of the leaflets.

OTHER COMMON NAMES Hartford fern

Vegetative and fertile leaflets of American climbing fern.

Japanese Climbing Fern
Lygodium japonicum (Thunberg) Swartz

DESCRIPTION Leaves vinelike with elongated rachises, climbing over other plants, to 6 m long; leaflets compound, of two somewhat different types: completely vegetative leaflets each with two 2- to 3-pinnate segments to 15 cm long, fertile leaflets similar to those but with slightly smaller segments and fingerlike marginal projections bearing the sori; completely vegetative leafl occur on the lower portion of leaf, fertile on the upper portion.

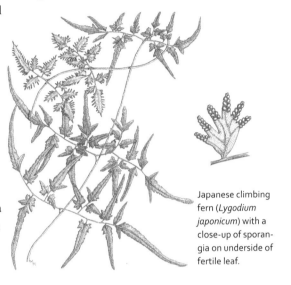

HABITAT Grows in woods, clearings, roadsides, stream banks, and swamp margins, often in partial sun.

RANGE Frequent in the Coastal Plain of Alabama, scattered in the Piedmont. A native of eastern Asia that is naturalized in Coastal Plain of the southeastern United States from Texas to Florida and north to North Carolina.

Japanese climbing fern (*Lygodium japonicum*) with a close-up of sporangia on underside of fertile leaf.

COMMENTS This fern has long been grown in outdoor gardens throughout the South and was first reported to have escaped from cultivation in Thomasville, Georgia, in the early 1900s (Nelson 2000). It has become naturalized and well established in the southeastern states.

Like so many non-native plants, this fern tends to be extremely weedy. In southern Alabama it may grow so thickly as to completely cover the shrubs and small trees on which the vinelike leaves climb. The growth may occasionally be so thick as to shade out and kill the underlying brush. This would suggest that an appropriate common name might be kudzu fern. It is considered a pest by the US Department of Agriculture.

The specific epithet *japonicum* means "of Japan" and refers to the native land of this fern.

Japanese climbing fern growing in a suburban yard in Jefferson County, 2010.

Southern Maidenhair Fern
Adiantum capillus-veneris Linnaeus

DESCRIPTION Rhizome short-creeping on surface of ground or rock, leaves closely spaced. Leaves spearhead-shaped to nearly ovate, 2- to 3-pinnate, blades to 30 cm long and 15 cm wide; leaf stalk not forking, with a single rachis present and primary leaf divisions arising from two sides of rachis, rachis and leaf stalk smooth and hairless, dark brown to black; Leaflets fan-shaped, outer margins deeply notched. Sori oblong, at margins of blade segments, covered by reflexed margins.

HABITAT Grows on damp calcareous rocks, ledges, and cliffs on stream banks and in ravines in full shade.

RANGE Scattered throughout the limestone regions of the Coastal Plain of Alabama, including the Black Belt; rare in the highland provinces in the Highland Rim, the Ridge and Valley, and the limestone slopes of the Cumberland Plateau. Occurs nearly throughout the southern half of the United States from California east to Virginia and southward, also northward along the coasts to southern British Columbia in the west and southern New England in the east; also in tropical regions throughout the world.

Southern maiden-hair fern (*Adiantum capillus-veneris*) with close-up of leaf underside showing sori arrangement.

COMMENTS This fern is often found growing on steep wet limestone banks of rivers and creeks in the Coastal Plain. It is also sometimes found in old wells or on damp, shaded stone walls, growing in cracks of the mortar. The leaves arch gracefully outward from the rock wall with their tips hanging downward.

Like *Adiantum pedatum*, this fern is commonly cultivated in gardens; it is also frequently grown as a house plant.

The genus is from the Greek *adiantos*, meaning "unwetted," for the hairless leaves that shed raindrops. The species epithet *capillus-veneris* means "hair of Venus" in Latin. In the United States, this fern

is called the southern maidenhair since it is more common in the southern part of the country, although it does occur as far north as southern Canada. It has been called the Venus-hair fern since ancient times and is known by that name through most of the rest of its worldwide range. The common name "maidenhair" is said to be an allusion to the slender black leaflet stalks of this fern.

OTHER COMMON NAMES Venus-hair fern, Venus maidenhair fern

Left: Close-up of sori on reflexed margins.

Below: Southern maidenhair fern growing in the Fern Glade at the Birmingham Botanical Gardens.

Rough Maidenhair Fern
Adiantum hispidulum Swartz

DESCRIPTION Rhizome short-creeping on surface of ground or rock, leaves spaced at short intervals. Leaves asymmetrically ovate to circular, 2- to 3-pinnate, blades to 20 cm long and wide; leaf stalk not forking, with a single rachis with primary leaf divisions arising from two sides of rachis, rachis and leaf stalk dark brown and covered with short stiff hairs; leaflets obliquely fan-shaped, outer margins nearly smooth, not obviously notched, with fine bristles underneath. Sori oblong, at margins of blade segments, covered by reflexed margins.

HABITAT Grows on damp shaded banks and old walls.

RANGE Known in Alabama from a few collections in the Coastal Plain. Occurs rarely in Florida and southern Georgia west to Louisiana. A native of Asia and Australia that has escaped from cultivation and possibly become naturalized.

Rough maidenhair fern (*Adiantum hispidulum*) with close-up of leaf underside showing sori arrangement.

COMMENTS This fern is commonly cultivated in pots and gardens. It has been found growing under apparently wild conditions in four southeastern states. It often becomes a weed in greenhouses and can contaminate other pots and be distributed in this way.

The first Alabama collection of this species was made in 1959 on a steep shady road bank near the junction of US Highways 90 and 98 on the eastern shore of Mobile Bay in Baldwin County. It is not known whether the fern persists at this locality. The roads have been reworked since 1959, and the fern may have been destroyed.

The specific epithet *hispidulum* means "minutely bristly" and refers to the fine bristly hairs on the leaf stalk and the undersides of the leaflets; so does the common name.

OTHER COMMON NAMES Rosy maidenhair fern, garden maidenhair fern

Rough maidenhair fern growing in a private garden in Jefferson County.

American Maidenhair Fern
Adiantum pedatum Linnaeus

DESCRIPTION Rhizome creeping, at or near ground surface, leaves spaced at short intervals. Leaves fan-shaped, 2-pinnate, blades to 25 cm long and 40 cm broad; leaf stalk forking into two nearly equal curving rachises, primary leaf divisions arising from one side of each rachis, rachis and leaf stalk smooth and hairless, dark brown to black; leaflets oblong or obliquely fan-shaped, with shallowly notched outer margins. Sori oblong, at margins of leaflets, covered by reflexed margins.

HABITAT Grows in rich, moist but well-drained deciduous woods, usually on slopes and often near rocks or in soils that contain rocks, frequently limestone; always in full shade.

RANGE Frequent throughout the highland provinces of Alabama except the Piedmont where it is present but uncommon, rare in the Coastal Plain. Occurs throughout most of northern North America, in the southeastern Unites States to the Gulf and Atlantic Coasts and possibly northern Florida; rare below the Fall Line except on the loess bluff of western Mississippi and eastern Louisiana where it is frequent.

American maidenhair fern (*Adiantum pedatum*) with close-up of leaf underside showing sori arrangement.

COMMENTS Because it is beautiful and easy to grow, this is one of the most popular native ferns with gardeners.

According to Clute (1938) this fern was once made into a tea and used as a cure-all.

Several subspecies have been described for this species. All Alabama occurrences belong to the type subspecies *A. pedatum* ssp. *pedatum*. The other subspecies occur in the northern and western parts of North America, nowhere near Alabama.

The specific epithet *pedatum* means "decreasing outward like

toes" and refers to the decreasing size of the primary leaf divisions toward the sides of the blade.

OTHER COMMON NAMES Common maidenhair fern, northern maidenhair fern

American maidenhair fern growing in the Fern Glade at the Birmingham Botanical Gardens.

Ladder Brake
Pteris vittata Linnaeus

DESCRIPTION Rhizome short-creeping, leaves crowded. Leaves spearhead-shaped, but widest above the middle, 1-pinnate, to 60 cm long and 25 cm wide; rachis and leaf stalk straw-colored, covered with fine scales; leaflets narrow and unlobed, margins without sori finely toothed; sori long and narrow, in continuous strips inside curls of rolled-under margins.

HABITAT Grows on limestone and on mortar of brick and stone walls, and under bridges and buildings, in full or partial shade.

RANGE Known in Alabama only from a few widely scattered localities, mostly in the Coastal Plain. Occurs sporadically in the southeastern United States from Florida north along and near the coast to South Carolina and west to southeastern Louisiana, also in southern California. A native of Asia that has escaped from cultivation and become naturalized in many parts of the world.

Ladder brake (*Pteris vittata*) with close-up of leaf underside showing sori arrangement.

COMMENTS Many of the places from which this species is known in the United States are in coastal, usually older, cities where it typically grows in mossy crevices in old walls and cemetery monuments. It is frequent in southeastern Louisiana and is easily found in the older parts of New Orleans, where it often grows in the ground along the edges of unenclosed crawl spaces beneath houses as well as on masonry. In Mobile, it has been found on masonry in a number of places in the older sections of the city.

This fern has been recently found growing on old masonry at Sloss Furnaces in Birmingham, Jefferson County. This is the only site for this fern presently known in the southeastern United States that is not in the Coastal Plain.

The genus name *Pteris* is a Greek word that means "fern." The specific epithet *vittata* means "striped" and refers to the long, continuous sori along the leaf margins. The common name refers to the ladderlike appearance of the leaves.

OTHER COMMON NAMES Chinese brake

SYNONYMS *Pycnodoria vittata* (Linnaeus) Small

Ladder brake growing on an old brick wall.

Spider Brake
Pteris multifida Poiret

DESCRIPTION Rhizome short-creeping, leaves crowded. Leaves ovate to spearhead-shaped to nearly circular, 1- to 2-pinnate, to 30 cm long and 25 cm wide; rachis and leaf stalk straw-colored, leaf stalk reddish at base, scales lacking; primary leaf segments at the base of the blade compound or deeply lobed, each with one or two pairs of lobes or leaflets that appear on both sides; lower leaf segments curved toward the leaf tip; sterile margins jaggedly toothed; sori long and narrow, in continuous strips inside curls of rolled-under margins.

Spider brake (*Pteris multifida*).

HABITAT Grows in moist shady locations on limestone rocks, mortar of masonry walls, and steep stream banks.

RANGE Occasional and widely scattered in Alabama in the Coastal Plain to the Fall Line with a few localities in the highland provinces. Well established along the Gulf Coast from eastern Texas to Florida; scattered along the Atlantic Coast as far north as Maryland; known from a few places in the highland regions of Alabama and Georgia; also known from southern California. A native of Asia that has escaped from cultivation and become naturalized.

COMMENTS This non-native fern is well established in the flora of the Southeast; it is the most common species of *Pteris* in the region.

This fern is abundant at Noccalula Falls, in the Cumberland Plateau near Gadsden in Etowah County. There it grows behind the waterfall underneath a deep rock overhang. It may be that the sheltered location and the spray from the waterfall protect the fern from the hard freezes that would otherwise kill it.

The specific epithet *multifida* means "cut into many segments" and refers to the many divisions of the leaf. The common name spider break comes from the spidery appearance of the leaf; another one, Huguenot fern, is derived from the place of its first North American discovery, a Huguenot cemetery in Charleston, South Carolina.

OTHER COMMON NAMES Wall brake, Huguenot fern

SYNONYMS *Pycnodoria multifida* (Poiret) Small

Spider brake growing in the mortar of Dexter Avenue Baptist Church, Montgomery.

Cretan Brake

Pteris cretica Linnaeus

DESCRIPTION Rhizome short-creeping, leaves crowded. Leaves ovate to nearly circular, 1- to 2-pinnate, to 30 cm long and 25 cm wide; rachis and leaf stalk straw-colored, leaf stalk reddish at base, scaly at base only; primary leaf divisions narrow and unlobed except at the base of the leaf, each with a single lobe or leaflet on the downward side, the leaf appearing palmately compound; lower leaflets straight; margins lacking sori, margins inconspicuously toothed; sori long and narrow, in continuous strips inside curls of rolled-under margins.

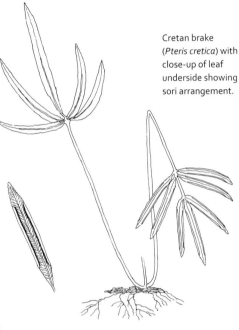

Cretan brake
(*Pteris cretica*) with close-up of leaf underside showing sori arrangement.

HABITAT Grows on steep limey creek and river banks, and on mortar of shaded old masonry.

RANGE Known in Alabama only from a few isolated localities in the Coastal Plain. Occasional along the Gulf Coast of the southeastern United States from Florida to Louisiana; also in southern California, Mexico, and the West Indies; a native of the Old World tropics that has escaped from cultivation and become naturalized.

COMMENTS This fern is very common in cultivation and has occasionally escaped to the wild. In the southeastern United States, it has been found growing naturally only in a few localities along the Gulf Coast.

Both the type variety and variety *albolineata* Hooker have been collected in Alabama. Variety *albolineata* is distinguished by light-colored stripes along the midveins of the leaflets and lobes. It, like the type variety, has become naturalized in the southern states and is called the white-lined Cretan brake.

The specific epithet *cretica* and the common name both refer to the Mediterranean island of Crete, where the fern was once thought to be native. The varietal epithet *albolineata* means "white-lined" and refers to light-colored stripes on the leaves.

OTHER COMMON NAMES Table fern

SYNONYMS *Pycnodoria cretica* (Linnaeus) Small

Cretan brake growing in Coastal Plain soils.

Southwestern Cloak Fern
Notholaena integerrima (Hooker) Hevly

DESCRIPTION Rhizomes compact; leaves crowded at tip. Leaves linear, 1-pinnate, blades to 23 cm long and to 2 cm wide, tapering gradually at the base and apex; undersurfaces densely covered with reddish brown, star-shaped scales and scattered whitish scales on the upper surfaces; leaflets unlobed to broadly and shallowly lobed. Sori scattered along the veins at leaflet margins, covered by rolled-under margins of the leaflets.

HABITAT Grows on limestone or dolomite rocks, ledges, and cliffs; occasionally growing on mortar of brick and stone walls; tolerates both shade and sun.

RANGE Known in Alabama only from the dolomite glades in central Bibb County along the Little Cahaba River. Occurs primarily in the southwestern United States, disjunct in Alabama.

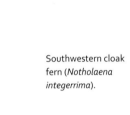

Southwestern cloak fern (*Notholaena integerrima*).

COMMENTS This is one of several western ferns that occur in isolated localities in the eastern United States. Because of their tiny size, the wind can carry fern spores long distances. That is probably how this fern got to Alabama.

This species was found in Alabama in the early 1990s growing on dolomite outcrops (Allison and Stevens 2001). Many other unusual plant species, some new to science, have been found in the dolomite glades of central Bibb County.

According to Lellinger (1985), this fertile fern is apparently an apogamous triploid derived from the hybridization of *Notholaena cochisensis* Goodding, Cochise's cloak fern, and *Notholaena sinuata* (Lagasca *ex* Swartz) Kaulfuss, wavy cloak fern. Other authors (Benham and Windham 1993) believe that it is a hybrid between *N. cochisensis* and an unnamed Mexican species. See chapter 1 of this book, "About Ferns and Fern Allies," for an explanation of apogamous triploids.

This species and seven others placed traditionally in *Notholaena* have been recently put in a separate genus, *Astrolepis*, which is from the Greek and means "star scale," referring to the starlike scales on the top surface of leaf blade. Some consider this genus to be more closely related to *Pellaea* and *Cheilanthes* than to *Notholaena* (Weakley 2010).

The genus name *Notholaena* is from the Greek and means "false cloak"; it refers to the reflexed leaflet margins that cover the sori like indusia. The species epithet *integerrima* means "entire" and refers to the uncut leaflets.

OTHER COMMON NAMES Star-scale cloak fern, hybrid cloak fern, false cloak fern, whole-leaf cloak fern

SYNONYMS *Astrolepis integerrima* (Hooker) Benham and Windham

Above left: Herbarium specimen of southwestern cloak fern collected by James R. Allison on September 28, 1992, on a Ketona Dolomite outcrop near the Little Cahaba River in Bibb County.

Above right: Southwestern cloak fern growing in highly xeric thin glade soils of Bibb County upslope from the Cahaba River.

Woolly Lip Fern
Cheilanthes tomentosa Link

DESCRIPTION Rhizomes creeping, short, often with short branches, leaves crowded at rhizome tip. Leaves narrowly spearhead-shaped, 3-pinnate, to 25 cm long; leaflets ovate but attached at the narrow end of the oval, densely hairy; rachis brown, densely hairy. Sori in continuous strips along rolled-under leaflet margins.

HABITAT Grows on hard noncalcareous rocks or boulders, ledges, and cliffs, often in full sun.

RANGE Occasional throughout much of the Alabama highland provinces. Occurs in the highland regions of the southeastern United States north to Pennsylvania and Kentucky and west to New Mexico and northern Mexico.

COMMENTS: This fern is most frequent in Alabama on the high ridges of the Appalachian Ridges and on the escarpments of the Cumberland Plateau. It is occasional in other areas of the Cumberland Plateau and in the upper Piedmont and rare elsewhere in its range in the state. Although *Cheilanthes tomentosa* and *C. lanosa* grow on similar rock types, they are rarely found growing together.

The generic name *Cheilanthes* is from the Greek words *cheilos*, "margin," and *anthus*, "flower," referring to the sporangia located at the leaflet margins. The specific epithet *tomentosa* means "densely woolly" and refers to the dense matted hairs on the leaf. The common name for the genus, lip fern, refers to the in-rolled margins of the leaflets, which can resemble a pair of lips when looking at the undersides of the smaller leaflets or lobes.

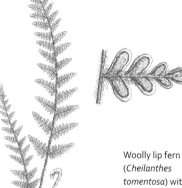

Woolly lip fern (*Cheilanthes tomentosa*) with close-up of leaf underside showing sori arrangement.

Top: Woolly lip fern growing in the Fern Glade at the Birmingham Botanical Gardens.

Bottom: Close-up to show the densely matted hairs on the leaves and rachis.

Alabama Lip Fern
Cheilanthes alabamensis (Buckley) Kunze

DESCRIPTION Rhizomes creeping, short, rarely branched, leaves crowded at rhizome tip. Leaves narrowly spearhead-shaped, 2-pinnate, to 15 cm long; leaflets oblong, usually lobed, with few or no hairs; rachis black, with few or no hairs. Sori in continuous strips along rolled-under leaflet margins.

HABITAT Grows in shaded crevices of limestone rocks and cliffs, and in soil around limestone rocks and boulders; rarely on noncalcareous rocks.

RANGE Occasional in limestone regions of the Alabama highland provinces; also known from a single collection in the Coastal Plain. Occurs in the highland regions of the southeastern United States, from Alabama and Georgia north to Virginia and west to New Mexico and northern Mexico; also in the West Indies.

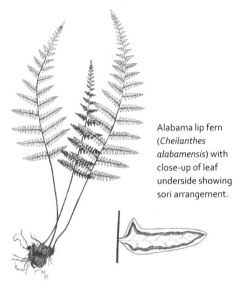

Alabama lip fern (*Cheilanthes alabamensis*) with close-up of leaf underside showing sori arrangement.

COMMENTS Samuel Buckley described this fern in 1843 as *Pteris alabamensis*. According to Small (1938), the place where it was first found, on the banks of the Tennessee River at Muscle Shoals, is now under Wilson Lake. Recent collections have shown that the fern is still present in the vicinity, if not in Buckley's original locality.

This species is easy to distinguish from the other Alabama members of *Cheilanthes* since the leaves are almost completely hairless. The leaves of the other members of the genus found in the state, *Cheilanthes lanosa* and *C. tomentosa*, are densely covered with hairs.

The specific epithet *alabamensis* and the common name, of course, refer to Alabama, where this fern was first discovered.

OTHER COMMON NAMES Smooth lip fern

Alabama lip fern in the Fern Glade at the Birmingham Botanical Gardens, grown from spores by the Birmingham Fern Society.

Hairy Lip Fern
Cheilanthes lanosa (Michaux) D. C. Eaton

DESCRIPTION Rhizomes creeping, short, rarely branched, leaves crowded at rhizome tip. Leaves spearhead-shaped, 2-pinnate, to 25 cm long; leaflets oblong, usually lobed, to 5 mm long, densely hairy beneath; rachis dark brown, densely hairy. Sori in confluent strips along rolled-under leaflet margins.

HABITAT Grows in thin soil on dry noncalcareous rocks often in only partial shade; seeming to prefer rocks that are level or only mildly sloped.

RANGE Frequent in the highland provinces of Alabama except areas dominated by limestone, rare in the Coastal Plain. Occurs throughout the highland regions of the eastern United States south of New England and the Great Lakes and east of the Great Plains; rare and widely scattered in the southeastern Coastal Plain south to northern Florida.

Hairy lip fern (*Cheilanthes lanosa*) with close-up of leaf underside showing sori arrangement.

COMMENTS This fern seems to be particularly abundant in the Piedmont, growing on the many granitic flat rocks. In dry weather, the leaflets curl up and the leaves appear withered and dead.

This species is sometimes confused with *Cheilanthes tomentosa*, the woolly lip fern, which grows in similar habitats. The leaves of *C. lanosa* are 2-pinnate, and the leaflets are oblong with wavy to lobed margins; the leaves of *C. tomentosa* are 3-pinnate, and the leaflets are oval with smooth margins.

The specific epithet *lanosa* means "woolly" and refers to the dense hairs on the leaf, as does the common name.

Top: Hairy lip fern growing in the Fern Glade at the Birmingham Botanical Gardens.

Bottom: Close-up showing individual hairs on the leaves and rachis.

Purple Cliff-Brake
Pellaea atropurpurea (Linnaeus) Link

DESCRIPTION Rhizomes short, creeping to ascending, occasionally branched; leaves crowded at rhizome tip. Leaves spearhead-shaped to oblong, 2-pinnate, to 50 cm long, of two slightly dissimilar kinds: the fertile leaves larger and with narrower leaflets than the purely vegetative ones; leaflets oblong on fertile blades and elliptical on purely vegetative ones, with smooth margins, hairless; leaf stalk and rachis purplish black, moderately covered with short hairs. Sori continuous at leaflet margins, partially covered by margins that are somewhat rolled under.

HABITAT Grows on limestone rocks, ledges, and cliffs; occasionally growing on mortar of brick and stone walls; tolerates both shade and sun.

Purple cliff-brake (*Pellaea atropurpurea*) with close-up of leaf underside showing sori arrangement.

RANGE Frequent in Alabama in the Highland Rim and Ridge and Valley, and on the limestone slopes of the Cumberland Plateau escarpments. Occurs throughout highland provinces of the United States and southern Canada east of the Rocky Mountains.

COMMENTS The colonial plant collector John Clayton (1694–1773) first discovered this species in the early 1700s on the Rappahannock River in Virginia (Snyder and Bruce 1986).

This fern is believed to have arisen from the hybridization of *Pellaea glabella* and *P. ternifolia*, neither of which is known from Alabama. The first named species has four sets of chromosomes, while the latter has two. The hybridization of these two produced an offspring that has three sets and is a triploid. Most hybrids are sterile, and triploids almost always are because three sets of chromosomes cannot pair up during meiosis, the chromosome-separating reduction division that produces the spores. This species does reproduce by spores, however; it does so by apogamy, which is explained in chapter 1 of this book.

The generic name *Pellaea* is from the Greek *pellos*, "dark," possibly referring to the bluish gray leaves. The specific epithet *atropurpurea* is also from the Greek and means "dark purple"; it refers to the color of the rachis and leaf stalk, which is also the basis for the common name.

OTHER COMMON NAMES Purple-stem cliff-brake, hairy cliff-brake

Purple cliff-brake at Monte Sano State Park in Madison County, 2011.

Appalachian Shoestring Fern
Vittaria appalachiana Farrar & Mickel

DESCRIPTION Plant thin, leaflike, only one cell thick in most places, up to 2 cm long and 1 cm broad, irregular in shape, attached to the substrate along an edge by root-hair-like rhizoids, deeply lobed elsewhere, lobes raised from the ground. Lobes usually producing small club-shaped buds or gemmae, which are a means of vegetative reproduction.

Found almost exclusively as a gametophyte; sporophyte very rarely produced and not persistent.

HABITAT Dark, moist cavities and crevices of sandstone bluffs and grottoes.

Appalachian shoestring fern (*Vittaria appalachiana*).

RANGE Known in Alabama from only a few collections in the Sipsey Gorges and Plateau Mountains of the Cumberland Plateau. Occurs in the eastern United States from New York to Indiana south to Alabama and Georgia.

COMMENTS Dense colonies of this gametophyte often coat deeply shaded rock surfaces. *Vittaria appalachiana*, the first-known fern species found primarily as a gametophyte, was actually discovered sixty years before it was confirmed to be identifiably distinct from sporophyte-producing species of *Vittaria*.

Since this plant is minute and not fernlike, it is easily overlooked and is likely to be more common than is presently known.

The upturned lobes of the plant are usually oriented so that they are perpendicular to the direction of the strongest light.

This plant superficially resembles a liverwort, but it is only one cell thick in most places, while liverworts are several cells thick. The root-hair-like rhizoids of the *Vittaria appalachiana* gametophyte are produced along one edge of the plant, but liverworts have rhizoids covering their undersurfaces. It also produces tiny club-shaped buds called gemmae, but liverworts produce none of these.

The sporophyte of this fern is almost never seen in nature. Attempts to produce sporophytes in the laboratory have succeeded, but the plants have always died in infancy (Farrar 1978).

The genus name *Vittaria* is from a Greek word that means "stripe," possibly referring to the narrow leaves of the sporophytes of other species of the genus. These long, very narrow leaves give members of this genus the common name shoestring fern. The specific name *appalachiana* and part of the common name refer to the Appalachian region of North America, where the plant is usually found.

OTHER COMMON NAMES Appalachian Vittaria

Gametophyte stage of Appalachian shoestring fern living in a dark recess of a rock shelter.

Taylor's Filmy Fern
Hymenophyllum tayloriae Farrar & Raine

DESCRIPTION Plant ribbonlike, only one cell thick and branching, producing spoon-shaped buds or gemmae that serve as a means of vegetative reproduction; root-hair-like rhizoids present along the margins of the plants only.

Almost always found as a gametophyte, sporophytes rarely produced. Sporophyte, if present, diminutive with a short stem bearing four leaves, the largest of which is less than 1 cm long. Leaves only one cell thick between veins, with starlike branched hairs and no sori.

HABITAT Deeply shaded, moist crevices in acidic rock, often in narrow gorges and behind waterfalls.

Taylor's filmy fern
(*Hymenophyllum
tayloriae*).

RANGE Currently known in Alabama only from the Sipsey Gorges of southern Lawrence County. Occurs in the southeastern United States in eastern Tennessee, western North Carolina, and northern Georgia and Alabama.

COMMENTS Recent findings show that this species is likely to be more abundant than current herbarium records indicate.

This plant resembles a liverwort, but it is only one cell thick and has no midrib, while liverworts are usually more than one cell thick and often have distinct midribs. Liverworts do not produce budlike gemmae, but this plant does. This species can be distinguished from the similar-looking *Vittaria appalachiana* by its flattened spoon-shaped gemmae, while those of *V. appalachiana* are round in cross section. The gametophytes of *Hymenophyllum tayloriae* have essentially parallel margins and are branched but unlobed, but those of *V. appalachiana* are variously lobed and of irregular shapes.

Paul G. Davison recently discovered sporophytes of this species growing with the gametophyte in Lawrence County, Alabama, in the Sipsey Wilderness.

If a mature sporophyte of this species were to be found, its leaves would probably superficially resemble those of either *Trichomanes boschianum* or *T. petersii* except that they would have the starlike hairs characteristic of *Hymenophyllum*. If sori were present, they would be at the leaf margins and would have funnel-like indusia like those of *Trichomanes*, but the indusium would have two liplike lobes and the sporangia would be borne within the indusium cup, not on a bristle.

The genus name *Hymenophyllum* means "membrane leaf" and refers to the leaves of the sporophytes of this genus. The leaves of both *Hymenophyllum* and *Trichomanes* are only one cell thick between the veins; for this reason, members of these and a number of related genera are known as filmy ferns. The specific epithet *tayloriae* honors Mary S. Taylor, who first discovered gametophytes of this species in South Carolina in 1936.

OTHER COMMON NAMES Gorge filmy fern

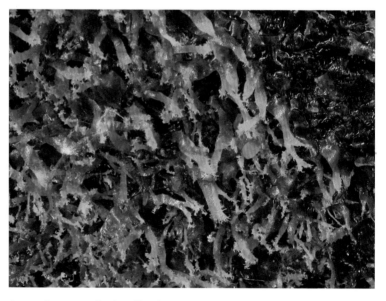

Gametophyte stage of Taylor's filmy fern growing in a sheltered habitat.

Appalachian Filmy Fern
Trichomanes boschianum Sturm *ex* Bosch

DESCRIPTION Rhizomes long-creeping, thin and wiry, with many branches, covered with black hairs, leaves widely spaced; leaves deeply and complexly lobed and appearing 2-pinnate, to 15 cm long; blade tissue between veins only one cell thick, nearly transparent; sori at leaf margins, indusia tubular to funnel-like, sporangia borne on bristles arising from the bases of the indusia.

HABITAT Grows underneath wet overhanging cliffs and ledges of acid rocks, chiefly sandstone, in deep shade.

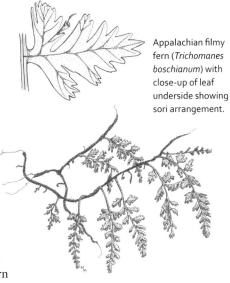

Appalachian filmy fern (*Trichomanes boschianum*) with close-up of leaf underside showing sori arrangement.

RANGE Frequent in the Sipsey Gorges region of Alabama and the rocky gorges of the adjacent Fall Line Transition Zone, rare in the rest of the Cumberland Plateau; seemingly disjunct in northern Hale County. Occurs in the southeastern United States from northern Alabama and Georgia and the mountains of North Carolina, north to the Ohio Valley, and west to the mountains of Arkansas. Most abundant in northwestern Alabama and eastern Kentucky.

COMMENTS Most authorities consider this fern to be rare, but it is actually rather common in the Sipsey Gorges region of Alabama. As one of the delicate filmy ferns, it needs deep shade and constant humidity in order to survive. Deep, often seeping, sandstone overhangs are abundant in the ravines of the Sipsey Gorges, and *Trichomanes boschianum* may be found in a great many of these places. It is usually seen hanging downward from the "ceiling" at or near the back of the overhang.

The Hale County locality is at the site near Havana that is famous for being the only place where *Asplenium tutwilerae* is found. The pebbly conglomerate rock forms substantial cliffs there, and several of these cliffs have deeply shaded overhangs suitable for the filmy fern.

This is one of two *Trichomanes* species Judge Thomas M. Peters discovered in Winston County in 1853. Peters sent specimens to Asa Gray at Harvard University, the foremost botanist in North America at the time, who determined that one of them was a new species and named it after Peters (*T. petersii*). The other specimen was the present species, but it was not recognized as new by Gray, who identified it as the tropical American *T. radicans* (Gray 1853). About ten years later, this species was recognized as different and Sturm named it *T. boschianum*. The type locality for both species is at the Sipsey River Picnic Area in the Bankhead National Forest; *T. boschianum* is still present and abundant there.

The genus name *Trichomanes* is from the Greek *thrix*, "hair," and *manes*, "cup," alluding to the hairlike bristle that extends from the cuplike indusium and bears the sporangia. The specific epithet *boschianum* honors Roelof van den Bosch, a nineteenth-century botanist who studied this group of ferns. This and other species of the genus are known as filmy ferns because of their thin, nearly transparent leaves; they are also called bristle ferns from the bristles that bear the sporangia. The rest of the common name refers to the Appalachian region, where this fern is usually found.

OTHER COMMON NAMES Appalachian bristle fern

SYNONYMS *Vandenboschia boschiana* (Sturm) Ebihara & K. Swastika

Above left: Appalachian filmy fern growing underneath a sandstone boulder in the Sipsey Wilderness, Winston County.

Above right: Close-up showing veins and bristles.

Peters's Filmy Fern
Trichomanes petersii A. Gray

DESCRIPTION Rhizomes long-creeping, thin and wiry, profusely branched and forming mats, covered with black hairs, leaves spaced; leaves undivided, to 2 cm long; blade tissue between veins only one cell thick, nearly transparent; sori at leaf margins, indusia tubular to funnel-like, sporangia borne on bristles arising from the bases of the indusia.

HABITAT Grows on sheltered sandstone and other acidic rocks in deep shade under moist overhangs and near waterfalls; also found on the bases of trees near swamps and streams.

RANGE Occasional in the Sipsey Gorges and adjacent Fall Line Transition Zone of Alabama, rare and widely scattered in the rest of the Cumberland Plateau and the Appalachian Ridges. Occurs in much of the southeastern United States from Louisiana to Florida and north to Arkansas and North Carolina; also in Central America.

Peters's filmy fern (*Trichomanes petersii*) with close-up of leaf underside showing sori arrangement.

COMMENTS This is historically one of the most renowned of Alabama's ferns. It was found in 1853 in Winston County (then known as Hancock County) by Judge Thomas M. Peters, a noted amateur collector of lichens, from nearby Moulton.

Peters was searching for his usual quarry on sandstone cliffs when he found two ferns that he could not identify. He sent specimens to Asa Gray at Harvard University for identification. Gray recognized one of the specimens as being a new species and named it *Trichomanes petersii* in Peters's honor (Gray 1853). The other specimen was later named *T. boschianum*.

One of the smallest and most inconspicuous of ferns, *T. petersii* was not found anywhere else until 1880, when Charles Mohr found

it at Noccalula Falls near Gadsden. By the turn of the century it was known from a total of three localities, all in Alabama (Mohr 1901). At that time it still had not been found outside of Alabama.

Trichomanes petersii is now known from many localities throughout much of the southeastern United States. It is best known growing on rocks in highland provinces, especially the Cumberland Plateau, but it has been discovered more recently growing on trees in the Coastal Plain. The trees are mainly evergreen hardwoods like magnolia and holly that are growing next to streams and swamps. The fern grows near the base of the tree trunk on the side facing the water, always in deep shade.

Although it is traditionally considered very rare, this fern is actually fairly frequent on trees in Louisiana and southern Mississippi. It has also been found growing on trees in Florida and southern Georgia. Although it has not yet been found in the Coastal Plain of Alabama, a thorough search of the region should yield *T. petersii* there as well.

The type locality for *T. petersii* is at the Sipsey River Picnic Area in the Bankhead National Forest. Unfortunately, this fern is no longer found there. Unlike *T. boschianum*, which is present in profusion at the site, *T. petersii* was present in only one spot, next to a small waterfall that was destroyed about 1960 when the parking lot for the picnic area was enlarged (Dean 1969).

OTHER COMMON NAMES Dwarf bristle fern, dwarf filmy fern

SYNONYMS *Didymoglossum petersii* (A. Gray) Copeland

Close-up of Peters's filmy fern growing on the face of a moss-covered sandstone boulder in Winston County.

Weft Fern
Trichomanes intricatum Farrar

DESCRIPTION Plant filamentous, algalike, much branched and tangled, often forming mats. Vegetative reproduction by buds or gemmae consisting of short filaments of undifferentiated cells.

Found only as a gametophyte; sporophyte not produced.

HABITAT Deeply sheltered overhangs and shelters of noncalcareous rocks like sandstone. On ceilings or back walls of grottoes, especially in humid gorges or near or behind waterfalls.

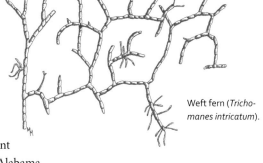

Weft fern (*Trichomanes intricatum*).

RANGE In Alabama, so far found only in Jackson and Winston Counties. Occurs in the eastern United States from Illinois to Vermont and south to northern Georgia and Alabama. Most likely present in Canada, but not reported.

COMMENTS Like the other gametophyte-only ferns, this species is diminutive and difficult to find and identify among the mosses and liverworts with which it grows. It, like the others, is probably more common than is presently known.

The filamentous algalike appearance of this plant distinguishes it from liverworts and from the other two gametophyte-only ferns found in Alabama, *Vittaria appalachiana* and *Hymenophyllum tayloriae*, which are broad and leaflike or ribbonlike.

The late Dr. Warren H. Wagner Jr. has described this plant as looking like "green steel-wool."

The specific epithet *intricatum* is Latin for "intricate" and apparently refers to the profusely branching and tangled filaments.

OTHER COMMON NAMES Grotto-felt

SYNONYMS *Crepidomanes intricatum* (Farrar) Ebihara & Weakley

Weft fern growing on sandstone rock taken from the back of a high-humidity, dimly lit sandstone overhang crevice in Winston County.

Hay-Scented Fern
Dennstaedtia punctilobula (Michaux) Moore

DESCRIPTION Rhizomes thin, long-creeping, shallowly buried, branched; leaves spaced apart. Leaves 2-pinnate with deeply lobed leaflets, spear-head-shaped to narrowly triangular, to 80 cm tall; rachis, leaf stalk, and undersides of veins with fine hairs. Sori round, less than 0.5 mm broad, at margins of leaflets at or near the bottoms of notches in leaflet margins, surrounded by cuplike indusia.

HABITAT Found in Alabama usually at the bases of damp shaded cliffs of sandstone and similar rocks; occurs farther north in acid soil on wooded or open hillsides, often in full sun.

RANGE Rare in Alabama, occurring primarily in the ravines of the Cumberland Plateau and at high elevations in the Appalachian Ridges. Occurs in eastern North America from eastern Canada south to northern Alabama and Georgia and west to the Great Lakes, the upper Mississippi Valley, and northern Arkansas.

Hay-scented fern (*Dennstaedtia punctilobula*) with close-up of leaf underside showing sori arrangement.

COMMENTS This is a very common fern in the northeastern United States; it spreads so aggressively by its widely creeping rhizomes that it is often considered a weed. It is rare in Alabama, where it is found only as small colonies at the bases of shaded cliffs.

For a fern that just barely occurs in Alabama, the range of altitudes at which *Dennstaedtia punctilobula* is found in the state is rather re-markable. It grows at 150–180 m (500–600 ft.) in the deep ravines of the Sipsey Gorges and at the Fall Line in Bibb County and at slightly higher elevations at the Narrows in Shelby County. In the Cumber-land Plateau of northeastern Alabama it grows at 450–550 m (1,500–1,800 ft.) on the upper slopes of the mountains and plateaus. It reach-es its highest altitudes on Mt. Cheaha, where *D. punctilobula* occurs just below the summit of the mountain at about 700 m (2,300 ft.).

The Cherokee Indians made a tea from this plant to help control chills (Dunbar 1989).

Johann Bernhardi named the genus in 1802 for August W. Dennstaedt, a German botanist. The specific epithet *punctilobula* means "with dotted lobes," referring to the sori on the surface of the leaflets. The leaves of this fern have the scent of newly mown hay, especially when crushed, giving it the common name hay-scented fern. Another common name, boulder fern, comes from the common association of this fern with rocky habitats.

OTHER COMMON NAMES Pasture fern, boulder fern

Hay-scented fern.

Spineless Bramble Fern
Hypolepis tenuifolia (G. Forster) Bernhardi

DESCRIPTION Rhizomes long-creeping, deeply buried; leaves very widely spaced. Leaves 2- or more pinnate, broadly triangular, the blades to 1 m or more long and broad, held horizontally on stiffly erect leaf stalks to 1 m or more tall; leaf stalk, rachis, and blade with stiff, prickly hairs. Sori round, at the margins of the leaflets, partially covered by reflexed margins.

HABITAT Escaping from cultivation into woods and vacant lots.

RANGE Known as an escape from cultivation in several places in Jefferson County, Alabama. A native of tropical eastern Asia and the South Pacific islands.

Spineless bramble fern (*Hypolepis tenuifolia*) with close-up of leaf underside showing sori arrangement.

COMMENTS This fern has been cultivated in and around Birmingham for several decades. It is the most common species of *Hypolepis* cultivated in the United States. Most horticultural material is misidentified as *H. repens* (Linnaeus) K. Presl, which has prickles on the leaf stalk, but it is actually *H. tenuifolia*, which lacks the prickles.

This large fern spreads aggressively by its rhizomes and has escaped into woods and vacant lots. The deeply buried rhizomes allow it to survive the winter cold even though this fern is of tropical origin. Growers report that they have not seen sori on *Hypolepis tenuifolia* in their gardens; therefore, it seems doubtful that this fern will become naturalized and establish itself in areas far from where it is cultivated.

Dean (1969) confused this fern with *Thelypteris torresiana*, the Mariana maiden fern. The drawing and description for *T. torresiana* in her book (pp. 103, 104, and 106) are actually of *Hypolepis*. Although *T. torresiana* and *H. tenuifolia* both have large triangular

blades, the former is somewhat smaller than the latter and its blades are erect or drooping on rather lax leaf stalks, and it has fine, soft hairs that can be seen but not felt. By contrast, the blades of *H. tenuifolia* are held nearly horizontally on stiff, erect leaf stalks; the hairs are stiff and prickly and give the leaf a decidedly scratchy feel.

The genus name *Hypolepis* is from the Greek words that mean "beneath" and "scale," referring to the sori being covered by a flap of leaf tissue. The specific epithet *tenuifolia* means "narrow-leaved" and appears to be a misnomer since the leaves of this fern are quite broad. Most species of *Hypolepis* bear prickles on the leaf stalk, giving them the common name bramble fern, but this species lacks the prickles and is therefore spineless.

OTHER COMMON NAMES Soft ground fern

Spineless bramble fern growing in the Fern Glade of the Birmingham Botanical Gardens in Jefferson County.

Bracken Fern
Pteridium aquilinum (**Linnaeus**) **Kuhn**

DESCRIPTION Rhizomes long-creeping, deeply buried; leaves widely spaced. Leaves 2- to 3-pinnate, broadly triangular, the blades to 70 cm or more long and broad, held horizontally on stiffly erect leaf stalks to 50 cm tall; hairs lacking or fine and sparse. Sori linear, continuous along margins, partially covered by rolled-under margins.

HABITAT Grows in open woods and pinelands, at margins of pastures and yards and on roadsides; often in full sun.

RANGE Occurs in every county of Alabama. Found throughout North America and worldwide except the polar regions and deserts.

Top left: Tailed bracken fern (*Pteridium aquilinium* var. *pseudocaudatum*) showing underside of leaf pinnule with sori.

Below left: Detail of eastern bracken fern (*Pteridium aquilinium* var. *latiusculum*) showing underside of leaf pinnule with sori.

COMMENTS This fern is very common in Alabama, as it is almost everywhere.

This is one of the few native ferns that is sometimes considered a noxious weed. It spreads rapidly and widely by its underground rhizomes. Because the rhizomes are so deep, it is very difficult to eradicate the fern once it is established.

The deeply buried rhizomes make this fern extremely resistant to fire. Since soil is a good insulator of heat, and since most woods and grass fires do not last long enough at any one location to heat the soil deeply, the rhizomes will usually survive a fire. If a fire occurs in any season but winter, the first green things to be seen in the burned area will be the fiddleheads of the fern.

Two varieties of this species are recognized in Alabama: var. *latiusculum* (Desvaux) Underwood *ex* A. Heller, eastern bracken fern, and var. *pseudocaudatum* (Clute) A. Heller, tailed bracken fern. The former is found mostly in the northern part of the state, while var. *pseudocaudatum* occurs throughout. They are distinguished by examining the tips of the leaflets. In var. *latiusculum*, they are less than four times as long as broad, but in var. *pseudocaudatum* they are

greater than six times as long as broad. However, these two varieties thoroughly intergrade in Alabama. It is common to see intermediates with leaflet tips greater than four and less than six times as long as broad.

This plant is poisonous and frequently grows in pastures; it is often a culprit in cases of livestock poisoning. Humans once considered the young fiddleheads edible, but it is now known that they contain a carcinogen and should not be eaten. It has been suggested that a high incidence of stomach cancer in Japan is the result of the popularity there of bracken fern fiddleheads as a vegetable (Thieret 1980).

Bracken fern is the host plant for the bracken borer moth (*Papaipema pterisii*).

The genus is named from the Greek *pteridion*, a diminutive of *Pteris*, an ancient name for a fern. The specific epithet *aquilinum* comes from the Latin *aquila*, "eagle," and refers to resemblance of the three-parted fiddleheads to the foot and talons of an eagle. "Bracken" or "brake" is from an Old Saxon word meaning a fallow or clearing, alluding to habitats of this fern.

OTHER COMMON NAMES Pasture brake, southern bracken fern

SYNONYMS *Pteridium latiusculum* (Desvaux) Hieronymus var. *latiusculum*, *Pteridium latiusculum* (Desvaux) Hieronymus var. *pseudocaudatum* (Clute) Maxon

Above: Growth habit of bracken fern.

Left: Sori on the undersides of leaves of ferns growing on dry, upland soils in Coosa County.

New York Fern
Thelypteris noveboracensis (Linnaeus) Nieuwland

DESCRIPTION Rhizomes long-creeping, shallowly buried; leaves mostly spaced several cm apart. Leaves 1-pinnate with deeply lobed leaflets; blades broadest in the middle and gradually tapering to a point at both ends, to 50 cm long, held erect on short leaf stalks to 10 cm long; leaves with fine hairs; veins all free. Sori round, located near the leaflet margins; indusia kidney-shaped, attached along the inner curve.

HABITAT Grows in damp open woods on stream banks, floodplains, and swamp margins.

RANGE Common throughout the highland provinces of Alabama, crossing the Fall Line into the rocky gorges of the Fall Line Transition Zone in the northwestern part of the state, absent from the rest of the Coastal Plain except for one locality in Clarke County. Occurs in eastern North America from southeastern Canada west to the Great Lakes and south to the Fall Line in Alabama, Georgia, and Arkansas; very rare in the Coastal Plain except close to the Fall Line.

New York fern (*Thelypteris noveboracensis*) with close-up of leaf underside showing sori arrangement.

COMMENTS The distribution of this fern is rather remarkable. It is abundant throughout the eastern United States in the highland regions, but its range stops almost abruptly at the Fall Line. It occurs only rarely in the Coastal Plain, usually in the bottoms of rocky ravines.

The tapering of the leaves at both ends is very distinctive and makes this one of the easiest species of *Thelypteris* to identify.

This fern is easily cultivated, but it spreads widely and may take over a shaded garden.

The genus name *Thelypteris* is from the Greek and means "female fern," and many other species in the genus are known as maiden ferns. The specific epithet *noveboracensis* is from Latin and means

"of New York," and the common name is derived from this. It is a mystery as to why Linnaeus gave the species this name since it is known that his specimen came from Canada.

Above: New York fern growing in rich, moist hardwood floodplain, DeKalb County.

Left: Close-up of single leaf.

Marsh Fern
Thelypteris palustris Schott

DESCRIPTION Rhizomes long-creeping, shallowly buried, leaves mostly spaced several cm apart. Leaves 1-pinnate with deeply lobed leaflets, occasionally barely 2-pinnate at base, spearhead-shaped to narrowly ovate; blades to 50 cm long and 20 cm broad, held erect on leaf stalks to 50 cm long; margins of fertile leaflets rolled under, margins of purely vegetative leaflets flat; rachis and midribs with a few fine hairs, leaf stalk smooth; veins not connected. Sori round, located between the midribs and margins of the leaflets; indusia kidney-shaped, attached along the inner curve.

Marsh fern (*Thelypteris palustris*) with close-up of leaf underside showing sori.

HABITAT Grows in swamps and marshes, on lake shores and stream banks, and in wet ditches, often in full sun.

RANGE Fairly frequent in the Alabama Coastal Plain, particularly in the southwestern part of the state; rare in the highland provinces. Occurs throughout eastern North America from Florida to Newfoundland and west to the eastern Great Plains; also in Europe and Asia.

COMMENTS The distribution of this fern in the southeastern United States is interesting. It is common in the Coastal Plain and frequent in the highland areas of Tennessee and North Carolina and northward, but *Thelypteris palustris* seems to be rather rare in the highland provinces of Alabama, Georgia, and South Carolina.

This is a worldwide species with several named varieties. All North American material belongs to var. *pubescens* (Lawson) Fernald.

Both the specific epithet *palustris*, meaning "of marshes," and the common name refer to the wet habitats in which this fern is usually found.

Linnaeus originally named this species *Acrostichum thelypteris*. Later, when botanists considered the ferns now known as *Thelypteris* to be a part of the genus *Dryopteris*, it was called *Dryopteris thelypteris* (Linnaeus) Gray. More recently, after *Thelypteris* was split from *Dryopteris*, the redundant combination *Thelypteris thelypteris* was deemed unacceptable even though it was duly published by Nieuwland, and Schott's later name was applied.

OTHER COMMON NAMES Eastern marsh fern

SYNONYMS *Thelypteris thelypteris* (Linnaeus) Nieuwland

Marsh fern growing at the edge of Weeks Bay pitcher plant bog boardwalk, Baldwin County.

Ovate Maiden Fern
Thelypteris ovata R. P. St. John

DESCRIPTION Rhizome long-creeping, shallowly buried; leaves in rows at rhizome tips. Leaves 1-pinnate with deeply lobed leaflets; blades broadly ovate with a long-tapering tip, to 75 cm long and 40 cm broad; leaf stalks to 35 cm long; veins and midveins moderately hairy below, hairless above; veins all free. Sori round, located near the margins; indusia kidney-shaped, attached along the inner curve.

HABITAT Grows on shaded damp limestone slopes and bluffs and in lime sinks.

RANGE Infrequent in the Coastal Plain of Alabama. Occurs in the southeastern United States from Florida north to South Carolina and west to southern Alabama; another variety is found in central Texas and Mexico.

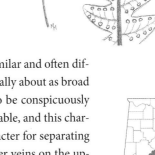

Ovate maiden fern
(*Thelypteris ovata*)
with close-up of
leaf underside
showing sori.

COMMENTS Two varieties of this species are known. All material from Alabama and eastward is variety *ovata*. The other variety, *Thelypteris ovata* var. *harperi* (C. Christensen) R. P. St. John occurs in Texas and Mexico.

This species and *Thelypteris kunthii* are very similar and often difficult to distinguish. The blades of *T. ovata* are usually about as broad as they are long, while those of *T. kunthii* tend to be conspicuously longer than broad. However, both species are variable, and this characteristic may be obscure. The most reliable character for separating the two is the form of the hairs found on the larger veins on the upper sides of the leaves. With *T. kunthii* these hairs are copious and are much longer than the width of the veins; *T. ovata* has veins that are hairless or have very sparse hairs that are only about as long as the width of the veins.

The specific epithet *ovata* and the common name both refer to the shape of the leaf blade.

SYNONYMS *Christella ovata* (R. P. St. John) Löve & Löve

Ovate maiden fern growing on a shaded damp limestone slope.

Widespread Maiden Fern
Thelypteris kunthii (Desvaux) Morton

DESCRIPTION Rhizomes short-creeping, shallowly buried; leaves in rows at rhizome tip. Leaves 1-pinnate with deeply lobed leaflets; blades broadly spearhead-shaped to narrowly triangular, to 60 cm or more long and 40 cm wide, occasionally larger; leaf stalks to 50 cm long; veins and midribs sparsely hairy above and thickly so below, hairs below of uniform length; veins all free. Sori round, midway between midribs and margins; indusia kidney-shaped, attached along the inner curve.

HABITAT Grows in wet woods on stream banks and swamp margins, in ditches and under bridges; also on damp limestone on bluffs and in ravines and sinks.

Widespread maiden fern (*Thelypteris kunthii*) with close-up of leaf underside showing sori.

RANGE Frequent in the Coastal Plain of Alabama, rare in a few limestone valleys of the highland provinces. Occurs in the southeastern United States from Florida north to South Carolina and west to eastern Texas, common in the Coastal Plain and rare above the Fall Line; also in tropical America.

COMMENTS This is one of the largest and one of the most common species of *Thelypteris* in the Coastal Plain of Alabama. It is particularly spectacular in the narrow limestone ravines of Little Stave Creek and its tributaries near Jackson in southern Clarke County. There, it is quite abundant and reaches its greatest size with leaf blades nearly one meter long.

Like so many species of *Thelypteris*, this one has gone through several nomenclatural changes. It was long known as *T. normalis* (Christensen) Moxley until the prior name *kunthii* was discovered in the 1960s.

The common name of this fern has evolved as well. It has been

known for years as the southern shield fern, which is the common name that Dean (1969) used, and it is still used by some in Alabama. However, the name shield fern properly belongs to the genus *Dryopteris*, to which this and most other *Thelypteris* species were once thought to belong.

The specific epithet *kunthii* honors Carl S. Kunth, a professor of botany in Berlin in the nineteenth century. This species is found throughout the Coastal Plain of the southeastern United States, and this wide distribution is the origin of the common name.

OTHER COMMON NAMES Common maiden fern, southern shield fern

SYNONYMS *Christella normalis* (Christensen) Holttum, *Thelypteris normalis* (Christensen) Moxley

Widespread maiden fern growing in a moist woodland.

Variable Maiden Fern

Thelypteris hispidula (Decaisne) Reed

DESCRIPTION Rhizomes short-creeping, shallowly buried; leaves clustered at rhizome tip. Leaves 1-pinnate with deeply lobed leaflets; blades broadly spearhead-shaped, to 50 cm long and 30 cm wide; leaf stalks to 30 cm long; blade, rachis, and leaf stalk with fine hairs, hairs on lower surface of a variety of lengths; pairs of veins occasionally uniting beneath notches in the leaflets into a single vein running to the bottom of the notch, some notches with nonunited veins beneath. Sori round, located near margins; indusia kidney-shaped, attached along the inner curve.

Variable maiden fern (*Thelypteris hispidula*) with close-up of leaf underside showing sori.

HABITAT Grows in moist woods on stream banks and bluffs, and in lime sinks.

RANGE Scattered throughout the Coastal Plain of Alabama up to the Piedmont Fall Line. Occurs in the Coastal Plain of the southeastern United States from Florida north to South Carolina and west to eastern Texas; also in the world tropics.

COMMENTS This is a chiefly tropical fern that is believed to occur naturally in the southeastern United States (Smith 1971).

This species has several named varieties; all material from the United States is variety *versicolor* (R. P. St. John) Lellinger. It has gone through several nomenclatural changes. Until recently it was usually known as *Thelypteris quadrangularis* (Fée) Schlepe var. *versicolor* (R. P. St. John) A. R. Smith.

Based upon recent collections, this fern seems to be becoming more common and expanding its range in Alabama.

The specific epithet *hispidula* means "with short hairs." The varietal epithet *versicolor* means "varying in color" and refers to the

leaves that are light green when young and mature to golden or gray; this is also the source of the common name.

OTHER COMMON NAMES Rough-hairy maiden fern, St. John's shield fern

SYNONYMS *Christella hispidula* (Decaisne) Holttum, *Thelypteris quadrangularis* (Fée) Schelpe var. *versicolor* (R. P. St. John) A. R. Smith, *Thelypteris versicolor* R. P. St. John

Variable maiden fern growing in mesic forest.

Downy Maiden Fern

Thelypteris dentata (Forsskål) E. P. St. John

DESCRIPTION Rhizome short-creeping, shallowly buried or on surface; leaves clustered at rhizome tip. Leaves 1-pinnate with lobed leaflets; blades spearhead-shaped, to 60 cm long and 25 cm broad, held erect or drooping; leaf stalks to 40 cm long; rachis and leaf stalk purplish in color and covered with short hairs; veins uniting beneath notches in the leaflets into a single vein running to the bottom of the notch, doing so beneath nearly every notch on a leaflet. Sori round, located between margins and midribs; indusia kidney-shaped, attached along the inner curve.

HABITAT Grows in damp woods, on roadsides and under bridges, in lime sinks, and rarely on sandstone cliffs.

RANGE Seemingly rare in Alabama, recorded from only a few scattered localities in the Coastal Plain up to the Fall Line and barely crossing it. Infrequent but not rare in the Coastal Plain of the southeastern United States from Florida north to South Carolina and west to Louisiana, with a few isolated localities in the highland regions. A native of the world tropics that has become naturalized in the southeastern United States.

Downy maiden fern (*Thelypteris dentata*) with close-up of leaf underside showing sori.

COMMENTS This fern was first collected in the United States at Mobile in 1904. Although *Thelypteris dentata* occurs in the tropics throughout the world, and its occurrence in the southeastern United States could be considered to be the natural northern limit of that range, it is believed that this fern is not native to the Southeast (Smith 1971).

The locality in Marion County, Alabama, is unusual for this species. There *Thelypteris dentata* grows on a shaded sandstone cliff

a few feet above the water of Bear Creek Lake. This species rarely grows on rocks except in lime sinks. It has been reported from masonry in Kentucky, but it is regarded as an ephemeral adventive there (Cranfill 1980). It has been found in two places in Lee County, on the sandy walls of an old well in the Coastal Plain and on the banks of a small brook in a residential neighborhood in Auburn, above the Fall Line in the Piedmont.

The specific epithet *dentata* means "toothed" and refers to the notched leaflets. The common name refers to the fine hairs on the rachis and leaf stalk.

OTHER COMMON NAMES Downy shield fern

SYNONYMS *Christella dentata* (Forsskål) Brownsey & Jermy

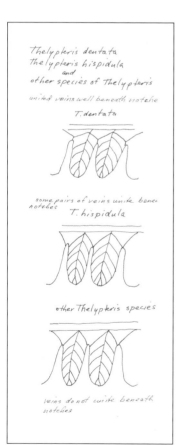

Above: Downy maiden fern volunteer in a shrubbery bed in Auburn, Lee County.

Left: Schematics of the leaf venation of the downy maidenhair fern (*Thelypteris dentata*), the variable maiden fern (*T. hispidula*), and the widespread maiden fern (*T. kunthii*) showing how the veins unite beneath the notches in some, but not in others.

Alabama Streak-Sorus Fern

Thelypteris pilosa (Martens & Galeotti) Crawford
var. *alabamensis* Crawford

DESCRIPTION Rhizomes short-creeping on the surface of thin soil, leaves clustered. Leaves spearhead-shaped, 1-pinnate below and decreasingly deeply lobed above; leaflets and larger lobes shallowly lobed; blade, rachis, and leaf stalk covered with fine, short hairs. Sori straight, conspicuously longer than wide, without indusia, arranged diagonally to the midribs and margins.

HABITAT Grows on thin, damp soil in pockets and overhangs of sandstone cliffs.

RANGE The variety *alabamensis* is known only from the gorge of the Sipsey Fork in Winston County, Alabama; other varieties are known from Mexico and Guatemala.

Alabama streak-sorus fern (*Thelypteris pilosa* var. *alabamensis*) with close-up of underside of leaf showing the sori.

COMMENTS Lloyd C. Crawford, then a student at the University of Alabama, first discovered this fern in 1950. Crawford found the fern on a sandstone cliff next to the Sipsey Fork near the US 278 highway bridge over that river, five miles east of Double Springs.

In about 1960, the cliff was destroyed when the highway bridge was rebuilt to make room for rising waters of the new L. M. Smith Lake. Since the fern was not found elsewhere for many years, it was assumed that *Thelypteris pilosa* was lost from the flora of Alabama (Dean 1969).

In the late 1970s, this fern was found growing under a scenic sixty-five-foot overhanging cliff where Alabama Highway 33 crosses the Sipsey five miles north of Double Springs and on several smaller cliffs downstream (Short and Freeman 1978). Recent searches have found the fern in seventeen places along a 4.25-mile stretch of the Sipsey (Gunn 1995).

Crawford thought some herbarium specimens from Mexico were var. *alabamensis*. Later studies showed no Mexican material is var. *alabamensis*, which has not been identified from outside Alabama.

Recent studies of this fern suggest that the Alabama material is distinct at the species level from Central American *Thelypteris pilosa*. It has been named as a separate species as *T. burksiorum* in honor of Mary Burks, a friend of Blanche Dean who helped with the preservation of the Sipsey Wilderness.

The federal government lists this species as threatened.

The specific epithet *pilosa* means "hairy" and refers to the fine hairs on the leaves.

SYNONYMS *Leptogramma pilosa* (Martens & Galeotti) Underwood var. *alabamensis* (Crawford) Wherry, *Thelypteris burksiorum* J. E. Watkins & D. R. Farrar

Left: Alabama streak-sorus fern growing in high-humidity/steep sandstone overhangs in Winston County.

Below: Wide-angle view of habitat showing sandstone rock overhanging the Sipsey Fork.

Mariana Maiden Fern

Thelypteris torresiana (Gaudichaud-Beaupré) Alston

DESCRIPTION Rhizomes short-creeping, shallowly buried, leaves in clumps at ends of rhizomes. Leaves triangular, 2-pinnate with lobed leaflets; blades to 75 cm long and 50 cm broad, covered with fine hairs, erect or drooping on lax leaf stalks to 50 cm long. Sori round, indusia attached along one side and not persistent.

HABITAT Grows on wooded stream banks and floodplains, in shaded ditches, under highway bridges, and on damp shaded boulders and masonry.

RANGE Common in most of the Coastal Plain of Alabama, occasional in the lower Piedmont and widely scattered in the rest of the highland provinces. A native of eastern Asia that is naturalized and well established in the Coastal Plain of the southeastern United States from Florida to eastern Texas and north to South Carolina and Arkansas.

Mariana maiden fern (*Thelypteris torresiana*) with close-up of leaf underside showing sori.

COMMENTS This is one of the most abundant of the naturalized ferns in the Alabama flora. It is probably present in every county of the Coastal Plain. Considered rare only a few years ago, this fern is apparently still spreading to new areas and becoming increasingly abundant where it is established.

First collection of this fern in the United States was in Florida in 1906. By the early 1960s it was known throughout northern Florida to southern Alabama and westward to eastern Texas. It is now known on the Atlantic Coast to the Carolinas and appears to be crossing the Fall Line in Alabama and Georgia.

Dean (1969) confused this fern with *Hypolepis tenuifolia*. Her description and the drawing (pp. 103–106) are both of *Hypolepis*.

The specific epithet *torresiana* honors Louis de Torres, a native of the Mariana Islands, where this fern was originally described and from which the common name is derived.

OTHER COMMON NAMES False maiden fern

SYNONYMS *Macrothelypteris torresiana* (Gaudichaud-Beaupré) Ching

Above: Mariana maiden fern growing in damp woods in northern Pike County.

Left: Close-up of sori on the underside of a leaf in Calhoun County.

Broad Beech Fern
Thelypteris hexagonoptera (Michaux) Weatherby

DESCRIPTION Rhizomes long-creeping, shallowly buried, leaves moderately separated. Leaves deeply 2-pinnatifid but not compound, except rarely with one pair of true leaflets at base, the lobes connected elsewhere by wings on what would be the rachis if the leaf were truly compound; blades broadly triangular, to 30 cm long and broad, held horizontally on erect leaf stalks to 40 cm tall; leaf stalk, rachis, and leaf margins with fine hairs. Sori round, without indusia, in irregular rows near the blade margins.

Broad beech fern (*Thelypteris hexagonoptera*) with close-up of leaf underside showing sori.

HABITAT Grows in rich deciduous woods in full shade, usually on slopes and other well-drained sites.

RANGE Common in the Alabama highland provinces, scattered but not rare in the Coastal Plain. Occurs in eastern North America from southern Canada south to northern Florida and west to the upper Mississippi Valley and eastern Texas.

COMMENTS This is one of several fern species that over recent years has been assigned by various authors to more than one genus. Many authors place this and similar species in the genus *Phegopteris*.

The specific epithet *hexagonoptera* refers to the six-angled appearance of the rachis wing. The common name reflects the broadly triangular blades and the sort of woodlands where it is generally found.

OTHER COMMON NAMES Southern beech fern

SYNONYMS *Phegopteris hexagonoptera* (Michaux) Fée

Broad beech fern growing in damp woods in northern Pike County.

Net-Vein Chain Fern

Woodwardia areolata (Linnaeus) Moore

DESCRIPTION Rhizome long-creeping, frequently branched; leaves widely spaced. Sterile and fertile leaves greatly dissimilar; vegetative leaves deeply lobed to 1-pinnate at base, with conspicuously netted veins; blade ovate to 35 cm long and 20 cm wide, lobes alternate, lobes to 15 mm or more broad, margins finely toothed, leaf stalk to 40 cm long, straw-colored above base; fertile blades 1-pinnate throughout, leaflets 5 mm or less wide, margins smooth, leaf stalk to 60 cm long, reddish brown to black throughout. Sori straight, conspicuously longer than wide, arranged end to end in chainlike rows along each side of midrib; indusium opening on side toward midrib.

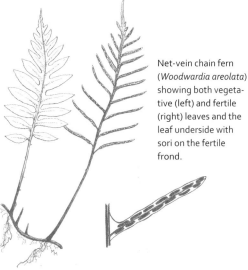

Net-vein chain fern (*Woodwardia areolata*) showing both vegetative (left) and fertile (right) leaves and the leaf underside with sori on the fertile frond.

HABITAT Grows in wet shaded soil in swamps and ditches, on stream banks and floodplains, and on wet rocks and seeping cliffs.

RANGE Common throughout Alabama, most frequent in the Coastal Plain. Occurs in eastern North America from Florida west to Texas and north to Nova Scotia and Michigan.

COMMENTS Sterile leaves of this fern are often difficult to distinguish from those of the sensitive fern, *Onoclea sensibilis*. The leaflets and lobes of *Woodwardia areolata* are alternate throughout the blade; the margins are finely toothed but are otherwise straight or gently curved. With *O. sensibilis* the segments are opposite, in pairs, or nearly so, at least at the base of the blade, and the margins are often shallowly lobed.

The genus name *Woodwardia* honors Thomas J. Woodward, an English botanist of the late eighteenth and early nineteenth centuries. The specific epithet *areolata* comes from the Latin word *areola*, which means a "small space"; it and the common name refer to the network of connected veins of the vegetative leaves.

OTHER COMMON NAMES Netted chain fern, netleaf chain fern

SYNONYMS *Lorinseria areolata* (Linnaeus) K. Presl

Sterile and fertile fronds of net-vein chain fern.

Virginia Chain Fern
Woodwardia virginica (Linnaeus) J. E. Smith

DESCRIPTION Rhizome long-creeping, leaves widely separated. Leaves 1-pinnate with deeply lobed leaflets; blades spearhead-shaped, to 70 cm long and 30 cm wide; leaflets narrowly spearhead-shaped; margins smooth; veins forming a single row of enclosed spaces on both sides of the midribs of the leaflets and lobes but unconnected elsewhere on the blade. Sori linear, arranged end to end in chainlike rows on both sides of and next to midribs; indusia opening on sides facing midribs.

HABITAT Grows in wet soil in swamps, wet meadows, and roadside ditches; often in full sun.

RANGE Frequent in the Alabama Coastal Plain; rare and widely scattered in the highland provinces, mostly in the Ridge and Valley. Occurs in eastern North America from Florida west to Texas and north to New Brunswick and Michigan; common in the Coastal Plain, infrequent inland.

Virginia chain fern (*Woodwardia virginica*) with close-up of the leaf underside showing sori.

COMMENTS This is one of the few ferns that is more commonly found in full sun than in shade. In the Alabama Coastal Plain it seems to be most abundant in roadside ditches and open wetlands.

Sterile leaves of this species resemble those of the cinnamon fern (*Osmunda cinnamomea*), but *Woodwardia virginica* can be distinguished by its blackish leaf stalk, the veins that are connected near the midrib, the absence of woolly brown hairs, and by its spreading growth pattern from its long horizontal rhizome. In *O. cinnamomea* the leaf stalk is brown to tan, no veins are connected, and there are reddish brown woolly hairs on the rachis, especially when young; its rhizome is short and erect and the plant does not spread.

This fern is used by the chain fern borer moth (*Papaipema stenocelis*) as a food source (Dunbar 1989).

The specific epithet *virginica* means "of Virginia," which is where the specimens Linnaeus saw came from.

OTHER COMMON NAMES Southern chain fern

SYNONYMS *Anchistea virginica* (Linnaeus) K. Presl

Virginia chain fern growing in swampy soils.

American Hart's Tongue Fern
Phyllitis scolopendrium (Linnaeus) Newman
var. *americana* Fernald

DESCRIPTION Rhizomes erect, at ground surface; leaves clustered at tip. Leaves undivided and unlobed, slightly eared at base; blades oblong to linear, to 30 cm long, margins smooth but slightly wavy; leaf stalks scaly, to 12 cm long; veins usually all free, but a few may unite. Sori straight and long, mostly in back-to-back pairs, nearly at right angles to midrib, of various lengths but the longest greater than half as long as the distance from the midrib to the margin; indusia linear, two per dual sorus.

HABITAT Grows in thin soil on ledges in cool moist lime sinks; on shaded limestone rocks in open woods in the northern part of its range.

American Hart's tongue fern (*Phyllitis scolopendrium*) with close-up of leaf section showing underside with sori.

RANGE Known from two localities in the Cumberland Plateau of northeastern Alabama. Rare in the northeastern United States and southern Canada from upstate New York to the upper peninsula of Michigan; disjunct in northeastern Alabama and southeastern Tennessee. Another variety is common in Europe.

COMMENTS Populations of this fern in the Southeast are believed to be leftovers from the Ice Ages when the climate was cooler and this fern occurred far to the south of its present main range. As the climate warmed, plants living in cool sinkholes were able to survive the increasing summer heat.

Frederick Pursh first discovered this fern in North America in 1807 near Syracuse, New York (Clute 1938). For many years it was known from the Southeast only from two places in Tennessee. One of these populations, discovered in Roane County in 1849, had disappeared by the turn of the twentieth century (Shaver 1954). The other Tennessee locality, in Marion County near the Alabama state line, has declined steadily since its discovery in the late 1870s until

only a few plants remain. It was assumed that this fern was dying out in its last remaining southern locality, but the decline of the Hart's tongue in this place was probably due to overcollecting by botanists.

A century after the last discovery in Tennessee, *P. scolopendrium* was found by spelunkers in northeastern Alabama. The first discovery was in 1978 in a Jackson County sinkhole. The cave at the bottom of the sinkhole is also the hibernating place of an endangered bat species, and that sinkhole is now protected as part of Wheeler National Wildlife Refuge. The population in Morgan County is much larger than the one in Jackson County, which may be on the decline.

Some of the specimens collected in Morgan County have a few veins that unite and form closed spaces. This feature has not been seen on this species from anywhere else.

The genus name *Phyllitis* is an ancient European name for this fern. The specific epithet *scolopendrium* is another ancient European word that means a "parallel-marked plant" and probably refers to the sori. The varietal epithet *americana* means, of course, "of America." The common name comes from the tonguelike appearance of the leaf blade.

Most authors now place this species in the genus *Asplenium* because the European variety frequently hybridizes with other *Asplenium* species.

The federal government lists this species as threatened.

OTHER COMMON NAMES Hound's-tongue fern, seaweed fern

SYNONYMS *Asplenium scolopendrium* Linnaeus var. *americanum* (Fernald) Kartesz & Gandhi

American Hart's tongue fern growing in a garden in Calhoun County.

Cut Spleenwort
Asplenium abscissum Willdenow

DESCRIPTION Rhizomes erect; leaves clustered at tip. Leaves 1-pinnate; blades spearhead-shaped to nearly triangular, to 18 cm long and 12 cm wide; rachis and leaf stalk green on upper surface, light gray-brown on the lower surface; leaflets alternate, narrowly spearhead-shaped, tapering bluntly at the base and gradually to the tip, widest near the base, veins not united. Sori spindle-shaped, borne along branch veins of the main vein, forming two chevronlike rows; indusium spindle-shaped, attached along the side of the sorus next to the vein.

HABITAT Grows on shaded limestone rocks and ledges.

RANGE Known in Alabama from a single locality in Jackson County. Known from a few places in central and southern Florida. Occurs in South and Central America, Mexico, the Caribbean islands, and the Florida peninsula, disjunct in northeastern Alabama.

Cut spleenwort (*Asplenium abscissum*) with close-up of leaf underside showing sori.

COMMENTS Wayne Barger found this fern in Alabama in 2009. He found a thriving colony of the fern growing on the walls of a vertical cave mouth near Stevenson in northeastern Jackson County.

It is remarkable that this tropical fern has established itself so far north of its usual range. At the time of this find, the northernmost known localities for *A. abscissum* were in central peninsular Florida, over 800 kilometers (500 miles) to the south.

The genus name *Asplenium* means "for the spleen" and was applied in ancient times to the members of this genus because of some supposed medicinal properties. Most members of the genus are called spleenworts; "wort" is an Old English word meaning "plant."

The specific epithet *abscissum* is a Latin word that means "cut off." The authors of this book do not know why that name was applied to this species.

OTHER COMMON NAMES Cutleaf spleenwort

Cut spleenwort growing in a vertical limestone cave entrance in Jackson County.

One-Sorus Spleenwort
Asplenium monanthes Linnaeus

DESCRIPTION Rhizomes erect; leaves clustered at tip. Leaves 1-pinnate; blades linear, to 25 cm long; rachis and leaf stalk dark brown to black, with bristly hairs; leaflets opposite, oblong, up to about 1 cm long, the main vein running along lower margin; veins not united. Sori spindle-shaped, borne parallel to and along the main vein on the side toward the outer leaflet margin, only one or rarely two or three sori per leaflet; indusium spindle-shaped, attached along the side of the sorus toward the main vein.

HABITAT Grows on shaded mossy rocks and ledges in deep ravines, in sinkholes, and around cave mouths.

RANGE Known from several localities in Jackson County, Alabama. Also known from a few places in the upper Piedmont of North and South Carolina. A species of tropical and subtropical highland regions throughout the world extending northward into the southwestern United States and disjunct in the southeastern United States.

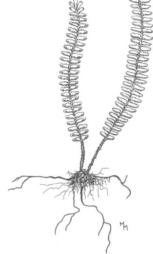

One-sorus spleenwort (*Asplenium monanthes*) with close-up of leaf underside showing sori.

COMMENTS Murray Evans first found this fern in the state in the mid-1980s. He has found it in at least three places in Jackson County, where it grows on rocks and boulders in sinkholes and at the mouths of caves, usually near the bases of the mountain slopes.

This fern was first discovered in the southeastern United States in 1946 in South Carolina. It is thought that hurricanes brought spores here from Mexico (Wherry 1964).

The specific epithet *monanthes* means "one-flowered" and refers to the solitary sori, as does the common name.

OTHER COMMON NAMES Single-sorus spleenwort

Above: One-sorus spleen-wort growing on thin soils of boulder-rich limestone woods at cave entrance in Jackson County.

Left: Close-up of the "single sorus" on the lower leaflet margins.

Black-Stemmed Spleenwort
Asplenium resiliens Kunze

DESCRIPTION Rhizomes nearly erect, at ground surface; leaves clustered at tip. Leaves 1-pinnate; blades linear, to 30 cm long; rachis and leaf stalk black, hairless; leaflets opposite, oblong with slight ears on the upper margins, up to a little more than 1 cm long; main vein running approximately through the center of each leaflet; upper leaflet margins wavy but not toothed; veins free. Sori spindle-shaped to crescent-shaped, four or more per leaflet, in diagonal rows on each side of the midrib and midway between the midrib and the margin; indusia spindle-shaped to crescent-shaped, attached along the side away from the main vein.

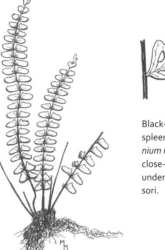

Black-stemmed spleenwort (*Asplenium resiliens*) with close-up of leaf underside showing sori.

HABITAT Grows on shaded limestone rocks, boulders, and cliffs.

RANGE Common in the limestone valleys of the Alabama highland provinces, chiefly in the Highland Rim, the Plateau Mountains, and the Ridge and Valley; rare in the limestone regions of the Coastal Plain. Widely distributed in the southern and eastern United States from Florida north to Pennsylvania and west to Arizona; also in tropical America.

COMMENTS Although *Asplenium resiliens* resembles the very common *A. platyneuron*, the two are easily distinguished by the fact that the leaflets in *A. resiliens* are opposite, in pairs, on the rachis, but those of *A. platyneuron* are alternate, attached singly to the rachis.

This species is triploid, with three sets of chromosomes, and reproduces by apogamy, which is explained earlier in this book in chapter 1, "About Ferns and Fern Allies." Even though the gametophytes produce sporophytes directly without producing gametes, somehow *A. resiliens* has managed to hybridize with *A. heterochroum*, a tetraploid, with four sets of chromosomes, of peninsular

Florida to produce *A. heteroresiliens*, which is pentaploid, with five sets of chromosomes. The latter also reproduces apogamously and occurs rarely in Georgia and the Carolinas, as well as in Florida. It has not been found in Alabama but may be present in the southeastern corner of the Coastal Plain.

The specific epithet *resiliens* means "springing back" and may refer to the flexible leaf stalks. The common name refers to the color of the rachis and the leaf stalk.

OTHER COMMON NAMES Black-stem spleenwort, little ebony spleenwort

SYNONYMS *Asplenium parvulum* Martens & Galeotti

Black-stemmed spleenwort growing on moss-covered limestone boulders in Jackson County.

Maidenhair Spleenwort
Asplenium trichomanes Linnaeus

DESCRIPTION Rhizomes short-creeping, frequently branched; leaves clustered at branch tips. Leaves 1-pinnate; blades linear, to 15 cm long and 1 cm broad; rachis and leaf stalk dark brown, hairless; leaflets opposite at leaf base, alternate near tip, to 0.5 cm long, oblong with rounded corners and wavy margins, asymmetrical about the midrib but not eared; veins free. Sori spindle-shaped to crescent-shaped, sparse, in diagonal rows on both sides of the midrib and midway between the midrib and the margin; indusia spindle-shaped to crescent-shaped, attached along the side away from the main vein.

Maidenhair spleenwort (*Asplenium trichomanes*) with close-up of leaf underside showing sori.

HABITAT Grows on shaded rocks of various types, in crevices, and on boulders and ledges.

RANGE Infrequent and widely scattered in the Alabama highland provinces, primarily the Cumberland Plateau and the Appalachian Ridges, extending south to northern Chilton and Hale Counties. Occurs throughout temperate North America except absent from the Great Plains and nearly so from the southeastern Coastal Plain; other varieties in Europe and Asia.

COMMENTS In Alabama this fern is most common on the Cumberland Plateau sandstone and shale, but it is occasionally found on limestone in both the Cumberland Plateau and the Ridge and Valley. In Hale County it is abundant on conglomerate rocks and cliffs at the site famous for *Asplenium tutwilerae* and in nearby ravines.

Two subspecies, ssp. *trichomanes* and ssp. *quadrivalens* D. E. Meyer, occur in North America. Only the type subspecies, ssp. *trichomanes*, is found in Alabama; it also occurs in Europe.

The species name *trichomanes* is from Greek *thrix*, "hair," and *manes*, "cup." Why Linnaeus applied that name to this species is unknown since this plant is hairless and has no cuplike features. The origin of the common name is also obscure, but it may have come from a superficial resemblance of the plant to some of the maidenhair ferns (*Adiantum*).

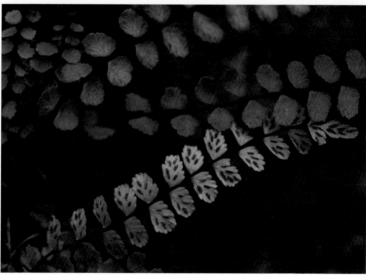

Top: Maidenhair spleenwort on moss-covered limestone boulders, Lauderdale County.

Bottom: Close-up of the sori on the underside of leaves.

Ebony Spleenwort
Asplenium platyneuron (Linnaeus) Britton, Sterns & Poggenburg

DESCRIPTION Rhizomes short-creeping, rarely branched; leaves clustered at tip. Leaves 1-pinnate throughout, of two similar types; purely vegetative leaves spreading and smaller than the erect fertile leaves; blades narrow, tapering at both ends, broadest above the middle; purely vegetative blades to 10 cm long and 3 cm broad, fertile blades typically to 35 cm long and 5 cm broad, occasionally to 60 cm or more long and 12 cm broad; rachis and leaf stalk brown throughout, hairless; leaflets alternate, oblong, stalkless, with bases overlapping the rachis, often with conspicuous ears on the upper margins; margins variable, finely toothed to deeply incised; veins all free. Sori spindle-shaped to crescent-shaped, numerous and crowded on fertile leaflets, in diagonal rows on both sides of the midrib, closer to the midrib than the margin; indusia spindle-shaped to crescent-shaped, attached along the side away from the midrib.

Ebony spleenwort (*Asplenium platyneuron*) with close-up of leaf underside showing sori.

HABITAT Grows in a wide variety of habitats: rocks, cliffs, and masonry; wooded slopes; shrubbery beds; roadside banks; and rarely flooded banks of streams.

RANGE Common and abundant throughout Alabama. Common throughout eastern North America from southern Canada and the Great Lakes region south to Florida and southwest to western Texas; also present in southern Africa.

COMMENTS This is one of the most common and abundant ferns in Alabama and has been collected in every county.

This is also one of the most variable of ferns. The smallest examples, from highland rocks and cliffs, may have the largest leaves less than 15 cm long. In some lowland woods of the Coastal Plain may be found individuals that are more than 50 cm tall.

The typical *Asplenium platyneuron* found throughout Alabama has fertile leaves that are usually no more than 35 cm tall and 5 cm broad. The leaflets are finely toothed but unlobed and have blunt or short-pointed tips. Many plants in the Coastal Plain have fertile leaves that can be over 50 cm tall and 10 cm broad. The leaflets are deeply and irregularly lobed with the lobes bearing fine teeth and have tips that are often narrow and long-pointed. This large Coastal Plain form has been named *A. platyneuron* var. *bacculum-rubrum* (Featherman) Fernald, the jagged spleenwort. It intergrades with typical *A. platyneuron*, and all sorts of intermediates may be found. Some of these have been called *A. platyneuron* var. *incisum* (Howe *ex* Peck) B. L. Robinson.

This fern hybridizes with many other *Asplenium* species.

The distribution of this fern is quite remarkable in that it occurs in eastern North America and in southern Africa, which are separated by thousands of kilometers and the Atlantic Ocean. Although the wind can carry fern spores vast distances, especially by strong storms like hurricanes, the patterns of the prevailing winds of the earth do not cross the equator, nor do major storms. This distribution is currently an enigma.

The specific epithet *platyneuron*, which means "broad-nerved," is a misnomer based on an early drawing with a large, exaggerated rachis. The varietal epithet *bacculum-rubrum* means "Baton Rouge" in Latin; *incisum* means "incised" or "cut." The common name refers to the color of the rachis and leaf stalk.

OTHER COMMON NAMES Brown-stem spleenwort

SYNONYMS *Asplenium ebeneum* Aiton

Ebony spleenwort in the Alabama Native Synoptic Garden at the Birmingham Botanical Gardens.

Walking Fern
Asplenium rhizophyllum Linnaeus

DESCRIPTION Rhizomes short, erect; leaves clustered at tip. Leaves un-divided and unlobed except occasionally with a pair of ears at the base; blades narrowly triangular, broadest at base, to 15 cm long and 4 cm wide, with thin prolonged tips that may root and form new plants where they touch the ground; leaf stalk brown at base, green at junction with blade; margins smooth or wavy; veins netted. Sori spindle-shaped to crescent-shaped, scattered throughout lower surface of blade; indusia spindle-shaped to crescent-shaped, attached along the side away from the midrib; spores fertile.

HABITAT Grows on shaded mossy boulders and ledges; primarily on limestone, but rarely on sandstone.

Walking fern (*Asplenium rhizophyllum*) with close-up of section of leaf underside showing sori and one leaf tip forming a new plant.

RANGE Frequent in the limestone regions of the Alabama highland provinces; also known from one locality in the Fall Line Hills of the Coastal Plain in northern Hale County. Occurs in the highland regions of eastern North America from southern Quebec south to northern Georgia and Alabama and west to the upper Mississippi Valley and the mountains of Arkansas and Oklahoma.

COMMENTS Because the leaf tips can take root and form new plants, dense colonies of this fern can form. Most other spleenworts occur singly, even where they are abundant.

The Hale County locality is the ravine famous for the descen-dant of this fern, *Asplenium tutwilerae*. Over the years, *A. rhizo-phyllum* has been variously reported as being present or absent at this locality, with recent reports indicating its absence (Walter et. al. 1982). On a Birmingham Fern Society field trip in June 1983, which included John T. Mickel of the New York Botanical Garden and

John W. Short, a small colony of *A. rhizophyllum* was found at the upper end of the ravine, somewhat removed from the bulk of the *A. tutwilerae* population.

This species hybridizes with other *Asplenium* species.

A number of authors follow the view that this fern is generically distinct from *Asplenium* and cite it as *Camptosorus rhizophyllus*; others do not. If this view is held, then the various hybrids and hybrid-derived species derived from it and various members of *Asplenium* proper are placed in the "hybrid genus" *Asplenosorus*. This matter is not universally agreed on by botanists, and the simpler view of including all of these ferns in *Asplenium* is taken here.

The specific epithet *rhizophyllum* means "rooting leaf" and refers to the leaf tips that can root to produce new plants. The common name walking fern comes from the way in which this characteristic makes the plants seem to "walk" from place to place.

SYNONYMS *Camptosorus rhizophyllus* (Linnaeus) Link

A grouping of walking fern growing among mosses on a boulder surface.

Tutwiler's Spleenwort
Asplenium tutwilerae B. R. Keener & L. J. Davenport

DESCRIPTION Rhizomes short and erect or ascending; leaves clustered at tip. Leaves mostly deeply lobed but 1-pinnate with only a few leaflets at base; blades spearhead-shaped, broadest near the base, to 20 cm long and 5 cm broad, with a prolonged tip that may occasionally root and form a new plant; leaf stalk brown; rachis brown below, green above; rachis and leaf stalk hairless; leaflets and lobes alternate to nearly opposite, oblong, stalkless, often of irregular lengths; margins smooth or wavy; veins all free. Sori spindle-shaped to crescent-shaped, in diagonal rows on both sides of the midrib; indusia spindle-shaped to crescent-shaped, attached along the side away from the midrib.

Above Left: Schematic of frond and sori placement on underside of fertile leaf.

Below right: Tutwiler's spleenwort (*Asplenium tutwilerae*) with close-up of leaf underside showing sori.

HABITAT Known only from mossy shaded acidic sand-and-gravel conglomerate ledges and boulders.

RANGE This species has been found only in a single ravine in northern Hale County, Alabama, in the Fall Line Hills of the Coastal Plain.

COMMENTS This is the most renowned of all of the ferns of Alabama. It is a fertile species that was derived by chromosome doubling in the sterile hybrid *Asplenium* × *ebenoides* R. R. Scott, Scott's spleenwort, which is the hybrid between *A. platyneuron* and *A. rhizophyllum*.

The sterile hybrid *Asplenium* × *ebenoides* occurs rarely throughout the Appalachian region of the eastern United States and west to the mountains of Missouri and Arkansas. It typically grows on shaded mossy rocks of various types, but usually limestone.

The chromosome doubling that produced this species apparently

occurred only once and seems to have done so recently since this fertile species can be found only in one small ravine.

Reports of *A.* × *ebenoides* from Marion County (Mohr 1901) and Jefferson County (Thomas 1976) may have been the sterile hybrid. Since there are no specimens to confirm these reports, we have excluded the hybrid from this book.

Brian Keener and Larry Davenport (2007) named this species *A. tutwilerae* only recently. Previously the fertile Hale County population was known simply as "fertile *A.* × *ebenoides*," with or without the ×.

The specific epithet *tutwilerae* honors Julia Tutwiler, a schoolteacher who discovered the Hale County ferns and reported that there were a great many more of them there than would seem likely for a sterile hybrid.

OTHER COMMON NAMES Scott's spleenwort, walking spleenwort

SYNONYMS *Asplenium* × *ebenoides* R. R. Scott, *Asplenosorus* × *ebenoides* (R. R. Scott) Wherry

Tutwiler's spleenwort growing in its natural habitat in conglomerate rocks containing pebbles of quartz and chert in Hale County, 2006.

Boydston's Spleenwort
Asplenium × *boydstoniae* (K. S. Walter) J. W. Short

DESCRIPTION Rhizomes short-creeping to ascending; leaves clustered at tip. Leaves 1-pinnate below, upper third to half of blade deeply lobed but not compound; blades narrow and nearly straight-sided, broadest near the base, to 20 cm long and 3 cm broad, tips narrow but with blunt ends; leaf stalk brown; rachis brown below, green above; rachis and leaf stalk hairless; leaflets alternate, oblong with blunt tips, stalkless, often with ears on the upper margins; margins finely toothed; veins all free. Sori spindle-shaped to crescent-shaped, in diagonal rows on both sides of the midrib; indusia similarly shaped, attached along the side away from the midrib; spores shrunken, abortive.

HABITAT Grows on shaded mossy conglomerate boulders and ledges.

RANGE Occurs naturally only in one ravine in northern Hale County, Alabama.

Boydston's spleen-wort (*Asplenium* × *boydstoniae*) with close-up of leaf underside showing sori.

COMMENTS This is one of the rarest of all ferns. It is the sterile hybrid between *Asplenium platyneuron* and *A. tutwilerae*. Since *A. tutwilerae* is found only in one ravine in Hale County, Alabama, this hybrid can not be expected to be found naturally anywhere else.

Asplenium × *boydstoniae* was found growing naturally for the first time in 1971 at the Hale County site by K. S. Walter, who found three plants growing together and took two of them back to the laboratory (Walter et. al. 1982).

In June of 1983, the Birmingham Fern Society made a field trip to the Hale County site; included in the group were John T. Mickel of the New York Botanical Garden and the senior author. On that occasion, two plants of *A.* × *boydstoniae* were found in separate places in the ravine. The ferns were photographed, but no collections were made.

This hybrid was first bred artificially in the 1950s at the University of Michigan by K. E. Boydston, for whom it is named.

SYNONYMS *Asplenosorus* × *boydstoniae* K. S. Walter

Boydston's spleenwort growing on a shaded conglomerate rock in Hale County.

Lobed Spleenwort
Asplenium pinnatifidum Nuttall

DESCRIPTION Rhizomes short, creeping to erect; leaves clustered at the tips. Leaves not compound but deeply lobed; blades narrowly triangular, broadest at base, with prolonged tips, to 12 cm long and 2 cm wide; leaf stalk brown at base, green at junction with blade; lobes asymmetrical, rounded; margins smooth or wavy; veins mostly free. Sori spindle-shaped to crescent-shaped, scattered on lower surfaces of lobes; indusia spindle-shaped to crescent-shaped, attached along the side away from the midrib; spores fertile.

HABITAT Grows on shaded but dry sandstone boulders, ledges, and cliffs.

RANGE Occasional throughout the Cumberland Plateau of Alabama. Occurs in the highland provinces of the eastern United States from New Jersey and Pennsylvania south to northern Alabama and Georgia and west to the Mississippi Valley and the mountains of Arkansas and Oklahoma.

Lobed spleenwort (*Asplenium pinnatifidum*) with close-up of leaf underside showing sori.

COMMENTS This is a fertile species derived from the hybridization of *Asplenium rhizophyllum* and *A. montanum* with subsequent chromosome doubling. It is the most common of the hybrid-derived spleenwort species of the Appalachian region. The sterile hybrid form is rarely found in nature and has not been reported from Alabama.

Some authors cite this species as *Asplenium pinnatifidum* (Muhlenberg) Nuttall (Wherry 1964) or *A. pinnatifidum* Muhlenberg (Lellinger 1985). Muhlenberg actually coined the epithet in 1813, five years before Nuttall described the species, but he did not include a description, so his name is considered invalid under the rules of nomenclature. Nuttall (1818) adequately described the species and noted that Muhlenberg had "apparently" referred to it in his 1813 work.

This species occasionally hybridizes with other spleenworts.

The specific epithet *pinnatifidum* means "pinnately lobed" and refers to the shape of the leaf blade, as does the common name.

Synonyms *Asplenosorus pinnatifidus* (Nuttall) Mickel

Lobed spleenwort growing in sandstone rock face in Cullman County, 2011.

Mountain Spleenwort
Asplenium montanum Willdenow

DESCRIPTION Rhizomes short, creeping to erect; leaves clustered at tip. Leaves 2-pinnate at base, 1-pinnate with lobed leaflets above; blades triangular to oblong, to 10 cm long and 6 cm wide; leaf stalk almost entirely green, brown only at the very base; pinnae triangular to oblong, narrowing toward the leaf tip; pinnae with short stalks; margins variable from evenly toothed to irregularly lobed; veins free. Sori few, spindle-shaped to crescent-shaped, scattered on lower surfaces of leaflets and lobes; indusia spindle-shaped to crescent-shaped, attached along the side away from the midrib; spores fertile.

HABITAT Grows in shaded crevices on sandstone and other acidic rocks.

RANGE Found in Alabama in the Cumberland Plateau and Appalachian Ridges. Occurs throughout the Appalachian region from northern Alabama and Georgia north to Ohio and Massachusetts.

Mountain spleenwort (*Asplenium montanum*) with close-up of leaf underside showing sori.

COMMENTS This is one of the most frequent of the many ferns in the southeastern United States that grow only on rocks. In Alabama, it is most abundant in the Sipsey Gorges of the northwest and on the Cumberland Plateau escarpments in the northeast; shaded sandstone cliffs and ledges are common in both regions.

This species hybridizes with other *Asplenium* species.

The specific epithet *montanum* means "of mountains"; it and the common name were bestowed because it was first collected in the Appalachian Mountains.

Mountain spleenwort growing on a sandstone cliff near Stevenson, Jackson County.

Cliff Spleenwort
Asplenium bradleyi D. C. Eaton

DESCRIPTION Rhizomes slender, short-creeping; leaves clustered at tip, leaf stalk bases persistent. Leaves mostly compound but lobed at the tip, 1-pinnate, occasionally barely 2-pinnate at base; blades narrow, oblong to spearhead-shaped, to 15 cm long and 4 cm wide; leaf stalk brown throughout, rachis brown at base, green in upper third to half; leaflets triangular at the base of the blade to oblong near the tip, lobed; lower leaflets with short stalks, with a conspicuous lobe at base and shallowly lobed farther out; margins with fine teeth; veins free. Sori spindle-shaped to crescent-shaped, along secondary veins of the leaflets; indusia spindle-shaped to crescent-shaped, attached along the side away from the midrib; spores fertile.

Cliff spleenwort (*Asplenium bradleyi*) with close-up of leaf underside showing sori.

HABITAT Grows in crevices on cliffs of acidic rocks, chiefly sandstone.

RANGE Found rarely in Alabama on Sand and Lookout Mountains in the Cumberland Plateau and in the Appalachian Ridges. Rare and scattered from central Georgia and northern Alabama north to New York and Ohio and west to Arkansas and eastern Oklahoma.

COMMENTS This fern arose from the hybridization of *Asplenium platyneuron* and *A. montanum* with subsequent chromosome doubling. It also hybridizes with these and other *Asplenium* species.

The sterile hybrid is unknown in nature, although it has been produced in the laboratory.

Some examples of this species closely resemble diminutive versions of *A. platyneuron*. They can be identified by examining the leaflets at and near the base of the blade. The leaflets of *A. bradleyi* will have tiny stalks connecting them to the rachis; those of *A. platyneuron* are completely stalkless.

The specific epithet *bradleyi* honors Frank Bradley, who first discovered this fern in Tennessee in 1870. The common name refers to its preferred type of habitat.

OTHER COMMON NAMES Bradley's spleenwort

Cliff spleenwort with leaf underside showing sori.

Graves's Spleenwort
Asplenium × gravesii Maxon

DESCRIPTION Rhizomes slender, creeping; leaves clustered at tip. Leaves 1-pinnate at base, lobed above; blades narrowly spearhead-shaped, to 15 cm long and 3 cm wide; leaf stalk brown throughout, rachis brown at base, green above; leaflets and lobes blunt, ovate to triangular, not further lobed or divided; lower leaflets with short stalks; margins with fine teeth; veins free. Sori spindle-shaped to crescent-shaped, scattered on lower surfaces of pinnae and lobes; indusia similarly shaped, attached along the side away from the midrib; spores sterile, shrunken.

HABITAT Grows on partially shaded sandstone cliffs and boulders.

RANGE E. T. Wherry made the only known collection of this fern from Alabama in 1930 at Noccalula Falls on Lookout Mountain in Etowah County. Rare in the Cumberland Plateau of northeastern Alabama and northwestern Georgia north to Kentucky and Pennsylvania.

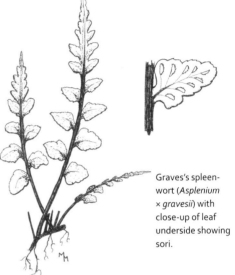

Graves's spleenwort (*Asplenium × gravesii*) with close-up of leaf underside showing sori.

COMMENTS This is the sterile hybrid between *Asplenium pinnatifidum* and *A. bradleyi*.

This is one of the rarest of the hybrid spleenworts. Thomas Darling made a thorough search for it in Georgia and Alabama in the 1950s and found it only at the type locality in Georgia (Darling 1957). E. W. Graves (1920) reported it from northeastern Jackson County, but there are no specimens to confirm this report.

The species name *gravessi* and the common name honor E. W. Graves, an avid student of Alabama ferns in the early twentieth century who first collected it in Dade County, Georgia, not in Alabama as Dean (1969) reported.

OTHER COMMON NAMES Sand mountain spleenwort

SYNONYMS *Asplenosorus × gravesii* (Maxon) Mickel

Herbarium specimen of Graves's spleenwort collected by
E. T. Wherry in Etowah County on April 22, 1930.

Trudell's Spleenwort
Asplenium × trudellii Wherry

DESCRIPTION Rhizomes short, creeping to erect; leaves clustered at tip. Leaves 1-pinnate at base, lobed above; blades narrowly spearhead-shaped to triangular, to 10 cm long and 2 cm wide; leaf stalk brown at base, turning green below junction with blade, rachis green; leaflets and lobes rounded, nearly triangular at blade base and narrowing above; lower leaflets with short stalks and often with a few lobes; margins with coarse teeth; veins free. Sori spindle-shaped to crescent-shaped, scattered on lower surfaces of pinnae and lobes; indusia spindle-shaped to crescent-shaped, attached along the side away from the midrib; spores sterile.

HABITAT Grows in shaded crevices in sandstone and other acidic rocks.

RANGE Rare and widely scattered in the Cumberland Plateau of Alabama. Occasional in the Appalachian Mountains and plateaus from New Jersey west to Ohio and south to northern Alabama and Georgia.

Trudell's spleenwort (*Asplenium × trudellii*) with close-up of leaf underside showing sori.

COMMENTS This is the sterile hybrid between *Asplenium pinnatifidum* and *A. montanum*. It has been found in only a few places in Alabama.

In Kentucky, *A. × trudellii* seems to be more frequent than it should be since it is sterile and should exist only by the chance of having spores from both parents fall very near to each other. It has been suggested that some sort of apogamy may be at work (Cranfill 1980).

The specific epithet *trudellii* and the common name honor Harry W. Trudell, an amateur botanist from Philadelphia and associate of E. T. Wherry, who first collected this fern in 1920.

SYNONYMS *Asplenosorus × trudellii* (Wherry) Mickel

Trudell's spleenwort growing in a shaded sandstone crevice.

Wall-Rue Spleenwort

Asplenium ruta-muraria Linnaeus

DESCRIPTION Rhizomes erect, short; leaves clustered at tip. Leaves 2-pinnate, dull gray-green; blades ovate to triangular, to 5 cm long and 4 cm wide; leaf stalk green, brown at base, rachis entirely green; pinnae triangular to oblong; primary leaf divisions with long stalks with only a few widely spaced leaflets; leaflets stalked, fan-shaped to diamond-shaped, many with a few sparse lobes; margins toothed; veins free. Sori spindle-shaped to crescent-shaped, scattered on lower surfaces of leaflets and lobes; indusia spindle-shaped to crescent-shaped, attached along the side away from the midrib; spores fertile.

HABITAT Grows on shaded limestone cliffs.

RANGE Rare in Alabama at widely scattered localities in the Cumberland Plateau, Highland Rim, and Ridge and Valley. Occurs in eastern North America from New England to the western Great Lakes and south to Missouri and along the Appalachian Mountains and plateaus to northern Georgia and central Alabama; also in Europe.

Wall-rue spleenwort (*Asplenium ruta-muraria*) with close-up of leaf underside showing sori.

COMMENTS This fern has not been collected in Alabama for many years. It is tiny and of a dull color that blends with the rock on which it grows; it is easily missed. In addition, it often grows in places like high cliffs that are difficult for collectors to access. It may be more common in Alabama, and elsewhere, than is presently known.

Some authors consider American examples of this species as var. *cryptolepis* (Fernald) Wherry, which only differs slightly from the European type variety.

The specific epithet *ruta-muraria* means "rue of walls" and refers to the fact that it commonly grows on walls in Europe, where it was first known, and to its resemblance to the flowering plant rue. This is also the source of the common name.

Herbarium specimen of wall-rue spleenwort collected first by Dr. E. A. Smith on the Sipsey Fork, Winston County, in July 1877, and described as inhabiting "upper districts in the mountains and northward to Kentucky"; then collected later by Dr. E. L. Lee near Bridgeport at the foot of the Cumberland Plateau in March 1908.

Sensitive Fern
Onoclea sensibilis Linnaeus

DESCRIPTION Rhizome long-creeping, shallowly buried, leaves widely separated. Leaves of two very dissimilar types. Vegetative blades deeply lobed, almost compound, ovate to triangular, to 35 cm long; lobes opposite or nearly so, narrow, oblong to spindle-shaped; margins toothless, varying from slightly wavy to lobed as much as halfway to the midrib, leaf stalk to 40 cm long, pale with dark base. Fertile blades 2-pinnate; primary segments ascending; leaflets rolled up, beadlike, with sporangia inside, leaf stalk to 25 cm long, stiff, dark brown.

HABITAT Grows in swamps, wet ditches, and meadows, and low stream and lake banks; occasional on low chalk or limestone river bluffs.

RANGE Common throughout Alabama. Occurs throughout much of eastern and central North America from the Atlantic Coast to the Great Plains and from the Gulf Coast of Texas to Labrador and Manitoba.

Sensitive fern (*Onoclea sensibilis*) showing both vegetative and fertile blades.

COMMENTS This fern is probably present in every Alabama county. It is probably slightly more abundant in the Coastal Plain than the highland provinces due to the greater frequency of wetland habitats there.

This is one of the few ferns that can survive in places that are frequently flooded. It grows mostly in swamps and other places with deep, wet soils.

In the Black Belt of Alabama and in the limestone areas of southwestern Alabama it is also found in an entirely different habitat. In these places *Onoclea* is often found growing on low chalk or limestone bluffs along the banks of rivers and streams. It grows with the rhizome in thin soil at the top edge of the bluff with the leaves hanging downward toward the water.

This is the host plant for the sensitive fern borer moth (*Papaipema inquesita.*)

This fern has caused poisonings in livestock. Animals that have ingested it become uncoordinated and are unable to walk or eat temporarily.

The genus name *Onoclea* is an ancient name for some plant, the identity of which is now unknown. The specific epithet *sensibilis* means "sensitive"; it and the common name were given because the vegetative leaves are very "sensitive" to cold and will die with the first frost, leaving only the upright fertile leaf with its beadlike leaflets.

OTHER COMMON NAMES Bead fern

Vegetative and fertile leaves of sensitive fern growing in the Birmingham Botanical Gardens.

Japanese False Spleenwort
Deparia petersenii (Kunze) M. Kato

DESCRIPTION Rhizomes creeping, leaves slightly separated. Leaves 1-pinnate with deeply lobed leaflets; blade broadly spearhead-shaped, to 40 cm long and 25 cm wide; leaf stalk to 30 cm long, rachis and leaf stalk light brown, with fine scales; leaflets distant, oblong to spearhead-shaped, deeply lobed, lowest few pairs ascending; veins free. Sori straight, side by side in two chevronlike rows along the midribs of the leaflet lobes; occasional pairs of sori lying back to back will be present in the rows; indusia attached along the side.

HABITAT Grows in moist, often disturbed soil on shaded stream banks, cypress swamps, and under bridges. Often found on limey or marly soils.

Japanese false spleenwort (*Deparia petersenii*) with close-up of section of leaf underside showing sori.

RANGE Scattered but apparently becoming more common in Alabama, mostly in the Coastal Plain but crossing the Fall Line in Lee County. A native of southeastern Asia that appears to be naturalized in southern Alabama and Georgia and in northern Florida.

COMMENTS This fern seems to be in the early stages of becoming part of our flora. It was first collected in the United States in northern Florida in 1957 and was not found elsewhere in this country until over twenty years later when it was found in Lee County, Alabama. It has since been found in a few more scattered localities in southern Alabama and Georgia. In some areas it is now quite common.

This is considered to be an edible fern.

This species has long been misidentified as another Asian species, the Japanese twin-sorus fern, *Diplazium japonicum*.

The genus name *Deparia* comes from a Greek word meaning "saucer"; it refers to the saucerlike indusium of the type species, *D. prolifera*, but this is different from the other members of the genus, including the present species. The specific epithet *petersenii* honors C. W. Petersen, a Danish botanist who collected the type specimen. The common name false spleenwort refers to the resemblance of the sori to those of the genus *Asplenium*, the spleenworts.

OTHER COMMON NAMES Petersen's spleenwort, Japanese lady fern

SYNONYMS *Diplazium japonicum* (Thunberg) Beddome, *Deparia japonica* (Thunberg) M. Kato, both misapplied

Japanese false spleenwort growing in damp woods in northern Pike County.

Glade Fern
Athyrium pycnocarpon (Sprengel) Tidestrom

DESCRIPTION Rhizome thick, short-creeping, covered with scales. Leaves 1-pinnate, of two slightly different types, the fertile narrower, longer, and with more widely spaced leaflets than the purely vegetative ones; blade to 75 cm long and 20 cm wide, spearhead-shaped; leaf stalk to 30 cm long, green, rachis green; leaflets not lobed or divided, narrowly spearhead-shaped; margins toothless and slightly wavy; veins free. Sori long and thick, straight or nearly so, crowded side by side in two rows on the leaflet undersurface, long axes of sori at a moderate angle to the midrib producing chevronlike rows.

HABITAT Grows in rich hardwood forests in moist soil near streams and cliff bases, seeming to prefer the proximity of limestone.

Glade fern (*Athyrium pycnocarpon*) showing vegetative and fertile fronds with close-up of leaf underside and sori.

RANGE Infrequent in Alabama in the Highland Rim, Cumberland Plateau, and Ridge and Valley, with one disjunct locality in the southwestern Coastal Plain. Occurs from southern Quebec west to Minnesota and south to Louisiana and Georgia; in the Southeast, most frequent in the Highland Rim and the Appalachian regions, rare in the Piedmont and Coastal Plain.

COMMENTS R. M. Harper found the Washington County locality in a limestone ravine on the bank of the Tombigbee River in the first decade of the twentieth century. This fern is found only rarely in the Coastal Plain of the southeastern United States except in the rich woods of the loess bluff of Mississippi and Louisiana, where it is locally abundant.

André Michaux originally described this fern in 1803 as a spleenwort because of its linear sori.

The genus name *Athyrium* means "without a door" and refers to the late-opening indusia of some members of the genus. The specific epithet *pycnocarpon* means "thick seed" and refers to the large sori.

OTHER COMMON NAMES Narrow-leaved spleenwort

SYNONYMS *Diplazium pycnocarpon* (Sprengel) M. Broun, *Homalosorus pycnocarpus* (Sprengel) Small

Glade fern growing in rich woods near a sandstone cliff at the Sipsey River Picnic Area, Bankhead National Forest, Winston County.

Silvery Glade Fern
Athyrium thelypterioides (Michaux) Desvaux

DESCRIPTION Rhizomes creeping, scaly, leaves narrowly spaced near the rhizome tip. Leaves 1-pinnate with deeply lobed leaflets; blade to 70 cm long and 25 cm wide, spearhead-shaped; leaf stalk and rachis green, with fine scales and hairs; leaflets narrowly oblong with tapering tips, deeply lobed with rounded oblong lobes; margins of lobes smooth to slightly toothed; veins free. Sori straight or nearly so, side by side in two chevronlike rows on either side of the lobe midrib; indusia attached along the side away from the lobe midrib.

HABITAT Grows in rich, moist hardwood forests, often in the close proximity of rocks or cliffs.

RANGE Rare and widely scattered in the Cumberland Plateau of Alabama. Occurs throughout the Appalachian region from Nova Scotia south to northern Georgia and Alabama and west to Arkansas and Minnesota.

Silvery glade fern (*Athyrium thelypterioides*) with close-up of leaf underside showing sori.

COMMENTS This is one of many plants that reach the southern limits of their distributions in Alabama. Because of this, it is quite rare here even though in other parts of its range it is considered frequent. In Alabama, it is generally confined to cool rocky ravines and sinkholes.

The specific epithet *thelypterioides* means "like a *Thelypteris*"; the 1-pinnate blades with deeply lobed leaflets resemble those of many species in that genus. Young indusia have a silvery appearance that gives the fern its common name.

OTHER COMMON NAMES Silvery spleenwort

Synonyms *Deparia acrostichoides* (Swartz) M. Kato, *Diplazium acrostichoides* (Swartz) Butters

Top: Silvery glade fern growing in a sink at the Nature Conservancy's Sharp Mountain Preserve, Jackson County.

Bottom: Close-up showing sori.

Southern Lady Fern
Athyrium filix-femina (Linnaeus) Roth

DESCRIPTION Rhizomes short-creeping to ascending, scaly. Leaves 2-pinnate, rarely 3-pinnate at base; blade spearhead-shaped to ovate, to 90 cm long and 40 cm broad, sometimes more; leaf stalk to 30 cm long, rachis and leaf stalk pale green to wine-red; pinnae oblong to spearhead-shaped with tapering tips; primary leaf segments oblong to spearhead-shaped, toothed to deeply lobed. Sori short, nearly straight to crescent-shaped, crowded side by side in rows on either side of the pinnule midrib; indusia attached along the side away from the pinnule midrib.

HABITAT Grows in shaded damp soil on stream banks and floodplains, swamp margins, cliff bases, and roadsides.

RANGE Common throughout Alabama. A worldwide species; the variety found in Alabama occurs along the Gulf Coast from Florida to Texas and north to Kansas and southeastern New England.

Southern lady fern (*Athyrium filix-femina*) with close-up of leaf underside showing sori.

COMMENTS This is one of the most variable ferns in Alabama. In its typical form the leaves are less than 65 cm tall, and the blades are spearhead-shaped in outline, more than twice as long as broad. The leaflets are oblong, straight-sided except for a tapering tip, and the leaflets are less than 1.5 cm long and are merely toothed.

Sometimes along rich stream banks in the Coastal Plain and along the Fall Line there are examples of this fern that have leaves over 1 meter tall with broad, ovate to nearly triangular blades. The pinnae are spearhead-shaped, broadest near the middle and tapering abruptly at the base. The longest leaflets are 2 to 3 cm long and are deeply lobed, occasionally all the way to the midrib to make the blade actually 3-pinnate.

Native Americans used the rhizome to make a tea to help stop breast pains in childbirth, induce lactation, and ease labor (Foster and Duke 1990).

Several varieties of this cosmopolitan species occur in North America, but only variety *asplenioides* occurs in Alabama. Some authors have separated it from *Athyrium filix-femina* as *A. asplenioides* (Michaux) A. A. Eaton.

The specific epithet *filix-femina* literally means "lady-fern"; it refers to the delicate and lacy appearance of the leaves. These ferns had traditionally been known as lady-ferns when Linnaeus named the species; he simply used a Latin form of that common name as its epithet. The varietal name *asplenioides* refers to its small crescent-shaped sori that resemble those of an *Asplenium*.

OTHER COMMON NAMES Lowland lady fern

SYNONYMS *Athyrium asplenioides* (Michaux) A. A. Eaton

Southern lady ferns growing in a moist boulder-strewn woodland.

Bulblet Bladder Fern
Cystopteris bulbifera (Linnaeus) Bernhardi

DESCRIPTION Rhizomes short-creeping, scaly; leaves clustered at end of rhizome. Leaves 2-pinnate with lobed leaflets; blade narrowly triangular, to 50 cm long and 15 cm wide, tip prolonged; leaf stalk to 15 cm long, rachis and leaf stalk pale; pinnae spearhead-shaped; leaflets oblong to spearhead-shaped and toothed or lobed; veins free.

Sori round, scattered on the lower surfaces of the leaflets; indusium hoodlike, attached at one side and arching over sorus. Round, fleshy bulblets are often present at the junctions of the rachis with the primary leaf divisions.

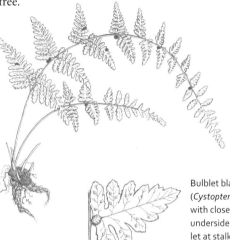

HABITAT Grows on moist, shaded limestone rocks, cliffs, ledges, and talus slopes.

Bulblet bladder fern (*Cystopteris bulbifera*) with close-up of leaf underside with bulblet at stalk juncture and showing sori.

RANGE Occasional in Alabama in the Highland Rim, Cumberland Plateau, and Ridge and Valley. Occurs in eastern North America throughout the Appalachians from Newfoundland south to Georgia and Alabama and west to eastern Oklahoma and South Dakota.

COMMENTS The leaves bear bulblets on the rachis that drop off and may grow to produce new plants. The bulblets are very rarely seen in herbarium specimens because they drop off very quickly after the plant is collected, before the collector has a chance to press and preserve it.

The narrow elongated triangular shape of the leaves is highly distinctive of this fern.

Some of the most luxuriant examples of this fern may be found at Noccalula Falls, near Gadsden in Etowah County. There, it is abundant and grows to a large size in the grotto behind the waterfall.

The genus name *Cystopteris* means "bladder fern" and refers to the bladderlike appearance of the indusia before they open. The common name comes from this and the bulblets that are present on the leaves.

Bulblet bladder fern growing on a shaded ledge at Wolf Den Mountain in southern Cherokee County.

Tennessee Bladder Fern
Cystopteris tennesseensis Shaver

DESCRIPTION Rhizomes short-creeping; leaves clustered at end of rhizome. Leaves 2-pinnate with lobed leaflets; blade narrowly triangular to spearhead-shaped, to 30 cm long and 15 cm wide; leaf stalk to 15 cm long, rachis and leaf stalk pale green, dark at leaf stalk base; primary leaf divisions broadly spearhead-shaped; leaflets spearhead-shaped, larger ones deeply lobed; veins free. Sori scattered on pinnule undersurface, round; indusia hoodlike, attached at one side and arching over sorus. Cylindrical scaly bulblets occasionally present at the junctions of the rachis with the primary leaf divisions.

HABITAT Grows on shaded limestone rocks, cliffs, and ledges.

RANGE Infrequent in Alabama in the Highland Rim and the Plateau Mountains. Occurs in eastern North America from Kentucky west to Iowa and Kansas and south to eastern Oklahoma and northern Alabama and Georgia; disjunct in the Coastal Plain of North Carolina.

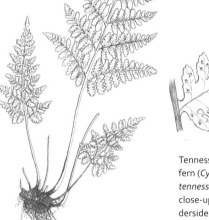

Tennessee bladder fern (*Cystopteris tennesseensis*) with close-up of leaf underside showing sori.

COMMENTS It is interesting that a fern that is as widespread as this one would for many years escape the notice of botanists, but it was unknown to science until Shaver described it in 1950. Prior to that time collections of this fern tended to be identified as *Cystopteris fragilis* (Linnaeus) Bernhardi. Old reports of that species from Alabama undoubtedly represent *C. tennesseensis* or *C. protrusa*.

This is a fertile species that was derived from the hybridization of *Cystopteris bulbifera* and *C. protrusa* with subsequent chromosome doubling. Since this species is of hybrid origin, it combines the characteristics of its parent species. It is also quite variable within the

range of those characteristics. Because of this, many examples are difficult to distinguish from one ancestor or the other.

The leaf blades of *C. bulbifera* are very narrow, and the tips are greatly elongated. They are usually four to five times as long as broad and are broadest at the very base. The blades of *C. tennesseensis* are usually fairly narrow, but the tips end abruptly. They are usually a little more than twice as long as broad and may be broadest slightly above the base. The blades of *C. protrusa* are spearhead-shaped, somewhat narrowed at the base, and are about twice as long as broad. The tip of the rhizome of *C. protrusa* extends beyond the bases of the leaf stalks; the leaves are in clusters at the tip of the rhizome in the other two species. Bulblets may be present in living plants of *C. bulbifera* or *C. tennesseensis*, but not in *C. protrusa*. Bulblets of *C. bulbifera* are round and fleshy; those of *C. tennesseensis* are spindle-shaped and scaly.

This fern was discovered in Tennessee by Jesse M. Shaver, who named it for that state in 1950. Shaver's book *Ferns of Tennessee* (1954) still stands as having some of the most detailed descriptions of ferns ever written.

Tennessee bladder fern growing on a shaded limestone ledge.

Lowland Brittle Fern
Cystopteris protrusa (Weatherby) Blasdell

DESCRIPTION Rhizome long-creeping; leaves clustered well behind the end of rhizome. Leaves 2-pinnate with lobed leaflets; blade spearhead-shaped to ovate, to 25 cm long and 15 cm wide; leaf stalk to 20 cm long, rachis and leaf stalk pale green, dark at leaf stalk base; pinnae broadly spearhead-shaped to ovate; leaflets spearhead-shaped, larger ones deeply lobed; veins free. Sori round, scattered on lower surfaces of the leaflets; indusia hoodlike, attached at one side and arching over sorus. Bulblets absent.

HABITAT Grows in moist soil in rich woodlands.

RANGE Occasional in the Alabama Highland Rim and Cumberland Plateau; rare in the rest of the highland provinces and the Coastal Plain. Occurs in eastern North America throughout the Appalachians from New York south to Georgia and Alabama and west to Louisiana, eastern Nebraska, and southeastern Minnesota.

Lowland brittle fern (*Cystopteris protrusa*) with close-up of leaf underside showing sori.

COMMENTS The tip of the rhizome of this fern extends 1 to 2 cm beyond the cluster of leaves. This is a very distinctive feature that makes this species easy to distinguish from similar-looking members of the genus.

This species was once thought to be a variety of the brittle fern, *Cystopteris fragilis*. Some old reports of that species in Alabama surely represent *C. protrusa*, while others are of *C. tennesseensis*. True *C. fragilis* is a northern species that is not likely to occur in Alabama.

The specific epithet *protrusa* refers to the rhizome tip that protrudes beyond the leaf bases. This species is the only *Cystopteris* that may be found in the Coastal Plain.

OTHER COMMON NAMES Lowland bladder fern, spreading bladder fern

SYNONYMS *Cystopteris fragilis* (Linnaeus) Bernhardi var. *protrusa* Weatherby

Lowland brittle fern growing in moist woodland soils.

Blunt-Lobed Cliff Fern

Woodsia obtusa (Sprengel) Torrey

DESCRIPTION Rhizome short-creeping, scaly; leaves closely spaced at rhizome tip. Leaves 1-pinnate with deeply lobed leaflets, may be 2-pinnate at base; blade spearhead-shaped, to 30 cm long and 10 cm wide; leaf stalk to 20 cm long, rachis and leaf stalk green to straw-colored, leaf stalk base dark; primary leaf divisions narrowly triangular to spearhead-shaped; leaflets and lobes oblong, margins toothed to moderately lobed; veins free. Sori round, in indistinct rows; indusium attached all around the sorus, splitting from the center into narrow segments that surround the sporangia, producing a starlike pattern in the mature sorus.

HABITAT Grows on and around shaded rocks, cliffs, and ledges, and on well-drained wooded hillsides, also on dry sandy roadside banks in full sun.

Blunt-lobed cliff fern (*Woodsia obtusa*) with close-up of leaf underside showing sori.

RANGE Frequent in the Alabama highland provinces, rare and widely scattered in the Coastal Plain. Frequent in eastern North America from New England south to Georgia and west to Texas and Minnesota.

COMMENTS Most ferns that grow on rocks, including the members of this genus, are specific either to acidic rocks like sandstone and granite or to alkaline calcareous rocks like limestone, but not both. *Woodsia obtusa* is unusual in that it is frequently found on rocks of both types; it also may grow in soil away from any rock outcrops.

This fern resembles some *Cystopteris* species but can be distinguished by the numerous scales on the leaf stalk and the star-shaped indusia.

The genus name *Woodsia* honors English botanist Joseph Woods of the late eighteenth and early nineteenth centuries. The specific epithet *obtusa* means "blunt" and refers to the tips of the lobes and leaflets. The common name refers to the blunt features and to one of the preferred habitats of the fern.

OTHER COMMON NAMES Blunt-lobed Woodsia, common Woodsia

Top: Blunt-lobed cliff fern in mixed pine-hardwood forest.

Bottom: Underside of leaflets showing sori.

Marginal Wood Fern
Dryopteris marginalis (Linnaeus) A. Gray

DESCRIPTION Rhizome thick, short-creeping, scaly; leaves at or near tip. Leaves 1-pinnate with deeply lobed leaflets to 2-pinnate; blade oblong to spearhead-shaped to 40 cm long and 25 cm wide, tapering abruptly at the tip, leathery; primary leaf divisions oblong with tapering tips, deeply lobed nearly to the midrib, occasionally all the way to the midrib; sori-bearing leaflets occurring mostly in upper half of blade, not different from the purely vegetative ones except for the presence of sori; margins shallowly toothed; veins free. Sori round, at the blade margins; indusia kidney-shaped, glandless. Spores fertile.

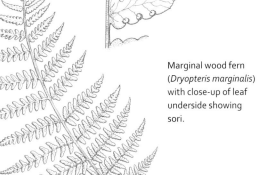

Marginal wood fern (*Dryopteris marginalis*) with close-up of leaf underside showing sori.

HABITAT Grows on shaded cliffs, boulders, and rocky slopes.

RANGE Frequent throughout the highland provinces of Alabama except seemingly absent from the Piedmont; barely crosses the Fall Line into the rock ravines of the Fall Line Transition Zone in northwestern Alabama. Occurs in eastern North America from Newfoundland west to Wisconsin and Kansas and south to northern Alabama and Georgia.

COMMENTS Although this fern has not been found in the Alabama Piedmont, it does occur sparingly in the Piedmont of Georgia and northward. The Hale County locality is in the rocky ravine in the Coastal Plain that is well known as the only place where *Asplenium tutwilerae* may be found. *Dryopteris marginalis* is one of several plants with northern affinities that reaches the southernmost limit of its distribution in that place.

This is one of the few rock-loving ferns that is commonly found on both alkaline rocks like limestone and on acidic rocks like sandstone.

The genus name *Dryopteris* means "oak fern" and refers to the wooded habitats, often with oak trees, in which these ferns grow. The specific epithet *marginalis* and part of the common name both refer to the location of the sori at the margins of the leaf blade. The rest of the common name, wood fern, refers to the habitat. Most species in this genus are called wood ferns, and they are also known as shield ferns because of their conspicuous shieldlike indusia.

OTHER COMMON NAMES Marginal shield fern, leather wood fern

Marginal wood fern growing in Jackson County.

Florida Wood Fern
Dryopteris ludoviciana (Kunze) Small

DESCRIPTION Rhizome thick, short-creeping, scaly; leaves separated but not distant. Leaves 1-pinnate with deeply lobed leaflets; blade spearhead-shaped, to 90 cm long and 30 cm wide, of two somewhat dissimilar types with the fertile blades longer than the purely vegetative ones, sori present only on upper portion of blade; leaflets narrow, oblong, with long-tapering tips; fertile leaflets occurring on upper half of blade, conspicuously narrower than the vegetative ones, with more widely separated lobes that are cut almost completely to the midrib; margins shallowly toothed; veins free. Sori round, well between midveins and margins; indusia kidney-shaped, glandless. Spores fertile.

Florida wood fern (*Dryopteris ludoviciana*) with coiled fiddlehead and close-up of leaf underside showing sori.

HABITAT Grows in shaded wet soil on stream banks and swamp margins, usually in the proximity of limestone.

RANGE Occasional in Alabama in the Coastal Plain. Infrequent from central Florida west to eastern Louisiana and north to southeastern North Carolina. Occurs only in the Coastal Plain of the southeastern United States.

COMMENTS *Dryopteris* is a genus of mostly cool-climate ferns. This is the only one of them that commonly occurs in the lower Coastal Plain.

The name *ludoviciana* means "of Louisiana." This fern was first collected in Louisiana in the 1790s and was named in 1848. This name was published in a little-known journal and botanists overlooked it for many years. In the meantime, the fern was discovered in Florida, where it is now known to reach its greatest abundance, and was given the name *floridana* in 1850. It became generally known by this name and by the common name Florida wood (or shield) fern.

When the name *ludoviciana* was rediscovered in the 1930s, it became necessary to reject the name *floridana* and use *ludoviciana* since it was published earlier. It has been suggested that because of this change in the scientific name, the common name Florida wood fern is no longer appropriate and the fern should be called the Louisiana wood fern (Thieret 1980). This species has also been called the southern wood (or shield) fern, but this name has been used for many years to refer to *Dryopteris* × *australis*, and southern shield fern has also been used to refer to *Thelypteris kunthii*. Although it no longer reflects the scientific name, Florida wood fern is unambiguous and is still the most frequently used common name. It also refers to the region with the greatest abundance of the fern.

OTHER COMMON NAMES Louisiana wood fern, Florida shield fern

SYNONYMS *Dryopteris floridana* (Hooker) Kuntze

Florida wood fern growing in a cypress swamp of northern Pike County.

Goldie's Wood Fern
Dryopteris goldiana (Hooker) A. Gray

DESCRIPTION Rhizome thick, short-creeping, scaly; leaves separated but close. Leaves 1-pinnate with deeply lobed leaflets; blade oblong, to 80 cm long and 40 cm wide, tapering abruptly at tip; leaflets broad, oblong with tapering tips, deeply lobed; fertile leaflets occurring over most of blade, not different from the purely vegetative ones except for the presence of sori; margins shallowly toothed; veins free. Leaf stalks tan with abundant scales at the base, the scales dark brown or brown with tan margins. Sori round, closer to midveins than margins; indusia kidney-shaped, glandless. Spores fertile.

HABITAT Grows in rich, damp woodlands, often around rocks and cliffs.

Goldie's wood fern (*Dryopteris goldiana*) with close-up of leaf underside showing sori.

RANGE Currently known in Alabama from a single collection in the Sipsey Gorges. Occurs from southern New England west to Minnesota and south to northern Alabama and Georgia.

COMMENTS Blanche Dean collected this fern in Sipsey Gorges of Winston County in 1969 and W. H. Wagner confirmed her identification. All other material from Alabama that has been identified as *Dryopteris goldiana* has turned out to be *D. celsa*.

This species and *D. celsa* are very similar appearing and are easily confused. In *D. celsa*, the sori are about halfway between the midvein and the margin; in *D. goldiana*, they are closer to the midvein than the margin. The blades of *D. goldiana* taper abruptly at the tip and are widest near the middle; the blades of *D. celsa* taper gradually at the tip and are widest below the middle. The leaf stalk of *D. goldiana* is tan with large and abundant shiny dark brown scales that have tan margins at the base. The leaf stalk of *D. celsa* is green and the scales are tan with a narrow dark brown stripe in the center.

The specific epithet *goldiana* and the common name honor John Goldie, a British traveler of the early nineteenth century who discovered the fern in Canada.

OTHER COMMON NAMES Giant wood fern

Herbarium specimen of Goldie's wood fern collected and identified by Blanche Dean in Winston County on May 12, 1969.

Log Fern

Dryopteris celsa (W. Palmer) Small

DESCRIPTION Rhizome thick, short-creeping, scaly; leaves separated but close together. Leaves 1-pinnate with deeply lobed leaflets; blade spearhead-shaped to oblong, to 80 cm long and 30 cm wide; leaflets spearhead-shaped, with long-tapering tips; sori-bearing leaflets occurring only on upper half of blade, not different from the vegetative ones except for the presence of sori; margins shallowly toothed; veins free. Leaf stalks light green with tan scales of varying widths at the base, each having a narrow dark central stripe. Sori round, well between midveins and margins; indusia kidney-shaped, glandless. Spores fertile.

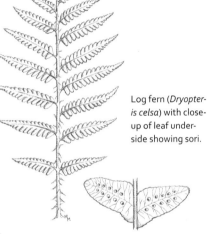

Log fern (*Dryopteris celsa*) with close-up of leaf underside showing sori.

HABITAT Grows in shade in organic soil and on rotting stumps and logs on the banks of streams and the margins of swamps, and in damp, sheltered coves of cliffs and hillsides.

RANGE Rare in Alabama, known from only a few sites widely scattered throughout the state. Rare and scattered in the eastern United States from New York west to upper Michigan and eastern Missouri and south to Louisiana and south Alabama.

COMMENTS This species is believed to have arisen as a hybrid between *Dryopteris ludoviciana* and *D. goldiana* with subsequent chromosome doubling to become fertile. One may wonder as to where this hybridization took place since the ranges of the two parents do not come anywhere near each other, much less overlap.

Dryopteris celsa is locally abundant in the Dismal Swamp of Virginia and North Carolina and rare elsewhere.

The specific epithet *celsa* means "high" and possibly refers to its habit of sometimes growing on logs, from which the common name is derived.

Top: Log fern growing in rich woods at Wolf Den Mountain in southern Cherokee County.

Bottom: Close-up of the leaf.

Southern Wood Fern
Dryopteris × australis (Wherry) Small

DESCRIPTION Rhizome thick, short-creeping, scaly; leaves separated but close. Leaves 1-pinnate with deeply lobed leaflets; blade spearhead-shaped to oblong, to 90 cm long and 30 cm wide; leaflets oblong to spearhead-shaped, with long-tapering tips; sori-bearing leaflets occurring only on upper half of blade, slightly narrower than the vegetative leaflets with somewhat more widely separated lobes; margins shallowly toothed; veins free. Sori round, well between midveins and margins; indusia kidney-shaped, glandless. Spores shrunken, sterile.

HABITAT Grows in wet soil on the margins of shallow swamps.

RANGE Known from a few localities in Alabama in the Ridge and Valley, in the Piedmont Fall Line, and in the Coastal Plain. Rare and widely scattered in the southeastern United States from eastern North Carolina south to east-central Alabama and west to Louisiana, mostly in the Coastal Plain.

Southern wood fern (*Dryopteris × australis*) with close-up of leaf underside showing sori.

COMMENTS This is the sterile hybrid between *Dryopteris ludoviciana* and *D. celsa*. Its distribution is remarkable in that, though a sterile hybrid, it is almost never found in the proximity of either parent.

E. T. Wherry named this fern *D. clintoniana* var. *australis* in 1937 from material he collected in Cherokee County, Alabama. It was actually first collected in Alabama in Lee County by L. M. Underwood, but he identified it as *D. floridana*, which is now known as *D. ludoviciana*. Wherry saw Underwood's specimens and recognized them to be his new variety *australis*.

As of 1977 the type locality in Cherokee County was still in existence, but attempts to find it have failed until very recently when Wayne Barger found it again in that place.

In Lee County the fern is abundant despite having been disturbed by logging and cattle. It grows over an area of an acre or so in a small swamp formed by a tiny stream that flows into a larger creek that flows out of the Piedmont rocks into the Coastal Plain sands, thus crossing the Fall Line, almost within sight of the swamp.

The name *australis* means "southern" and Wherry applied it because he thought it to be a variety of the northern *D. clintoniana*. The common name is derived from the epithet.

OTHER COMMON NAMES Dixie wood fern

SYNONYMS *Dryopteris clintoniana* (D. C. Eaton) Dowell var. *australis* Wherry

Southern wood fern growing in rich floodplain in Cherokee County.

Evergreen Wood Fern
Dryopteris intermedia (Muhlenberg) A. Gray

DESCRIPTION Rhizome short, thick, ascending, scaly; leaves clustered at tip. Leaves 2-pinnate with deeply lobed leaflets, occasionally 3-pinnate; blade oblong to spearhead-shaped, to 60 cm long and 30 cm wide; leaf stalk to 30 cm long, rachis and leaf stalk pale and scaly, upper part of rachis with minute stalked glands; primary leaf divisions spearhead-shaped, basal ones nearly symmetrical; leaflets spearhead-shaped, deeply lobed to pinnately divided, margins toothed; veins free. Sori round, between midveins and margins; indusia kidney-shaped to nearly round, covered with minute stalked glands. Spores fertile.

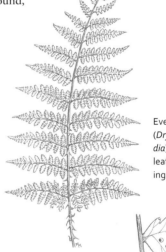

HABITAT In Alabama, restricted to shaded rocks and cliffs in cool ravines and around cave mouths; habitat more varied farther north to include rich woods, swamp margins, and rocky hillsides.

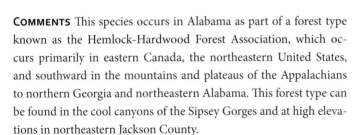

Evergreen wood fern (*Dryopteris intermedia*) with close-up of leaf underside showing sori.

RANGE Rare in Alabama, found in the Sipsey Gorges and Plateau Mountains. Occurs from Newfoundland south to northern Georgia and Alabama and west to eastern Missouri and Minnesota.

COMMENTS This species occurs in Alabama as part of a forest type known as the Hemlock-Hardwood Forest Association, which occurs primarily in eastern Canada, the northeastern United States, and southward in the mountains and plateaus of the Appalachians to northern Georgia and northeastern Alabama. This forest type can be found in the cool canyons of the Sipsey Gorges and at high elevations in northeastern Jackson County.

The spinulose wood fern, *Dryopteris carthusiana* (Villars) H. P. Fuchs, has been reported from the Bankhead National Forest in Winston County (Dean 1969), but no specimens have been seen. *Dryopteris intermedia* has clear glands on the blade, and the two innermost leaflets on each of the bottom pair of primary leaf divisions are usually of about the same size. The blades of *Dryopteris carthusiana* have no glands; the lower innermost leaflet on each of the bottom pair of primary leaf divisions is conspicuously longer than the upper innermost leaflet.

Muhlenberg apparently named this fern *D. austriaca* var. *intermedia, intermedia* is Latin for "intermediate," because it had similarities to two other ferns now known as *D. carthusiana* and *D. expansa*. The common name refers to the leaves that do not die back in winter, unlike many other species of *Dryopteris*.

OTHER COMMON NAMES Common wood fern, fancy fern

Evergreen wood fern growing near sandstone cliffs at the Sipsey River Picnic Area, Bankhead National Forest, Winston County.

Hybrid Wood Fern
Dryopteris intermedia × marginalis

DESCRIPTION Rhizome thick, short-creeping, scaly; leaves separated but close. Leaves 2-pinnate; blade spearhead-shaped to ovate, to 80 cm long and 50 cm wide; major leaf divisions and leaflets well separated; leaflets oblong with rounded tips; sori-bearing leaflets occurring over most of blade, not different from the purely vegetative ones except for the presence of sori; margins shallowly toothed; veins free. Sori round, at or very close to the margins; indusia kidney-shaped, with a few stalked glands. Spores sterile, shrunken.

HABITAT Grows in rich woods on cool rocky slopes and at cave mouths.

RANGE Known in Alabama from a single locality in Jackson County. Rare and scattered in the highland regions of the eastern United States and southeastern Canada.

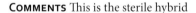

Hybrid wood fern (*Dryopteris intermedia × marginalis*) with close-up of leaf underside showing sori.

COMMENTS This is the sterile hybrid between *Dryopteris intermedia* and *D. marginalis*.

The Jackson County locality is at the mouth of a blowing cave at the base of a mountain in the Paint Rock Valley. The fern is growing on a mossy limestone boulder. Both parents are nearby.

This fern is large and spectacular and is not easily mistaken for either parent.

Rare sterile hybrid wood fern with a multicrowned rhizome growing in Jackson County.

Christmas Fern
Polystichum acrostichoides (Michaux) Schott

DESCRIPTION Rhizome thick, short-creeping to erect; leaves crowded at tip. Leaves 1-pinnate, dark shiny green, of two kinds: short and purely vegetative or tall with sori-bearing leaflets on the upper half or less of the blade; blade oblong to narrowly spearhead-shaped, to 50 cm long and 15 cm wide; leaf stalk to 20 cm long, rachis and leaf stalk green and scaly, leaf stalk base brown; leaflets narrow and straight, with ears that point toward the leaf tip, otherwise unlobed except in occasional unusual examples, margins with bristly teeth; sori-bearing leaflets conspicuously narrower and shorter than purely vegetative leaflets; blade tissue stiff, leathery; veins free. Sori round, crowded in two rows along the midribs of leaflets and larger ears; indusium attached in the center of the sorus and opening from around the edges, producing an umbrella-like structure over the sporangia.

Christmas fern (*Polystichum acrostichoides*) with close-up of leaf underside showing sori.

HABITAT Grows in rich hardwood and mixed forests in moist but well-drained soil, frequently on hillsides and near small streams.

RANGE Common throughout Alabama. Common throughout eastern North America from Nova Scotia south to northern Florida and west to Texas and Minnesota.

COMMENTS This is one of the most common ferns in Alabama and is one of the most likely to be encountered in the woodlands. Since the leaves are evergreen, this fern is especially conspicuous in winter when it may be one of only a few green things to be seen on the forest floor.

This fern can be grown as a house plant and is often cultivated in moist shaded gardens. It can be quite variable in the wild, and various forms with rolled, ruffled, or deeply incised leaflets are occasionally found growing naturally in Alabama.

The Cherokee Indians used the rhizomes of this fern as an ingredient in medicines for ailments such as toothaches and stomachaches (Dunbar 1989).

The genus name *Polystichum* means "many rows" and refers to the arrangement of the sori. The specific epithet *acrostichoides* means "like an *Acrostichum*," another genus of ferns that Michaux thought this species resembled.

The evergreen nature of this fern may be what gives it the common name Christmas fern. Another possibility is that the leaflet with its "ear" at the base was thought to resemble a Christmas stocking or Santa in his sleigh. It also is sometimes used in Christmas wreaths and decorations.

OTHER COMMON NAMES Dagger fern

Above: Christmas fern growing in rich woods on a bluff of the Conecuh River near Linwood, Pike County.

Left: Fiddleheads unfurling in early spring.

Japanese Tassel Fern
Polystichum polyblepharum (Roemer *ex* Kunze) C. Presl

DESCRIPTION Rhizome thick, short-creeping to erect; leaves crowded at tip. Leaves 2-pinnate; blades oblong to spearhead-shaped, to 50 cm or more long and 15 cm or more wide; leaf stalk and rachis densely covered with brown scales; leaflets rectangular to diamond-shaped, 0.5 to almost 1 cm long, unlobed except for slight ears that point toward the margin of the leaf; tips of leaflets and ears with stiff bristles; blade tissue stiff and leathery; veins free. Sori round, about 1 mm in diameter, in two unequal rows near the leaflet margins; indusium attached in the center of the sorus and opening from around the edges, producing an umbrella-like structure over the sporangia.

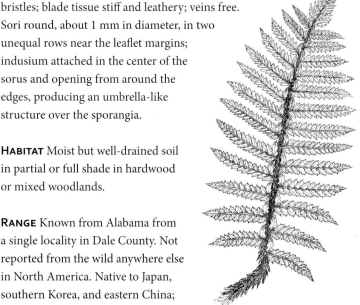

HABITAT Moist but well-drained soil in partial or full shade in hardwood or mixed woodlands.

RANGE Known from Alabama from a single locality in Dale County. Not reported from the wild anywhere else in North America. Native to Japan, southern Korea, and eastern China; naturalized and weedy in New Zealand.

Japanese tassel fern (*Polystichum polyblepharum*) with close-up of leaf underside showing sori.

COMMENTS The Dale County site is in disturbed woodland near a small naturally occurring pond. Its origin is unknown, but it may have appeared naturally from spores blown there from a garden.

This species was apparently introduced to cultivation in the United States only recently. It is commonly grown in the Birmingham area and is often sold to gardeners at fern shows. The fern is winter-hardy and may be in the early stages of becoming naturalized in Alabama.

The specific epithet *polyblepharum* means "many eyelashes" and refers to the abundant scales on the leaf stalk and rachis. The young fiddleheads bend over backward and resemble tassels, giving the fern part of its common name, the rest of which refers to its native land.

OTHER COMMON NAMES Korean tassel fern

SYNONYMS *Polystichum setosum* (Wallich) Schott

Above: Japanese tassel fern in the Fern Glade of the Birmingham Botanical Gardens.

Left: Close-up made in March showing "tassel" or fiddlehead emerging from the leaf litter.

Japanese Holly Fern
Cyrtomium falcatum (Linnaeus f.) K. Presl

DESCRIPTION Rhizome short, erect or ascending, densely scaly; leaves clustered at tip. Leaves 1-pinnate with usually four to ten pairs of leaflets; dark shiny green on both surfaces, blade tissue thick and leathery; blade oblong, to 60 cm long and 15 cm wide; leaf stalk scaly, to 20 cm long, rachis and leaf stalk green; leaflets asymmetrically ovate with elongate tips, curving toward leaf tip, margins coarsely toothed; veins netted. Sori round, abundant, scattered over lower surface of leaflet and essentially covering the surface; indusium attached in the center of the sorus and opening from around the edges, producing an umbrella-like structure covering the sporangia.

Japanese holly fern (*Cyrtomium falcatum*) with close-up of leaf underside showing sori.

HABITAT Grows on a variety of shaded cliffs, rocks, and masonry, also under bridges, in ravines, and in clay soils on wooded stream banks.

RANGE Presently known from a few localities in the Alabama Coastal Plain and in the Piedmont near the Fall Line. A native of eastern Asia that is commonly cultivated outdoors and is escaped or possibly naturalized in Florida and northward to South Carolina and west to Louisiana, seemingly rare.

COMMENTS This fern was first collected in Montgomery County before 1900 and soon after the turn of the century in Mobile County (Graves 1920). It has been collected in both places since then but not recently. It has been collected recently at several locations in the Coastal Plain of southeastern Alabama and has been found growing on the banks of a small stream in Lee County, above the Fall Line.

This fern is likely to be present almost anywhere in the Alabama Coastal Plain. It is cultivated throughout the lower Southeast in shrubbery beds and may spread by spores.

The genus name *Cyrtomium* means "cut in a curve." The specific epithet *falcatum* means "scythe-shaped." Both names refer to the slightly curved shape of the leaflets. The common name refers to the hollylike appearance of the leaflets.

OTHER COMMON NAMES Japanese net-vein holly fern, Asian net-vein holly fern

Japanese holly fern growing in the Fern Glade of the Birmingham Botanical Gardens, Jefferson County.

Fortune's Holly Fern
Cyrtomium fortunei J. Smith

DESCRIPTION Rhizome short, erect or ascending, densely scaly; leaves clustered at tip. Leaves 1-pinnate with ten to twenty-five pairs of leaflets; dark green but not shiny on upper surface, blade tissue papery; blade oblong, to 90 cm long and 15 cm wide; leaf stalk scaly, to 20 cm long, rachis and leaf stalk green; leaflets asymmetrically ovate with elongate tips, margins with fine rounded teeth; veins netted. Sori round and scattered over lower surface of the leaflet; indusium attached in the center of the sorus, opening from around the edges producing an umbrella-like structure covering the sporangia and shriveling at maturity.

Fortune's holly fern (*Cyrtomium fortunei*) with close-up showing leaf underside with sori.

HABITAT Clay banks, damp ravines, and brick or stone walls.

RANGE Currently known from Alabama from a single locality in Jefferson County, probably present at scattered locations in the Coastal Plain. Sparingly naturalized in the Southeast from Florida to South Carolina and Louisiana in the Coastal Plain. A native of eastern Asia.

COMMENTS This holly fern is also from Asia, and it resembles *Cyrtomium falcatum* except the upper surfaces of the leaflets of *C. fortunei* are dull pale green, while the leaflets of *C. falcatum* are dark green above. The blade tissue of *C. fortunei* is thin and papery, but that of *C. falcatum* is thick and leathery.

This fern has been recently collected in Jefferson County, Alabama, in a disturbed ravine in Birmingham; so far this is the only record for the state. This occurrence is unusual in that it is in the highland provinces far from the Fall Line. It probably represents an escape from cultivation.

This fern is commonly cultivated and will probably be found in more locations, especially in the Coastal Plain.

The specific epithet *fortunei* and the common name honor Robert Fortune, who brought a specimen to England from China in the 1860s.

OTHER COMMON NAMES Fortune's net-vein holly fern

Fortune's holly fern growing in the Fern Glade of the Birmingham Botanical Gardens, Jefferson County.

Tuber Sword Fern
Nephrolepis cordifolia (Linnaeus) Presl

DESCRIPTION Rhizome short-creeping, often producing thin, scaly stolons that can root and produce new plants; stolons often with scaly tubers up to 15 mm in diameter; leaves clustered at rhizome tip. Leaves 1-pinnate; blade swordlike, narrow, tapering at both ends, to 60 cm long and 7 cm wide; leaflets narrow with blunt tips and basal ears; margins smooth or slightly toothed; veins free. Sori round, near the margins; indusia kidney-shaped.

HABITAT Grows in the ground or on old walls; or in trees, mostly on palmettos.

RANGE Previously known from Alabama by a single collection on Dauphin Island, Mobile County. Recently collected in Baldwin County at Foley. Well established in central and southern Florida. Abundant on the west side of the Escambia River in Pensacola, Florida. A native of Asia and Africa that has escaped from cultivation; seemingly naturalized in Florida.

Tuber sword fern (*Nephrolepis cordifolia*) showing tubers on the stolons and with close-up of leaf underside showing sori.

COMMENTS J. S. White made the Mobile County collection in 1953 at Fort Gaines on Dauphin Island. The collector did not note the habitat on the label, but it is likely that the fern was found growing on the stone walls of the fort. The Baldwin County specimen was found growing on a cabbage palmetto.

According to Dean (1969), this fern may be found in a number of places on Dauphin Island, but this is not documented by specimens except for the one collection mentioned above.

This species is similar to other *Nephrolepis* ferns, like the commonly cultivated Boston fern, *N. exaltata*, but is easily distinguished from the others by the presence of tubers on its stolons.

The genus name *Nephrolepis* means "kidney-shaped scale" and refers to the indusia. The specific epithet *cordifolia* comes from the Latin and means "heart-leaf" and obviously does not refer to the

shape of the leaves; Linnaeus may have thought the sori to be heart-shaped. The common name comes from the tubers on the stolons and the sword-like shape of the leaf.

OTHER COMMON NAMES Narrow sword fern, wild Boston fern

Herbarium specimen of tuber sword fern collected by Dan Spaulding et al. in Baldwin County in 2005.

Rock Cap Fern
Polypodium virginianum Linnaeus

DESCRIPTION: Rhizome creeping on surface, thin, profusely branched, densely covered with small brown scales, leaves widely spaced; leaves spearhead-shaped to oblong, deeply lobed, to 20 cm long, smooth and without scales on both surfaces; lobes oblong to linear, as many as eighteen pairs per leaf. Sori round, without indusia, in rows between the margins and the midribs of the lobes.

HABITAT: Grows on shaded mossy rocks and ledges of various types but usually sandstone or similar acid rocks.

RANGE: Infrequent in Alabama in the Cumberland Plateau and Appalachian Ridges. Occurs in eastern North America from central Canada south to the highland regions of northern Alabama and Georgia and west to the upper Mississippi Valley. This is a northern species reaching its southern limits in northern Alabama and Georgia.

Rock cap fern (*Polypodium virginianum*) with close-up of leaf underside showing sori.

COMMENTS: Typical *Polypodium virginianum* is tetraploid, meaning that it has four sets of chromosomes. Some plants identified as this species have been determined to be diploid, with two sets of chromosomes. Some authors have recognized this diploid form as a separate species, known as *P. appalachianum* Haufler & Windham, the Appalachian rock cap fern.

These two forms are very similar in appearance and difficult to separate. The scales on the rhizome of *P. appalachianum* are often uniformly golden brown, sometimes weakly two-colored, the leaves have blades that average 5.8 cm wide and are usually widest near the base, the spores are less than 52 micrometers in diameter, and there are usually more than forty clusters of sporangia per sorus. Typical

P. virginianum usually has two-colored scales with a dark central stripe, the leaves smaller, with blades averaging 4.5 cm wide, and tend to be widest near the middle, the spores are more than 52 micrometers in diameter, and there are fewer than forty clusters of sporangia per sorus.

Both forms occur in Alabama. Specimens identifiable as *P. appalachianum* have been collected in Pisgah Gorge, on the escarpment of Sand Mountain in Jackson County. A thorough study of herbarium specimens labeled as *P. virginianum* will probably yield more occurrences of this form.

Since *Polypodium appalachianum* is arguably not distinct from *P. virginianum*, and since it is currently so poorly known, we have chosen to treat both of them as *P. virginianum* here.

This species has been used medicinally for various ailments, especially coughs and other respiratory problems (Dunbar 1989). Ashes from burning this fern contain large amounts of potash and were once used in the manufacture of glass (Abbe 1981).

The genus name *Polypodium* means "with many feet" and refers to the many branches of the rhizome. The specific epithet *virginianum* means "of Virginia," which is where the specimens Linnaeus saw supposedly came from. This fern grows on top of rocks and ledges, which gives it its common name.

OTHER COMMON NAMES Rock polypody, common polypody

SYNONYMS *Polypodium vulgare* Linnaeus var. *virginianum* (Linnaeus) A. Eaton

Rock cap fern growing from pine-hardwood humus, an unusual habitat for this fern.

Resurrection Fern
Polypodium polypodioides (Linnaeus) Watt

DESCRIPTION Rhizome creeping on surface, thin, profusely branched and forming mats, densely covered with small dark scales, leaves widely spaced; leaves narrowly triangular to oblong, deeply lobed, to 15 cm long, smooth on upper surface and densely scaly on lower surface; lobes oblong to linear, as many as fifteen pairs per leaf. Sori round, without indusia, in short rows near the margins of the lobes.

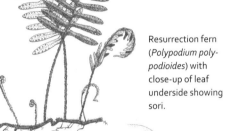

HABITAT Usually found growing on oaks and other hardwood trees with rough bark and occasionally on eastern red cedar; occasional on rocks of various types in the highland provinces and on roadside banks in the Coastal Plain.

Resurrection fern (*Polypodium polypodioides*) with close-up of leaf underside showing sori.

RANGE Abundant throughout Alabama. Common in the southeastern United States from Florida north to Maryland and the Ohio Valley and west to eastern Texas and Oklahoma; also in tropical America.

COMMENTS This is one of the most common ferns in Alabama. It is especially luxuriant on old trees with many large spreading limbs in parks and clearings and along city streets.

Indians made an ointment from the leaves and rhizome for treatment of sores and ulcers (Foster and Duke 1990).

The specific epithet *polypodioides* means "like a *Polypodium*"; this is redundant, but Linnaeus had originally put this species in a different genus, naming it *Acrostichum polypodioides*. The common name, resurrection fern, refers to the fact that the leaves curl up and appear dead during dry weather but come back to life with rain.

Several varieties of this species are known, but only var. *michauxianum* Weatherby occurs in North America. This variety is named in honor of André Michaux, a French naturalist of the late eighteenth century who collected plants in North America and first discovered this fern.

OTHER COMMON NAMES gray polypody, scaly polypody

SYNONYMS *Marginaria polypodioides* (Linnaeus) Tidestrom, *Pleopeltis polypodioides* (Linnaeus) Andrews & Windham var. *michauxiana* (Weatherby) Andrews & Windham

Above: Resurrection fern growing on a rock ledge in the Kaul Wildflower Garden of the Birmingham Botanical Gardens.

Left: Desiccated specimen on a dead log in Tallapoosa County.

Gold-Foot Fern
Phlebodium aureum (Linnaeus) J. Smith

DESCRIPTION Rhizome creeping on surface, stout, with many branches, densely covered with large reddish brown to golden scales; leaves oblong to spearhead-shaped, deeply lobed, to 50 cm long, without scales; lobes oblong to linear, fewer than ten pairs per leaf; veins netted. Sori round, without indusia, widely spaced in rows near the midveins of the lobes.

HABITAT Usually grows on palmettos and oaks, also on crumbly limestone and on old walls.

RANGE Known in Alabama from a few collections made in the Coastal Plain. Frequent in peninsular Florida, rare northward to coastal Georgia and southern Alabama; known primarily from tropical America.

Gold-foot fern
(*Phlebodium aureum*)
with close-up of leaf
underside showing
sori.

COMMENTS This species is commonly cultivated, and many of the records from north of peninsular Florida, where it is native, may represent escapes from cultivation. It is often present on the trunks of palms brought to Alabama from Florida, but these plants rarely persist for any length of time.

The genus name *Phlebodium* means "with prominent veins" and refers to the many netted veins of the blade. The specific epithet *aureum* means "golden"; it and the common name refer to the color of the rhizome scales.

OTHER COMMON NAMES Golden polypody, golden serpent fern, cabbage palm fern

SYNONYMS *Polypodium aureum* Linnaeus

Gold-foot fern growing on a planted palm tree in a shopping center complex, Daphne, Baldwin County.

Big-Foot Water-Clover

Marsilea macropoda Engelmann *ex* A. Braun

DESCRIPTION Rhizomes thin, long-creeping; leaves clustered on short side branches; roots present only at nodes or on branch points of the rhizome. Leaves cloverlike with four leaflets attached at the top of the leaf stalk; blades approximately circular, to 2.5 cm or more broad; leaflets with wedgelike bases and rounded outer margins, hairy, margins smooth; veins free; leaf stalks to 20 cm long. Spores of two types, borne inside hard pill-like sporocarps that are held low to the ground on short stalks. Sporocarp stalks usually branched; sporocarps mostly elliptic with a blunt lower tooth and an inconspicuous or absent upper tooth.

HABITAT Usually grows in wet soil, often rooted in shallow water. At the Mobile location the plant is a weed in lawns and cemeteries, and along roads and sidewalks. There, it grows in moist to dry sandy soil, often in full sun.

Big-foot water-clover (*Marsilea macropoda*).

RANGE Known in Alabama from the city of Mobile. Native to southern Texas and Mexico. Occurrences in Louisiana and Alabama probably brought there by humans or birds.

COMMENTS This fern is found growing in an area of several city blocks on the south side of the city of Mobile. It grows in vacant lots, in cracks in sidewalks, and in grassy areas between buildings. It is abundant and forms thick patches of "four-leaved clover" in the vacant lots.

When first found in Mobile in the 1970s, this fern was misidentified as *Marsilea vestita* Hooker & Greville, which is also known as *M. mucronata* A. Braun.

The genus name *Marsilea* honors Luigi Marsigli, an Italian naturalist of the late seventeenth and early eighteenth centuries. The specific epithet *macropoda* means "with big feet," but the reason Engelmann gave it to this plant is not known to the authors. Part of the common name is derived from the specific epithet; the rest refers to the cloverlike appearance of the plant and the fact that it usually grows in or near water.

OTHER COMMON NAMES Clover fern, large-foot pepperwort

Big-foot water-clover growing in vacant lot of downtown Mobile.

Dwarf Water-Clover
Marsilea minuta Fournier

DESCRIPTION Rhizomes floating, creeping, or underground; roots present along the entire length of the stem. Leaves cloverlike with four leaflets attached at the top of the leaf stalk; blades evenly green, up to 1.7 cm broad; leaflet bases wedge-shaped with outer margins rounded and often shallowly lobed; leaf stalks up to 22 cm long. Spores of two types, borne inside hard pill-like sporocarps that are held low to the ground on short stalks. Sporocarp stalks frequently branched; sporocarps oval to oblong and have one conspicuous tooth on top.

HABITAT Ditches, canals, ponds, and other wetland habitats. Grows best in full sun.

RANGE Recently found in Pike County, Alabama, at several locations in the Conecuh River drainage. Recently appearing in the southeastern United States and documented for Tennessee, Alabama, Georgia, and Florida. Native and weedy in India and Africa; also introduced into the New World tropics, Southeast Asia, and Australia.

Dwarf water-clover
(*Marsilea minuta*).

COMMENTS Though tending to be weedy, this fern appears to be susceptible to being killed by drought. The senior author visited a locality just west of Troy in 2004 and found the fern abundant and indeed weedy in the sloughs and backwaters of the Conecuh River. He visited the site again in 2009 and found that there was almost none left. Only a very few isolated plants remained. Apparently the severe drought of 2006 and 2007 nearly wiped out the colony.

This fern was first found in the United States in a roadside ditch in Escambia County, Florida, near Pensacola. It is ranked as one of the worst rice paddy weeds in Southeast Asia (Jacono and Johnson 2006).

Water birds such as ducks eat the sporocarps of this species, and it is believed that it is spread in this manner.

The specific epithet *minuta* means "minute"; it and the common name refer to the small size of the leaf blades as compared to other species in the genus.

OTHER COMMON NAMES Small clover fern, small water-clover

Dwarf water-clover growing in a backwater off the Conecuh River near Troy, Pike County.

Australian Water-Clover
Marsilea mutica Mettinius

DESCRIPTION Rhizomes floating, creeping, or underground; leaves clover-like with four leaflets attached at the top of the leaf stalk; leaflets two-toned green, usually 1.7 cm broad, up to 4 cm when aquatic; leaflet bases wedge-shaped with outer margins rounded and smooth; leaf stalks about 18 cm long, up to 100 cm when aquatic. Spores of two types, borne inside hard pill-like sporocarps that are held low to the ground on short stalks. Sporocarps nearly spherical and lacking teeth.

HABITAT Shorelines of ponds and lakes.

RANGE Recently found around some ponds in Marion County, Alabama. Introduced to the southeastern United States; also from Virginia to Mississippi south to Florida and in Oklahoma. Native to Australia and New Caledonia.

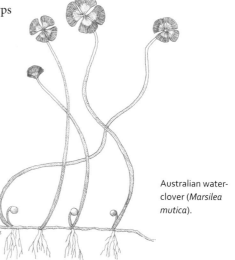

Australian water-clover (*Marsilea mutica*).

COMMENTS Because the apex of the leaf stalk is inflated and functions as an air bladder, the plants are able to float in water (Jacono and Johnson 2006).

This species can be easily distinguished from others by its two-toned leaflets and lack of teeth on the sporocarp.

This fern is often sold at nurseries and garden centers for water gardens and aquariums. It is likely to become more widespread in Alabama as people dispose of excess plant material by dumping it in streams, ponds, and lakes.

This fern was first reported for North America from Virginia in 2002.

The specific epithet *mutica* means "blunt-tipped" and refers to the round, toothless sporocarps. The common name refers to the native land of this fern.

OTHER COMMON NAMES Banded nardoo

Herbarium specimen of Australian water-clover collected on a Hamilton farm pond in Marion County in 2001 by J. Chris Greene.

American Pillwort
Pilularia americana Linnaeus

DESCRIPTION Rhizome long-creeping, thin; leaves clustered on short side branches. Leaves bladeless, consisting only of green leaf stalks that are 1–7.5 cm long. Spores of two types, borne inside hard sporocarps that are held low to the ground on short stalks. Sporocarps globular and tiny.

HABITAT Grows in mud in temporary pools and on pond margins.

RANGE Known from Alabama from two collections, one in northwestern Lauderdale County, the other in northwestern Winston County. Primarily a western species occurring from California to Oregon and east to Nebraska and Texas; disjunct populations known in Alabama, Arkansas, Georgia, and Tennessee.

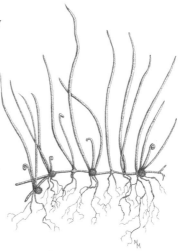

American pillwort
(*Pilularia americana*).

COMMENTS This fern is extremely inconspicuous due to its grasslike appearance and small size. The best characteristics to distinguish it from other grasslike plants are the curled tips, typical fern fiddle-heads, of the young leaves and, if they are present, the sporocarps.

The hard pill-like sporocarps that contain the spores allow the plant to survive droughts (Dean 1969).

The genus *Pilularia* means "little ball" and refers to the sporo-carps. This American species was named for the continent to distinguish it from a European species.

Herbarium specimen of American pillwort collected by Al Schotz in 2001 on a muddy bank of Bear Creek in Winston County.

Water-Spangles
Salvinia minima Baker

DESCRIPTION Rhizomes horizontal, branching, floating just below the water surface, rootless; leaves produced in threes, two floating or emergent, the third submersed. Floating leaves circular to oval in shape, with heart-shaped bases and rounded to notched tips, 0.4 to 1.0, sometimes 2.0, cm in length, the larger ones often folding upward into the air, emerald green to rusty brown; submersed leaves dissected into rootlike filaments. Upper surfaces of floating leaves covered with rows of white bristly hairs, each dividing into four thin spreading branches with free tips. Submersed filaments, rhizomes, and undersides of floating leaves covered with long chestnut-colored hairs. Spores of two types, borne in hard nutlike sporocarps that are borne on the rootlike submersed leaves.

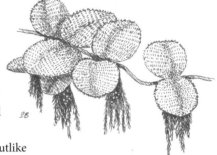

Water-spangles
(*Salvinia minima*).

HABITAT Floating in stagnant water of ponds, canals, and slow streams.

RANGE Known in Alabama from a few localities in the Coastal Plain. Introduced to the southeastern United States from Georgia west to Louisiana and south to Florida, also in the West Indies. Native to Mexico and Central and South America.

COMMENTS The continuous branching and fragmentation of the rhizomes creates a large number of daughter plants throughout the growing season.

Plants have been seen on boats, trailers, alligators, turtles, and even dogs leaving the water. The copious hairy coverings minimize the drying of the fern when out of the water. The fern can be spread from one body of water to another in this way.

This fern may seem to disappear during cold weather or droughts, but lateral buds deeply imbedded in the rhizome may lie dormant during these times. Small rhizome fragments are commonly sheltered by other vegetation and provide material for the reappearance of the fern upon the return of favorable growing conditions.

This fern has been cultivated in greenhouses and gardens in the United States since the late 1880s. *Salvinia minima* is still widely available in the water garden trade, either as a sale item or a contaminant.

This introduced species can be weedy and is considered a pest in some places. Early plants in Florida likely entered natural areas from flooding of cultivated pools or through intentional release (Jacono et al. 2001). Although it continues to infest new regions, it is not included on the Federal Noxious Weeds List, but it is prohibited to bring it into the states of Texas and Louisiana.

The branching hairs on the upper surfaces of the leaves provide a water-repellent shield. They also help distinguish the fern from duckweed, which the plant superficially resembles but which lacks the branched hairs.

The genus *Salvinia* was named for the seventeenth-century Italian naturalist A. M. Salvini. The specific epithet *minima* means "smallest"; apparently it was the smallest *Salvinia* known to John Baker, who named it in 1886.

OTHER COMMON NAMES Common salvinia, floating fern

SYNONYMS *Salvinia rotundifolia* Willdenow, misapplied

Close-up of water-spangles.

Kariba-Weed
Salvinia molesta D. S. Mitchell

DESCRIPTION Rhizomes horizontal, rootless, floating just below the water surface; leaves produced in threes, two floating or emergent, the third submersed. Floating and emergent leaves green, ovate to oblong, 1.5 to 3.5 cm in length; submersed leaves brown, highly divided and dangling into the water, rootlike in appearance.

Upper surfaces of floating leaves covered with white, bristly hairs, each dividing into four thin branches that spread and then converge and rejoin at the tips, forming a cagelike structure that resembles a tiny eggbeater. Spores of two types, borne in hard nutlike sporocarps. Sporocarps borne on the rootlike submersed leaves.

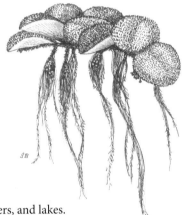

Kariba-weed (*Salvinia molesta*).

HABITAT Ditches, canals, ponds, rivers, and lakes.

RANGE Found in Alabama, so far, at two localities near the Fall Line in the eastern part of the state. Known to occur in the United States from Florida north to Virginia and west to Texas; also in southern California and Arizona. Believed to have been introduced into the United States through the aquarium trade. Native to southern Brazil and introduced to many places around the world.

COMMENTS This species grows rapidly, doubling in numbers in little more than two days under ideal conditions. It produces dense floating mats on the water surface and aggressively spreads by vegetative fragments. These floating mats shade out native submersed vegetation and degrade water quality; they also impede boating, fishing, swimming, and clog water intakes for irrigation and electrical generation.

Considered one of the world's most noxious weeds, this plant has the potential to become a major pest in the United States. It has caused severe economic and environmental problems in many countries, including New Zealand, Australia, and southern Africa.

In the United States, authorities are usually quick to eradicate this fern whenever it appears. This has been done with the two documented Alabama occurrences.

The rootlike submersed leaves may grow to great lengths and act to stabilize the plant by creating drag. The specialized cagelike hairs on the upper leaf surfaces provide a water-repellent, protective covering. These hairs may be damaged on mature leaves and not appear cagelike; however, young unfolding leaves will have intact structures.

The specific name *molesta* is a Latin word that means "annoying," "troublesome," or "tiresome." This species was named based on material collected from Lake Kariba in Zimbabwe, even though it is not native there, and this is the source of the common name. Apparently the plant was already a problem in the lake when it was collected, hence the specific name.

OTHER COMMON NAMES Aquarium water-moss, giant salvinia

Herbarium specimen of kariba-weed collected in a golf course pond in Lee County by W. D. Bryant in 1999.

Eastern Mosquito Fern

Azolla caroliniana Willdenow

DESCRIPTION Plants tiny, 1 cm or less broad. Stems floating on water, threadlike, forking, with thin roots hanging into the water, essentially clothed with leaves. Leaves in two rows along the stem, overlapping, each with two rounded lobes, less than 1 mm long and broad; upper lobe floating or held above water, green to reddish; lower lobe submerged, colorless. Spores of two types, borne in globular sporocarps in the axils of leaves; sporocarps rarely produced.

HABITAT Floating on still water in ponds, lake backwaters, bayous, ditches, and borrow pits.

RANGE Scattered, possibly frequent, in the Coastal Plain of Alabama, also found in the valley of the Tennessee River in the north. Occurs in the eastern United States primarily in the Coastal Plain from Florida to New England, west along the Gulf Coast to Louisiana and inland up the Mississippi Valley to western Kentucky.

Eastern mosquito fern (*Azolla caroliniana*).

COMMENTS This fern is tiny and un-fernlike; it is easily overlooked even though it can cover large surfaces of water. From a distance, it looks like pond scum or duckweed, but if the "scum" is red or bronze in color, it is probably *Azolla*. It may be more common than is presently known. It seems to be most abundant in areas underlain by limestone such as the Black Belt and in areas adjacent to limestone springs.

These ferns are economically important because of their symbiotic relationship with the nitrogen-fixing blue-green alga, *Anabaena azollae*. They are used in southeastern Asia as "green" fertilizer with crops such as rice or as a nutritional supplement when mixed with livestock feed.

Plants turn red when under stress from factors such as high temperatures or poor nutrition.

The valley of the Tennessee River in northern Alabama appears to be the only place in the highland regions of the Southeast where this fern occurs; it is otherwise found only in the Coastal Plain. It may be that *Azolla* was introduced to northern Alabama after the construction of the Tennessee Valley Authority (TVA) lakes in the early twentieth century, and the backwaters of these lakes provided the still-water habitats that the fern needs.

The genus name *Azolla* means "killed by drought"; the plants die when the water upon which they live dries up. The specific epithet *caroliniana* refers to the Carolinas, where this fern was originally discovered. The common name comes from the growth of this fern that can be so dense over the water surface as to exclude mosquito larvae.

OTHER COMMON NAMES Carolina mosquito fern, water fern

Colorful eastern mosquito fern.

Appendix A

Checklist

This checklist of ferns and fern allies is arranged in the same order as the species descriptions in chapter 4.

☐ **Whisk plant** (*Psilotum nudum*)
  Date: Location:

☐ **Shining clubmoss** (*Lycopodium lucidulum*)
  Date: Location:

☐ **Rock clubmoss** (*Lycopodium porophilum*)
  Date: Location:

☐ **Bartley's clubmoss** (*Lycopodium × bartleyi*)
  Date: Location:

☐ **Ground-pine** (*Lycopodium obscurum*)
  Date: Location:

☐ **Running-cedar** (*Lycopodium digitatum*)
  Date: Location:

☐ **Ground-cedar** (*Lycopodium tristachyum*)
  Date: Location:

☐ **Staghorn clubmoss** (*Lycopodium cernuum*)
  Date: Location:

☐ **Slender clubmoss** (*Lycopodium carolinianum*)
  Date: Location:

☐ **Tight-leaf clubmoss** (*Lycopodium appressum*)
  Date: Location:

☐ **Foxtail clubmoss** (*Lycopodium alopecuroides*)

Date: Location:

☐ **Feather-stem clubmoss** (*Lycopodium prostratum*)

Date: Location:

☐ **Copeland's clubmoss** (*Lycopodium × copelandii*)

Date: Location:

☐ **Hybrid clubmoss** (*Lycopodium alopecuroides × prostratum*)

Date: Location:

☐ **Bruce's clubmoss** (*Lycopodium × brucei*)

Date: Location:

☐ **Riddell's spikemoss** (*Selaginella arenicola* ssp. *riddellii*)

Date: Location:

☐ **Rock spikemoss** (*Selaginella rupestris*)

Date: Location:

☐ **Blue spikemoss** (*Selaginella uncinata*)

Date: Location:

☐ **Braun's spikemoss** (*Selaginella braunii*)

Date: Location:

☐ **Gulf spikemoss** (*Selaginella ludoviciana*)

Date: Location:

☐ **Meadow spikemoss** (*Selaginella apoda*)

Date: Location:

☐ **Florida quillwort** (*Isoëtes flaccida*)

Date: Location:

☐ **Engelmann's quillwort** (*Isoëtes engelmannii*)

Date: Location:

☐ **Louisiana quillwort** (*Isoëtes louisianensis*)
Date: Location:

☐ **Strong quillwort** (*Isoëtes valida*)
Date: Location:

☐ **Limestone quillwort** (*Isoëtes butleri*)
Date: Location:

☐ **Black-foot quillwort** (*Isoëtes melanopoda*)
Date: Location:

☐ **Piedmont quillwort** (*Isoëtes piedmontana*)
Date: Location:

☐ **Field horsetail** (*Equisetum arvense*)
Date: Location:

☐ **Tall scouring-rush** (*Equisetum hyemale*)
Date: Location:

☐ **Ferriss's scouring-rush** (*Equisetum × ferrissii*)
Date: Location:

☐ **Rattlesnake fern** (*Botrychium virginianum*)
Date: Location:

☐ **Winter grape fern** (*Botrychium lunarioides*)
Date: Location:

☐ **Sparse-lobed grape fern** (*Botrychium biternatum*)
Date: Location:

☐ **Alabama grape fern** (*Botrychium jenmanii*)
Date: Location:

☐ **Cutleaf grape fern** (*Botrychium dissectum*)
Date: Location:

☐ **Bulbous adder's-tongue** (*Ophioglossum crotalophoroides*)
Date: Location:

☐ **Limestone adder's-tongue** (*Ophioglossum engelmannii*)
Date: Location:

☐ **Least adder's-tongue** (*Ophioglossum nudicaule*)
Date: Location:

☐ **Stalked adder's-tongue** (*Ophioglossum petiolatum*)
Date: Location:

☐ **Southeastern adder's-tongue** (*Ophioglossum pycnostichum*)
Date: Location:

☐ **Royal fern** (*Osmunda regalis*)
Date: Location:

☐ **Cinnamon fern** (*Osmunda cinnamomea*)
Date: Location:

☐ **Interrupted fern** (*Osmunda claytoniana*)
Date: Location:

☐ **Drooping forked fern** (*Dicranopteris flexuosa*)
Date: Location:

☐ **American climbing fern** (*Lygodium palmatum*)
Date: Location:

☐ **Japanese climbing fern** (*Lygodium japonicum*)
Date: Location:

☐ **Southern maidenhair fern** (*Adiantum capillus-veneris*)
Date: Location:

☐ **Rough maidenhair fern** (*Adiantum hispidulum*)
Date: Location:

☐ **American maidenhair fern** (*Adiantum pedatum*)
Date: Location:

☐ **Ladder brake** (*Pteris vittata*)
Date: Location:

☐ **Spider brake** (*Pteris multifida*)
Date: Location:

☐ **Cretan brake** (*Pteris cretica*)
Date: Location:

☐ **Southwestern cloak fern** (*Notholaena integerrima*)
Date: Location:

☐ **Woolly lip fern** (*Cheilanthes tomentosa*)
Date: Location:

☐ **Alabama lip fern** (*Cheilanthes alabamensis*)
Date: Location:

☐ **Hairy lip fern** (*Cheilanthes lanosa*)
Date: Location:

☐ **Purple cliff-brake** (*Pellaea atropurpurea*)
Date: Location:

☐ **Appalachian shoestring fern** (*Vittaria appalachiana*)
Date: Location:

☐ **Taylor's filmy fern** (*Hymenophyllum tayloriae*)
Date: Location:

☐ **Appalachian filmy fern** (*Trichomanes boschianum*)
Date: Location:

☐ **Peters's filmy fern** (*Trichomanes petersii*)
Date: Location:

☐ **Weft fern** (*Trichomanes intricatum*)
Date: Location:

☐ **Hay-scented fern** (*Dennstaedtia punctilobula*)
Date: Location:

☐ **Spineless bramble fern** (*Hypolepis tenuifolia*)
Date: Location:

☐ **Bracken fern** (*Pteridium aquilinum*)
Date: Location:

☐ **New York fern** (*Thelypteris noveboracensis*)
Date: Location:

☐ **Marsh fern** (*Thelypteris palustris*)
Date: Location:

☐ **Ovate maiden fern** (*Thelypteris ovata*)
Date: Location:

☐ **Widespread maiden fern** (*Thelypteris kunthii*)
Date: Location:

☐ **Variable maiden fern** (*Thelypteris hispidula*)
Date: Location:

☐ **Downy maiden fern** (*Thelypteris dentata*)
Date: Location:

☐ **Alabama streak-sorus fern** (*Thelypteris pilosa* var. *alabamensis*)
Date: Location:

☐ **Mariana maiden fern** (*Thelypteris torresiana*)
Date: Location:

☐ **Broad beech fern** (*Thelypteris hexagonoptera*)
Date: Location:

☐ **Net-vein chain fern** (*Woodwardia areolata*)
Date: Location:

☐ **Virginia chain fern** (*Woodwardia virginica*)
Date: Location:

☐ **American Hart's tongue fern** (*Phyllitis scolopendrium*)
Date: Location:

☐ **Cut spleenwort** (*Asplenium abscissum*)
Date: Location:

☐ **One-sorus spleenwort** (*Asplenium monanthes*)
Date: Location:

☐ **Black-stemmed spleenwort** (*Asplenium resiliens*)
Date: Location:

☐ **Maidenhair spleenwort** (*Asplenium trichomanes*)
Date: Location:

☐ **Ebony spleenwort** (*Asplenium platyneuron*)
Date: Location:

☐ **Walking fern** (*Asplenium rhizophyllum*)
Date: Location:

☐ **Tutwiler's spleenwort** (*Asplenium tutwilerae*)
Date: Location:

☐ **Boydston's spleenwort** (*Asplenium × boydstoniae*)
Date: Location:

☐ **Lobed spleenwort** (*Asplenium pinnatifidum*)
Date: Location:

☐ **Mountain spleenwort** (*Asplenium montanum*)
Date: Location:

☐ **Cliff spleenwort** (*Asplenium bradleyi*)

Date: Location:

☐ **Graves's spleenwort** (*Asplenium × gravesii*)

Date: Location:

☐ **Trudell's spleenwort** (*Asplenium × trudellii*)

Date: Location:

☐ **Wall-rue spleenwort** (*Asplenium ruta-muraria*)

Date: Location:

☐ **Sensitive fern** (*Onoclea sensibilis*)

Date: Location:

☐ **Japanese false spleenwort** (*Deparia petersenii*)

Date: Location:

☐ **Glade fern** (*Athyrium pycnocarpon*)

Date: Location:

☐ **Silvery glade fern** (*Athyrium thelypterioides*)

Date: Location:

☐ **Southern lady fern** (*Athyrium filix-femina*)

Date: Location:

☐ **Bulblet bladder fern** (*Cystopteris bulbifera*)

Date: Location:

☐ **Tennessee bladder fern** (*Cystopteris tennesseensis*)

Date: Location:

☐ **Lowland brittle fern** (*Cystopteris protrusa*)

Date: Location:

☐ **Blunt-lobed cliff fern** (*Woodsia obtusa*)

Date: Location:

☐ **Marginal wood fern** (*Dryopteris marginalis*)
Date: Location:

☐ **Florida wood fern** (*Dryopteris ludoviciana*)
Date: Location:

☐ **Goldie's wood fern** (*Dryopteris goldiana*)
Date: Location:

☐ **Log fern** (*Dryopteris celsa*)
Date: Location:

☐ **Southern wood fern** (*Dryopteris × australis*)
Date: Location:

☐ **Evergreen wood fern** (*Dryopteris intermedia*)
Date: Location:

☐ **Hybrid wood fern** (*Dryopteris intermedia × marginalis*)
Date: Location:

☐ **Christmas fern** (*Polystichum acrostichoides*)
Date: Location:

☐ **Japanese tassel fern** (*Polystichum polyblepharum*)
Date: Location:

☐ **Japanese holly fern** (*Cyrtomium falcatum*)
Date: Location:

☐ **Fortune's holly fern** (*Cyrtomium fortunei*)
Date: Location:

☐ **Tuber sword fern** (*Nephrolepis cordifolia*)
Date: Location:

☐ **Rock cap fern** (*Polypodium virginianum*)
Date: Location:

☐ **Resurrection fern** (*Polypodium polypodioides*)
Date: Location:

☐ **Gold-foot fern** (*Phlebodium aureum*)
Date: Location:

☐ **Big-foot water-clover** (*Marsilea macropoda*)
Date: Location:

☐ **Dwarf water-clover** (*Marsilea minuta*)
Date: Location:

☐ **Australian water-clover** (*Marsilea mutica*)
Date: Location:

☐ **American pillwort** (*Pilularia americana*)
Date: Location:

☐ **Water-spangles** (*Salvinia minima*)
Date: Location:

☐ **Kariba-weed** (*Salvinia molesta*)
Date: Location:

☐ **Eastern mosquito fern** (*Azolla caroliniana*)
Date: Location:

Appendix B

On Taxonomic Change

ALAN WEAKLEY

One frequently hears among botanists (defined for my purposes here as "any and all regular users of botanical taxonomy and nomenclature") the suggestion—one might say "complaint"—that taxonomic changes are occurring at a rapid and unprecedented level. There are several variations to this charge:

- "I just wish the names would stay the same as they were when I was in college and first learned them" (*The Wistful*).
- "I know that names have to change because of improvements in our taxonomic understanding, but I just wish there weren't quite so many changes" (*The Rationalist*).
- "I just wish the new names weren't always longer and harder to pronounce than the old ones" (*The Frustrated*).
- "What the heck have they done now?" (*The Angry and Bewildered*).
- "What the heck have those Know-nothing, Molecular / DNA / Phylogeny people done now?" (*The [Angry] Traditionalist*).

Whatever the philosophic bent of the complainant, a frequent part of all the complaints is the idea that back in the good old days, taxonomic change occurred at a stately pace, following careful deliberation, and botanists were therefore able to absorb the (more carefully thought out and therefore clearly correct) changes more readily.

I thought it would be interesting to analyze the actual pace of taxonomic change in the eastern North American vascular plant flora to see if the perception that changes are more rapid now was true. To do so, I selected a series of influential floras and compared taxonomic usage in them, since floras summarize and synthesize taxonomic information and then serve as the primary source of taxonomic information for most users. Generally, a particular flora then serves as a sort of taxonomic standard for a generation. For comparison, I selected Weakley (2009), Radford, Ahles, & Bell (1968)(RAB), Fernald (1950), Small (1933), and Chapman (1883), a set of regional floras in use over a 126-year period, and selected a random sample

313

	RAB Weakley	Fernald RAB	Small Fernald	Chapman Small
intervening years	41	18	17	50
% species changed	42.3%	43.2%	51.8%	65.1%
% species changed/year	1.0%	2.4%	3.0%	1.3%
% genus changed	13.2%	3.3%	23.2%	28.8%
% genera changed/year	0.32%	0.18%	1.37%	0.58%
% family changed	9.7%	2.2%	33.3%	36.9%
% family changed/year	0.24%	0.12%	1.96%	0.74%

Table 1. Comparison of change in the taxonomy used in some eastern North American regional floras from 1883 to the present.

of 350 species (ca. 5 percent of the collective flora of the region) currently recognized in Weakley (2009), and compared their taxonomic treatment at species, genus, and family levels (see Table 1).

Of the random sample, a few examples will help illustrate the degree and nature of changes.

Diphasiastrum tristachyum

Chapman: *Lycopodium complanatum* (Lycopodiaceae). Not distinguishing "*tristachyum*" from "*digitatum/flabelliforme.*"

Small, Fernald, RAB: *Lycopodium tristachyum* (Lycopodiaceae). Recognizing two species in eastern North America.

Weakley: *Diphasiastrum tristachyum* (Lycopodiaceae). Segregate genera recognized based on lineages of great antiquity and fundamental differences in all ways.

Ilex amelanchier

Chapman, Small, Fernald, RAB, Weakley: *Ilex amelanchier* (Aquifoliaceae). No change at any taxonomic level from its naming by the Rev. Moses Ashley Curtis.

Platanthera lacera

Chapman: *Platanthera lacera* (Orchidaceae).

Small: *Blephariglottis lacera* (Orchidaceae). Genus change.

Fernald: *Habenaria lacera* var. *lacera* (Orchidaceae). Genus change again, and new variety recognized.

RAB: *Habenaria lacera* (Orchidaceae). Variety not recognized.

Weakley: *Platanthera lacera* (Orchidaceae). Genus change again . . . back to Chapman!

Galax urceolata

Chapman: *Galax aphylla* (Ericaceae).

Small: *Galax aphylla* (Galacaceae). Family change.

Fernald, RAB: *Galax aphylla* (Diapensiaceae). Family change again.

Weakley: *Galax urceolata* (Diapensiaceae). Change in specific epithet based on nomenclatural factors.

Ptelea trifoliate

Chapman, Small: *Ptelea* several species (Rutaceae).

Fernald: *Ptelea trifoliata* several varieties (Rutaceae).

RAB, Weakley: *Ptelea trifoliata* s.l. (Rutaceae).

The results show a generally high (though variable) level of taxonomic change throughout the past 126 years' time, and at all levels (species, genus, and family). Certainly, there seems to be no basis for the belief that taxonomic changes at any taxonomic level are at unprecedented (or even unusual) levels in recent years. Without considering the differences in time intervals between these floras, change at all taxonomic ranks was greatest between Chapman and Small. When compensating for intervals by calculating a change per year value, per year change at all taxonomic ranks was greatest from Small to Fernald. It is not clear to me which offers the better index of "psychological impact of taxonomic change," more simply labeled Taxonomic Whiplash (TW): normalizing by annual rate makes sense in some ways, but for a southeastern botanist born in 1840, who had used Chapman's various editions all of his life, the degree of change represented by Small's 1903 flora would surely have hit like a ton of bricks!

The mention of the names Small and Fernald has to suggest the possibility that change is not necessarily a directional, even, and inspirational story of the steady onward march of scientific progress, but rather a reticulating process, with some streams antagonistic to one another, and some changes circling back by reversal. Small and Fernald were from opposing camps, centered at the New York Botanical Garden and the Gray Herbarium at Harvard University, respectively (Yankees and Red Sox, anyone?). Small and his colleague Per Axel Rydberg became famous (or notorious, depending on your camp) for taxonomic opinions at odds with the prevailing and dominant Harvard camp (so maybe the Yankees and Red Sox analogy should be reversed).

So, it is worthwhile to look at the degree of change spanning over that period, thus ignoring change from Chapman to Small that was then reversed by the time of Fernald and RAB. From Chapman to RAB, the level of family change was 7.9 percent (0.09 percent per year), genus change was 19.5 percent (0.23 percent per year), and species change 59.8 percent (0.7 percent per year), so the longer view does smooth out some level of Taxonomic Whiplash. My colleague Rogers McVaugh's one-hundredth birthday is in May 2009. In his professional career, he has seen the taxonomic standard for eastern North America start with Robinson and Fernald (1908) and Small (1903), published about one hundred years ago, and go through a series of shifts. When I ask him about some taxonomic issue, he often will say things like "well, I always thought Small was probably right about that."

But whatever the era in which we live, or our lifespan, change (and overall, improvement, despite occasional blind alleys and reversals) in the taxonomic understanding of our flora is the order of the day.

ALAN WEAKLEY is the curator of the University of North Carolina Herbarium (NCU) of the North Carolina Botanical Garden and adjunct assistant professor of biology at the University of North Carolina at Chapel Hill.

REFERENCES

Chapman, A. W. 1883. Flora of the southern United States: containing an abridged description of the flowering plants and ferns of Tennessee, North and South Carolina, Georgia, Alabama, Mississippi, and Florida: arranged according to the natural system, second edition. American Book Company, N.Y.

Fernald, M. L. 1950. Gray's manual of botany, eighth (centennial) edition. Corrected printing, 1970. D. Van Nostrand Co., New York, N.Y.

Radford, A. E., H. E. Ahles, and C. R. Bell. 1968. Manual of the vascular flora of the Carolinas. University of North Carolina Press, Chapel Hill, N.C.

Robinson, B. L., and M. L. Fernald. 1908. Gray's new manual of botany. 7th edition. American Book Company, New York, N.Y.

Rose, P. M. 1984. In S. M. Sulgrove. The great ivy debate: the status of *Hibernica*. The Ivy Journal 10:33–49.

Small, J. K. 1903. Flora of the southeastern United States, being descriptions of the seed-plants, ferns and fern-allies growing naturally in North Carolina, South Carolina, Georgia, Florida, Tennessee, Alabama, Mississippi, Arkansas, Louisiana, and in Oklahoma and Texas east of the one hundredth meridian. Published by the author, New York, N.Y.

———. 1933. Manual of the southeastern flora, being descriptions of the seed plants growing naturally in Florida, Alabama, Mississippi, eastern Louisiana, Tennessee, North Carolina, South Carolina, and Georgia. University of North Carolina Press, Chapel Hill, N.C.

———. 1938. Ferns of the southeastern states. The Science Press, Lancaster, Pa.

Weakley, A. S. 2009. Flora of the Carolinas, Virginia, Georgia, northern Florida, and surrounding areas, working draft of 3 March 2008. University of North Carolina Herbarium, North Carolina Botanical Garden, Chapel Hill, N.C.

Appendix C

Alternative Keys to the Ferns and Fern Allies of Alabama

Appendix C contains a key to the ferns and fern allies using the family classification system of *Flora of North America North of Mexico*, Volume 2 (1993), and the species nomenclature follows "Flora of the Southern and Mid-Atlantic States" (Weakley 2010).

KEY TO FAMILIES

1a Plant filamentous, ribbonlike, or resembling a liverwort; mostly the gametophyte generation only present or rarely with a very small sporophyte (lacking sporangia); mostly growing in noncalcareous rock crevices.

> **2a** Plant filamentous or ribbonlike. **Hymenophyllaceae** (in part)

> **2b** Plant leaflike, resembling a liverwort. **Vittariaceae**

1b Plant not filamentous and not resembling a liverwort; having a distinctive sporophyte generation; habitat various.

> **3a** Leaves absent, stems naked except for veinless scales; sporangia three-lobed. **Psilotaceae**

> **3b** Leaves present, having at least one vein each; sporangia not lobed.

>> **4a** Plant floating on water and roots dangling or plants stranded on moist substrate (but not rooted in soil).

>>> **5a** Leaves minute, much less than 5 mm broad, dark green to red-brown in color. **Azollaceae**

>>> **5b** Leaves distinct, rounded or oval and greater than 5 mm broad, bright green in color. **Salviniaceae**

>> **4b** Plant rooting in soil (even if in water) or growing on trees or rocks.

>>> **6a** Plants resembling four-leaved clovers on slender petioles (blades divided into four leaflets); sporangia borne inside hard roundish enclosures (sporocarps). **Marsileaceae** (*Marsilea*)

>>> **6b** Plants not resembling four-leaved clovers; sporangia variously borne.

>>>> **7a** Stems hollow and ridged; nodes conspicuous and jointlike, encircled by numerous tiny toothlike leaves; sporangia in conelike strobili terminating stem. **Equisetaceae**

>>>> **7b** Stems (rhizomes) mostly solid, not hollow, lacking ridges; nodes nonjointed, leaves conspicuous and not forming sheaths around stem; sporangia variously borne. Go to **Key A.**

Key A

1a Plant grasslike; sporangia borne at leaf base.

    2a Plant tufted, stems short and thick, cormlike; sporangia enclosed in a cavity at leaf base. **Isoetaceae**

    2b Plant on short creeping stems, not tufted; sporangia numerous in a sporocarp attached by short stalk (1–3 mm) at base of leaf. **Marsileaceae** (*Pilularia*)

1b Plant not grasslike; sporangia not borne at leaf base.

    3a Plants like large mosses or miniature evergreen trees; leaves simple and greatly reduced; blades bearing a single midvein or midvein absent; sporangia in axils of leaves or in conelike strobili.

        4a Strobili (cones) quadrangular (four-sided) or flattened and sessile at the tips of branches; spores of two distinct sizes. **Selaginellaceae**

        4b Strobili, if present, cylindric and either sessile or stalked at tips of branches; if absent, then sporangia solitary in axils of foliage leaves; spores all of one size. **Lycopodiaceae**

    3b Plant not mosslike; leaves often large and elaborate, simple or compound, usually with conspicuous stalks (stipes), typically greater than 10 mm long; blades often greater than 10 mm broad and with numerous lateral veins; sporangia borne on surfaces or appendages of leaves, exposed or at least only loosely covered by indusia (a protective covering) and/or rolled-up leaf margins.

        5a Leaves vinelike, twining, and usually climbing on shrubs, trees, and fences. **Lygodiaceae**

        5b Leaves not vinelike and not climbing.

            6a Sporangia borne on a separate specialized spikelike branch of the leaf (sporophore) arising from the stalk beneath the blade; plant usually producing only one or two (sometimes three) leaves per growing season; sporangia 1 mm or more in diameter. **Ophioglossaceae**

            6b Sporangia borne on the leaf blade or segments of the blade, not on a sporophore; plant usually producing many leaves per growing season; sporangia less than 1 mm in diameter. Go to **Key B.**

Key B

1a Leaves very thin, blade tissue between veins nearly transparent, only one cell thick; sporangia borne along margins of leaves in a tubular cuplike structure (involucre) with an exserted bristle; plant growing on acidic rock, such as sandstone. **Hymenophyllaceae** (in part)

1b Leaves much thicker and not transparent, blade tissue several cells thick; sporangia borne on the underside (abaxial surface) or margins of leaflets, but not in an involucre with an exserted bristle; plants growing in soil or on various types of rock (basic or acidic).

2a Leaves repeatedly branched or forked (forks often with hairy dormant buds); blades pinnatifid (leaflets deeply cut); sori round. **Gleicheniaceae**

2b Leaves not forked; blades simple, pinnatifid or pinnately compound; sori various.

3a Fertile portions of leaf segments lacking blade tissue; sporangia borne on naked veins; sterile and fertile leaves strongly dimorphic; flat stipules present at base of leaves; annulus (row of thick-walled cells on sporangia) not well defined. **Osmundaceae**

3b Fertile leaf segments with blade tissue; sporangia borne on the undersides or margins of segments; sterile and fertile leaves similar (monomorphic) or dimorphic; stipules lacking at leaf bases; sporangia with well developed annulus.

4a Sori elongate to linear in shape, arranged in chainlike rows close to and parallel with midveins; leaf blades pinnate-pinnatifid or pinnatifid (only deeply lobed); veins areolate (netted) along midveins of leaflets, forming a series of chainlike loops. **Blechnaceae**

4b Sori of various shapes, if linear then borne along margins or side by side or not parallel to midveins; leaves and venation various.

5a Leaves simple and unlobed except for basal ears. **Aspleniaceae** (in part)

5b Leaves either compound or deeply lobed, or both.

6a Leaves strongly dimorphic, fertile (sporulating) leaves greatly dissimilar to sterile (nonsporulating) leaves, only sterile blades pinnatifid (sometimes pinnate at base); sori borne inside beadlike rolled up pinnules. **Dryopteridaceae** (*Onoclea*)

6b Sterile and fertile leaves similar in appearance or only slightly dimorphic; leaves variously cut or lobed; sori borne on the back surfaces or margins of leaves that may have recurved or reflexed margins but are otherwise flat or nearly so.

7a Sori located along margins of leaf segments and at least partially covered by recurved or rolled under (revolute) leaf edges.

8a Leaves broadly triangular; rhizome deeply buried, widely creeping. **Dennstaedtiaceae** (in part)

8b Leaves of various shapes, but not broadly triangular; rhizome exposed on ground surface, erect or short-creeping. **Pteridaceae**

7b Sori positioned variously, but not covered by rolled under leaf margins. Go to **Key C.**

Key C

1a Sori located along margins of leaflets in cuplike indusia; leaf blades and rachises bearing gland-tipped whitish hairs (with a haylike fragrance); leaves mostly 2-pinnate-pinnatifid and pale green; rhizome hairy. **Dennstaedtiaceae** (*Dennstaedtia*)
1b Sori not located along the edge of leaflets in cuplike indusia (if sori marginal, then with kidney-shaped indusium or sori lacking an indusium); leaf blades glabrous or sometimes pubescent with glandular hairs; leaves pinnatifid, pinnate, or more than 1-pinnate and pale green to dark green; rhizome often scaly.

> **2a** Leaf blades mostly 1-pinnatifid (deeply lobed, but segments not lobed), sometimes pinnate (cut to the midrib) at base.
>
> > **3a** Sori round and lacking an indusium (a protective covering); leaf stalk green. **Polypodiaceae**
> > **3b** Sori elongate and with an indusium; leaf stalk brown, at least near base. **Aspleniaceae** (in part)
>
> **2b** Leaf blades 2-pinnatifid, pinnate, or more than 1-pinnate.
>
> > **4a** Leaf blades with transparent, needlelike hairs; sori with or without indusium; leaf stalks with few or no scales; rhizome creeping (mostly subterranean) and slender, often less than 1 cm in diameter. **Thelypteridaceae**
> > **4b** Leaf blades pubescent or glabrous, but lacking transparent, needlelike hairs; sori with indusium; leaf stalks lacking scales or with persistent scales at base; rhizome creeping to ascending and slender or robust.
> >
> > > **5a** Sori elongate and bordering veins only along one side; leaf blade narrow, usually less than 10 cm wide and evergreen (present and green in midwinter); leaf stalks wiry and dark brown or black, at least near base. **Aspleniaceae** (in part)
> > > **5b** Sori round or elongate but not bordering veins just along one side, usually partially covering veins; leaf blades often broader (except sometimes in *Cystopteris*), usually more than 10 cm wide and evergreen or deciduous (absent or dead in midwinter); leaf stalks wiry to stout and blackish to green. **Dryopteridaceae** (in part)

FERN ALLIES

Equisetaceae (Horsetail Family)
Equisetum Linnaeus 1753—Horsetails

1a Stems dimorphic (fertile and sterile stems of two kinds), less than 50 cm tall; sterile; stems green and bushy with whorls of branches at each joint; fertile (sporulating) stems brownish and unbranched; strobili ("cones") apex rounded, maturing early spring before sterile stems; aerial stems annual, flexuous. *E. arvense*

1b Stems monomorphic, 100 cm or more tall; fertile and sterile stems green and un-branched; strobili with pointed apex, maturing late spring through summer; aerial stems evergreen, rigid.

   2a Stems evergreen, persisting for two years; spores green and spherical; plants present throughout Alabama. *E. hyemale*

   2b Stems partially deciduous, the upper portions dying back in winter, the lower persistent until spring; spores white and shrunken; plants only historically collected in Alabama. *E. × ferrissii*

Equisetum arvense Linnaeus—Field horsetail

Equisetum × ferrissii Clute [*E. hyemale × laevigatum* A. Braun]—Ferriss's scouring-rush [*Hippochaete × ferrissii* (Clute) Škoda & Holub]

Equisetum hyemale Linnaeus ssp. *affine* Calder & Roy L. Taylor—tall scouring-rush, common scouring-rush [*Equisetum hyemale* Linnaeus var. *affine* (Engelmann) A. A. Eaton, *Equisetum hyemale* Linnaeus var. *elatum* (Engelmann) Morton, *Equisetum hyemale* Linnaeus var. *pseudohyemale* (Farwell) Morton, *Equisetum hyemale* Linnaeus var. *robustum* (A. Braun) A. A. Eaton, *Equisetum praealtum* Rafinesque, *Equisetum robustum* A. Braun, *Hippochaete hyemalis* (Linnaeus) Bruhin ssp. *affinis* (Engelmann) W. A. Weber]

Isoetaceae (Quillwort Family)
Isoëtes Linnaeus 1753—Quillworts

1a Plants aquatic (submerged or emergent), growing in persistently wet soils in or near streams, ponds, and swamps, typically not associated with rock outcrops.

   2a Sporangium covered by less than one-half of velum (membranous flap covering sporangia on the inner side at the bottom of the leaf).

   3a Megaspores mostly with unbroken honeycomb-like ridges (evenly reticulate); sporangium wall whitish (unpigmented); plants mostly of the highland provinces. *I. engelmannii*

   3b Megaspores with broken ridges (irregularly reticulate); sporangium wall often pigmented with brown streaks; plants mostly of the Coastal Plain. *I. engelmannii* complex: [*I. appalachiana, I. boomii, I. hyemalis, I. louisianensis*]

   2b Sporangium covered by more than one-half of velum.

   4a Leaves dark green and flaccid, 25–60 cm long; velum almost completely covering sporangium (80–100 percent); sporangium wall white or sparsely brown-streaked; megaspore ornamentation of low, broad tubercles or ridges. *I. flaccida*

   4b Leaves yellow-green and not flaccid, 15–40 cm long; velum covering less than three-fourths of sporangium (50–70 percent); sporangium wall white (unpigmented); megaspore ornamentation of a high ragged-reticulate pattern. *I. valida*

1b Plants terrestrial or amphibious in thin clay soils of ephemeral pools or on seeps of rock outcrops that are seasonally wet and dry; plants chiefly found outside the Coastal Plain.

5a Plant of granite outcrops (rarely sandstone); sporangium wall brown and less than 6 mm long. *I. piedmontana*

5b Plant of limestone outcrops or prairielike habitats; sporangium wall mottled with brown and usually more than 6 mm long.

6a Leaf bases pale to brown; leaves usually less than 1 mm wide at middle; megaspores with tiny wartlike bumps (papillate); plant of limestone outcrops. *I. butleri*

6b Leaf bases usually shiny black; leaves usually more than 1 mm wide at middle; megaspores obscurely wrinkled (rugulate) with low ridges; plant of prairielike habitats and not associated with limestone outcrops. *I. melanopoda*

Isoëtes appalachiana D. F. Brunton & D. M. Britton—Appalachian quillwort

Isoëtes boomii N. Luebke—Boom's quillwort

Isoëtes butleri Engelmann—Limestone quillwort, glade quillwort, Butler's quillwort

Isoëtes engelmannii A. Braun—Engelmann's quillwort

Isoëtes flaccida Shuttleworth *ex* A. Braun—southern quillwort, Florida quillwort

Isoëtes hyemalis D. F. Brunton—Evergreen quillwort, wintergreen quillwort

Isoëtes louisianensis Thieret—Louisiana quillwort

Isoëtes melanopoda Gay & Durieu *ex* Durieu—Black-foot quillwort, midland quillwort

Isoëtes piedmontana (N. E. Pfeiffer) C. F. Reed—Piedmont quillwort, black-based quillwort [*Isoëtes virginica* N. E. Pfeiffer var. *piedmontana* N. E. Pfeiffer]

Isoëtes valida (Engelmann) Clute—Carolina quillwort, true quillwort, mountain quillwort [*Isoëtes caroliniana* (A. A. Eaton) N. Luebke; *Isoëtes engelmannii* A. Braun var. *caroliniana* A. A. Eaton]

Lycopodiaceae (Clubmoss Family)

1a Strobili occurring along the length of the stem; sporophylls (fertile leaves) similar to sterile leaves. *Huperzia*

1b Strobili occurring terminally along upper one-third of stem; sporophylls distinctly different from sterile leaves.

2a Plants pale green, usually dying back during winter; principal leafy stems creeping or erect and repeatedly branched (in *L. cernuum*); spores rugulate; plants primarily of wetland communities.

3a Vegetative stems erect and repeatedly branched; strobili (cones) nodding at the ends of the branches; plants resembling miniature trees. *Palhinhaea*

3b Vegetative stems prostrate, or if aerial, merely arching, with few or no branches, the only truly erect branches being unbranched strobilar peduncles; strobili erect on upright shoots; plants resembling large mosses.

4a Vegetative leaves of two distinct sizes; leaves of the prostrate stems

1.3–2.1 mm wide, not toothed cones compact, sporophylls with short tips extending barely beyond sporangia. *Pseudolycopodiella*

4b Vegetative leaves all about the same size; leaves of the prostrate stems 0.5–1.2 mm wide, ciliate-toothed or not toothed; cones more or less diffuse, sporophylls with long tips extending far beyond sporangia. *Lycopodiella*

2b Plants shiny, dark green and evergreen; principle stems erect and often branching into several finger- or fanlike branchlets; spores reticulate; plants primarily of upland communities.

5a Leaves widely spreading in six rows from stem, obviously spirally arranged, bases separated; branches appearing bushy, usually 5 to 8 mm wide; strobili sessile at tips of upper branches. *Dendrolycopodium*

5b Leaves appressed to stem in four rows, spiral arrangement obscure, fused together at base; branches appearing flat, usually 3 mm or less wide; strobili borne on long stalks (peduncles). *Diphasiastrum*

Dendrolycopodium A. Haines 2003—Tree Clubmoss

Dendrolycopodium obscurum (Linnaeus) A. Haines—Princess-pine, tree clubmoss, common ground-pine [*Lycopodium obscurum* Linnaeus]

Diphasiastrum Holub 1975—Flat-Branched Clubmoss

1a Rhizomes close to ground surface (usually within 1 cm of surface or within leaf litter); underside two rows of sterile leaves shorter than two upperside rows; sterile leaves green. *D. digitatum*

1b Rhizomes well below ground surface (usually 1–6 cm below surface); underside two rows of sterile leaves similar in size to two upperside rows; sterile leaves bluish (glaucous). *D. tristachyum*

Diphasiastrum digitatum (Dillenius *ex* A. Braun) Holub—Running ground-pine, running-cedar, fan ground-pine [*Lycopodium complanatum* Linnaeus var. *flabelliforme* Fernald, *Lycopodium digitatum* Dillenius *ex* A. Braun *Lycopodium flabelliforme* (Fernald) Blanchard]

Diphasiastrum tristachyum (Pursh) Holub—Deep-root ground-pine, blue ground-cedar, deep-root clubmoss [*Lycopodium tristachyum* Pursh]

Huperzia Bernhardi 1801—Firmoss

1a Sterile leaves widest above middle, leaves of varying lengths resulting in a tufted (shaggy) appearance, leaves with toothed upper margins; main stem frequently branching so that plant often forms dense clumps; stomata (pores) present only on lower surfaces of leaves; plant mainly of soil in rich rocky woods. *H. lucidula*

1b Sterile leaves widest below middle, leaves of essentially same length, leaves typically with entire margins (sometimes toothed); main stem usually branching only two to three times; stomata abundant on both leaf surfaces; plant growing directly on acidic rocks. *H. porophila*

Note: The hybrid, *Huperzia × bartleyi,* is intermediate in characters between its two parents above. It has stomata present on both leaf surfaces, but they are sparse on the upper and abundant on the lower.

Huperzia × bartleyi (Cusick) Kartesz & Gandhi [*H. lucidula × porophila*]—Bartley's clubmoss, Bartley's firmoss [*Lycopodium × bartleyi* Cusick]

Huperzia lucidula (Michaux) Trevisan—Shining clubmoss, shining firmoss [*Lycopodium lucidulum* Michaux]

Huperzia porophila (Lloyd & Underwood) Holub—Rock clubmoss, rock firmoss [*Lycopodium porophilum* Lloyd & Underwood]

Lycopodiella Holub 1964—Bog Clubmoss

1a Vegetative leaves appearing more or less in two rows, spreading toward two sides of the stem (may be obscure in live plants and be evident only by a tendency of the leaves to lean to one side or the other).

   2a Vegetative stems arching slightly, with rootless zones. *L. alopecuroides × prostratum*

   2b Vegetative stems completely prostrate, rooted all along.

      3a Sporophylls spreading widely; two-rowed appearance of vegetative leaves obvious. *L. prostratum*

      3b Sporophylls ascending; two-rowed appearance of leaves obscure *L. × brucei*

1b Vegetative leaves appearing in many rows or in spirals, spreading to all sides of the stem except where it touches the ground.

   4a Vegetative stems arching slightly, with rootless zones. *L. alopecuroides × prostratum*

   4b Vegetative stems completely prostrate, rooted all along.

      5a Vegetative stems completely prostrate, rooted all along; sporophylls strongly ascending, appressed; strobili less than 1 cm broad. *L. appressum*

      5b Vegetative stems arching, at least slightly, with rootless zones; sporophylls strongly spreading or loosely ascending; strobili 1 cm broad or broader.

         6a Vegetative stems arching strongly, the arches about as tall as broad; sporophylls strongly spreading. *L. alopecuroides*

         6b Vegetative stems arching weakly, the arches less than one-half as tall as broad; sporophylls ascending. *L. × copelandii*

Lycopodiella alopecuroides (Linnaeus) Cranfill—Foxtail clubmoss, foxtail bog clubmoss [*Lycopodium alopecuroides* Linnaeus]

Lycopodiella alopecuroides × prostrata—Hybrid clubmoss

Lycopodiella appressa (Chapman) Cranfill—Tight-leaf clubmoss, southern club-moss, appressed bog clubmoss [*Lycopodium appressum* (Chapman) Lloyd & Underwood, *Lycopodium inundatum* Linnaeus var. *bigelovii* Tuckerman]

Lycopodiella × *brucei* Cranfill [*L. appressa* × *prostrata*]—Bruce's clubmoss [*Lycopodium* × *brucei* (Cranfill) Lellinger]

Lycopodiella × *copelandii* (Eiger) Cranfill [*L. appressa* × *alopecuroides*]—Copeland's clubmoss [*Lycopodium* × *copelandii* Eiger]

Lycopodiella prostrata (Harper) Cranfill—Feather-stem clubmoss, creeping club-moss, prostrate bog clubmoss [*Lycopodium pinnatum* (Chapman) Lloyd & Underwood, *Lycopodium prostratum* Harper]

Palhinhaea Vasconcellos & Franco 1967—Nodding Clubmoss

Palhinhaea cernua (Linnaeus) Vasconcellos & Franco—staghorn clubmoss, nodding clubmoss [*Lycopodiella cernua* (Linnaeus) Pichi Sermolli, *Lycopodium cernuum* Linnaeus]

Pseudolycopodiella Holub 1983—Carolina Bog Clubmoss

Pseudolycopodiella caroliniana (Linnaeus) Holub—Carolina bog clubmoss, slender clubmoss [*Lycopodiella caroliniana* (Linnaeus) Pichi Sermolli, *Lycopodium carolinianum* Linnaeus]

Psilotaceae (Whisk Fern Family)
Psilotum Swartz 1800—Whisk Ferns

Psilotum nudum (Linnaeus) Beauvois—Whisk fern

Selaginellaceae (Spikemoss Family)
Selaginella Palisot de Beauvois 1804—Spikemoss

1a Sterile leaves all about the same size; spirally arranged on all sides of the stem; leaves appearing round in cross section.

2a Stems erect or ascending (seldom decumbent or creeping); aerial roots present only at or near base; megaspores with honeycombed surfaces. *S. arenicola* ssp. *riddellii*

2b Stems decumbent or creeping (never erect); aerial roots present nearly entire stem; megaspores nearly smooth. *S. rupestris*

1b Sterile leaves of two distinct sizes; arranged in four ranks on stem (two medial, two lateral); lateral leaves appressed to stem; leaves flat in cross section.

3a Leaves bluish green; margins of lateral leaves entire; lateral branches of the stems further branching two to three times. *S. uncinata*

3b Leaves yellowish green; margins of lateral leaves dentate-serrate; lateral branches of the stems further branching one to two times.

    4a Vegetative stems erect, repeatedly branched in a single plane, arising from a subterranean rhizome; plant appearing fernlike. *S. braunii*

    4b Vegetative stems creeping or weakly arching, erect portions absent or very sparsely branched, all on or above the surface of the ground; plant appearing mosslike.

        5a Stems prostrate; aerial shoots lacking, only the tips of prostrate stems turned upward; leaf margins without fringes. *S. apoda*

        5b Stems weekly arching; lateral branches stiffly erect; leaf margins with membranous fringes. *S. ludoviciana*

Selaginella apoda (Linnaeus) Spring—Meadow spikemoss [*Diplostachyum apodum* (Linnaeus) Beauvois, *Lycopodioides apodum* (Linnaeus) Kuntze, *Selaginella apus* Spring]

Selaginella arenicola Underwood ssp. *riddellii* (Van Eseltine) Tryon—Riddell's spikemoss [*Selaginella corallina* (Riddell) Wilbur & Whitson, *Selaginella riddellii* Van Eseltine]

Selaginella braunii Baker—Braun's spikemoss, treelet spikemoss

Selaginella ludoviciana (A. Braun) A. Braun—Gulf spikemoss, Louisiana spikemoss [*Diplostachyum ludovicianum* (A. Braun) Small, *Lycopodioides ludovicianum* (A. Braun) Kuntze]

Selaginella rupestris (Linnaeus) Spring—Rock spikemoss, ledge spikemoss, dwarf spikemoss [*Bryodesma rupestre* (Linnaeus) J. Soják]

Selaginella uncinata (Desvaux *ex* Poiret) Spring—Blue spikemoss, peacock-moss

TRUE FERNS

Aspleniaceae (Spleenwort Family)
Asplenium Linnaeus 1753—Spleenworts

1a Leaves simple and unlobed except for basal ears.

    2a Leaf apex long-tapering (attenuate) and often rooting at tip; veins forming areoles; sori single along veins. *A. rhizophyllum*

    2b Leaf apex acute to acuminate and not rooting at tips; veins free; sori in pairs along veins. *A. scolopendrium*

1b Leaves either divided to midrib or deeply lobed, or both.

    3a Blade deeply lobed but not divided completely to rachis. *A. pinnatifidum*

    3b Blade divided at least at base, upper portion either completely divided or deeply lobed.

        4a Leaf blades 2- to 4-pinnate or leaflets deeply lobed (at least lower ones).

5a Blades with two to five pairs of leaflets; leaf stalks entirely green; plants usually on calcareous (usually limestone) rock. *A. ruta-muraria*

5b Blades with more than five pairs of leaflets; leaf stalks darkened, at least at base; plants on acidic (usually sandstone) rock.

> **6a** Leaf stalks dark brown only at base; most pinnae divided. *A. montanum*
>
> **6b** Leaf stalks and lower portion of midrib (rachis) dark brown; only the lower leaf segments divided (bipinnate), upper leaflets merely lobed. *A. bradleyi*

4b Leaf blades 1-pinnate at least at base and leaflets not lobed.

> **7a** Leaf blade more than 5 cm wide near the middle; lower leaflets over 2.5 cm long with sharp pointed or long tapering tips and a short petiole. *A. abscissum*
>
> **7b** Leaf blade less than 5 cm wide at the middle; lower leaflets less than 2.5 cm long with round or acute tips and mostly sessile.
>
>> **8a** Blade divided (1-pinnate) for essentially all of its length.
>>
>>> **9a** Leaflets mostly alternate; base of leaflets with auricles (lobes) that usually overlap rachis. *A. platyneuron*
>>>
>>> **9b** Leaflets mostly opposite; base of leaflets not overlapping rachis.
>>>
>>>> **10a** Leaflets strongly asymmetrical, midvein running along basal edge of blade; sori few (usually one) and located on only one side of main vein (costa). *A. monanthes*
>>>>
>>>> **10b** Leaflets symmetrical, midvein running along the middle of blade; sori numerous (more than four) and located on both sides of the main vein.
>>>>
>>>>> **11a** Leaflets oblong (longer than wide) and usually more than 9 mm long; auricles (lobes) present at base of leaflets. *A. resiliens*
>>>>>
>>>>> **11b** Leaflets mostly oval (almost as long as wide) and usually less than 9 mm long; auricles lacking at base of leaflets. *A. trichomanes*
>>
>> **8b** Blade compound only at base, the upper third or more only lobed.
>>
>>> **12a** Lowermost leaflets deeply lobed. *A. × trudellii*
>>>
>>> **12b** Lowermost leaflets not lobed or at most toothed.
>>>
>>>> **13a** Rachis (midrib) green throughout or brown only to the first or second pair of leaflets. *A. × gravesii*
>>>>
>>>> **13b** Rachis brown for a third or more of its length.
>>>>
>>>>> **14a** Blade compound only at its base, with only one or two pairs of true leaflets; blade tip very narrow, long-tapering. *A. tutwilerae*

14b Blade compound for about half of its length or more, with many pairs of leaflets; blade tip narrow, but ending abruptly. *A.* × *boydstoniae*

Asplenium abscissum Willdenow—Cut-leaf spleenwort, abscised spleenwort

Asplenium × *boydstoniae* (K. S. Walter) J. W. Short [*A. ebenoides* × *platyneuron*]—Boydston's spleenwort [× *Asplenosorus boydstoniae* K. S. Walter]

Asplenium bradleyi D. C. Eaton—Cliff spleenwort, Bradley's spleenwort

Asplenium × *gravesii* Maxon [*A. bradleyi* × *pinnatifidum*]—Grave's spleenwort

Asplenium monanthes Linnaeus—Single-sorus spleenwort

Asplenium montanum Willdenow—Mountain spleenwort

Asplenium pinnatifidum Nuttall—lobed spleenwort

Asplenium platyneuron (Linnaeus) Britton, Sterns & Poggenburg—ebony spleenwort, brown-stem spleenwort [*Asplenium platyneuron* (Linnaeus) Britton, Sterns & Poggenburg var. *bacculum-rubrum* (Featherman) Fernald; *Asplenium platyneuron* (Linnaeus) Britton, Sterns & Poggenburg var. *incisum* (Howe *ex* Peck) B. L. Robinson]

Asplenium resiliens Kunze—Black-stem spleenwort, little ebony spleenwort [*Asplenium parvulum* M. Martens & Galeotti]

Asplenium rhizophyllum Linnaeus—Walking fern [*Camptosorus rhizophyllus* (Linnaeus) Link]

Asplenium ruta-muraria Linnaeus var. *cryptolepis* (Fernald) Wherry—American wall-rue, wall-rue spleenwort [*Asplenium cryptolepis* Fernald var. *cryptolepis*, *Asplenium cryptolepis* Fernald var. *ohionis* Fernald, *Asplenium ruta-muraria* Linnaeus]

Asplenium scolopendrium Linnaeus var. *americanum* (Fernald) Kartesz & Gandhi—American Hart's tongue fern [*Phyllitis scolopendrium* (Linnaeus) Newman var. *americana* Fernald]

Asplenium trichomanes Linnaeus ssp. *trichomanes*—Maidenhair spleenwort

Asplenium × *trudellii* Wherry [*A. montanum* × *pinnatifidum*]—Trudell's Spleenwort [*Asplenium pinnatifidum* Nuttall var. *trudellii* (Wherry) Clute, × *Asplenosorus trudellii* (Wherry) Mickel]

Asplenium tutwilerae B. R. Keener & L. J. Davenport—Tutwiler's spleenwort [*Asplenium* × *ebenoides* R. R. Scott p.p.]

Azollaceae (Mosquito Fern Family)
Azolla Lamarck 1783—Mosquito Ferns

Azolla caroliniana Willdenow—Carolina mosquito fern, water fern, eastern mosquito fern

Blechnaceae (Chain Fern Family)
Woodwardia J. E. Smith 1793—Chain Ferns

1a Sterile and fertile leaves dissimilar; fertile leaves pinnate, sterile leaves mostly pinnatifid (deeply lobed); veins conspicuously netted. *W. areolata*
1b Sterile and fertile leaves alike; leaves pinnate with deeply lobed (pinnatifid) leaflets; veins mostly free. *W. virginica*
Woodwardia areolata (Linnaeus) T. Moore—Netted chain fern, netleaf chain fern, net-vein chain fern [*Lorinseria areolata* (Linnaeus) K. Presl]
Woodwardia virginica (Linnaeus) Smith—Virginia chain fern, southern chain fern, giant chain fern [*Anchistea virginica* (Linnaeus) K. Presl]

Dennstaedtiaceae (Bracken Fern Family)
Dennstaedtia Bernhardi 1801—Cuplet Ferns

Dennstaedtia punctilobula (Michaux) T. Moore—Hay-scented fern, pasture fern, boulder fern

Hypolepis Bernhardi 1806—Bramble Ferns

Hypolepis tenuifolia (G. Forster) Bernhardi—Spineless bramble fern, soft ground fern [*Hypolepis repens* auct. non (Linnaeus) K. Presl]

Pteridium Gleditsch *ex* Scopoli 1760—Bracken Ferns

1a Terminal pinnules (leaflets) six to fifteen times longer than wide, undersurface of leaflets (abaxial axes) remotely pilose to glabrous. *P. aquilinum* var. *pseudocaudatum*
1b Terminal pinnules two to four times longer than wide, undersurface of leaflets (abaxial axes) villous. *P. aquilinum* var. *latiusculum*
Pteridium aquilinum (Linnaeus) Kuhn var. *latiusculum* (Desvaux) L. Underwood *ex* A. Heller—Eastern bracken fern, pasture brake [*Pteridium latiusculum* (Desvaux) Hieronymus, *Pteris aquilina* Linnaeus, *Pteris latiuscula* Desvaux]
Pteridium aquilinum (Linnaeus) Kuhn var. *pseudocaudatum* (Clute) A. Heller—Tailed bracken fern, southern brake [*Pteridium latiusculum* (Desvaux) Hieronymus var. *pseudocaudatum* (Clute) Maxon, *Pteris aquilina* Linnaeus var. *pseudocaudata* Clute]

Dryopteridaceae (Wood Fern Family)

1a Leaves 1-pinnate (blade cut only once to midrib and leaflets not deeply lobed).
    2a Stolons present at the bottom of leaves (wiry rootlike stems); base of leaflets overlapping midrib (rachis). *Nephrolepis cordifolia*
    2b Stolons absent; base of leaflets not overlapping midrib.
        3a Leaflets thin, deciduous, and lacking basal lobes; sori elongate; indusium attached on one side of sorus, not umbrella-like. *Diplazium pycnocarpon*

3b Leaflets thick, evergreen, and with basal lobes; sori round; indusium attached at center of sorus, umbrella-like.

    4a Veins free; sori in distinct rows on upper most leaflets. *Polystichum acrostichoides*

    4b Veins netted; sori scattered, not arranged in any pattern and not localized just on the upper leaflets. *Cyrtomium*

1b Leaves pinnate-pinnatifid to tripinnate (leaflets deeply lobed or divided).

  5a Sori elongated (linear to crescent-shaped) and indusia attached along the side (flaplike).

    6a Leaves pinnate-pinnatifid (leaflets only deeply lobed); sori almost straight and parallel to veins. *Deparia*

    6b Leaves pinnate-pinnatifid to 3-pinnate (leaflets cut two or three times); sori crescent shaped and curved across veins. *Athyrium asplenioides*

  5b Sori round and indusia variously attached.

    7a Leaf stalk (stipe) and rachis densely scaly obscuring the undersurface. *Polystichum polyblepharum*

    7b Leaf stalk and rachis smooth or scaly but not obscuring the undersurface.

      8a Robust ferns with thick-textured leaves; larger pinnae (the main leaflets) mostly more than 8 cm long; leaf stalk distinctly scaly; rhizome thick; indusium kidney-shaped and attached on top of sorus. *Dryopteris*

      8b Smaller ferns with thin-textured leaves; larger pinnae mostly less than 8 cm long; leaf stalk with or without scales; rhizome slender; indusium not kidney-shaped, either hoodlike or cuplike and attached under sorus.

        9a Indusium hoodlike or pocketlike, attached along one side of sorus and arching over the sporangia; leaf stalks lacking scales or with just a few; old leaf stalks not persisting through the winter. *Cystopteris*

        9b Indusium not hoodlike, attached completely under sorus, covering sides and at maturity, separating into flaps, forming a star-shaped cup (these scalelike structures eventually fall off); leaf stalks usually distinctly scaly; old leaf stalks usually persisting into the next season. *Woodsia obtusa*

Athyrium Roth 1799—Lady Ferns

Athyrium asplenioides (Michaux) A. A. Eaton—Southern lady fern, lowland lady fern [*Asplenium filix-femina* (Linnaeus) Bernhardi, *Athyrium filix-femina* (Linnaeus) Roth *ex* Mertens var. *asplenioides* (Michaux) Farwell]

Cyrtomium K. Presl 1836—Asiatic Holly Ferns

1a Leaflets leathery, with shiny, dark-green lower surfaces, usually with four to ten pairs; margins wavy or coarsely toothed. *C. falcatum*

1b Leaflets papery (not as thick), with dull, light-green lower surfaces, usually with ten to twenty-five pairs; margins with small rounded teeth (crenulate-dentate). *C. fortunei*

Cyrtomium falcatum (Linnaeus f.) K. Presl—Japanese holly fern, Japanese net-vein holly fern

Cyrtomium fortunei J. Smith—Asian holly fern, Fortune's net-vein holly fern

Cystopteris Bernhardi 1806—Bladder Ferns

1a Rhizome elongated (internodes distinct), apex usually protruding more than 1 cm past leaves; pinnules near middle of blade dissected to midrib (pinnate); bulblets absent; leaf blades usually widest near middle. *C. protrusa*

1b Rhizome not elongated (internodes indiscernible due to closely overlapping nodes), leaves clustered near apex; pinnules near middle of blade not dissected to midrib (pinnatifid); bulblets often present (found on the underside of leaf); leaf blades usually widest near base.

    2a Leaf apex gradually long-tapered (attenuate), often very elongated; gland-tipped hairs scattered along rachis and leaflets or absent; bulblets smooth, 2–3 mm in diameter and found on rachis and leaflets. *C. bulbifera*

    2b Leaf apex not long-tapered (acute to acuminate), never greatly elongated; gland-tipped hairs absent or scarce; bulblets often absent, if present then deformed and densely scaly, 1.5 mm in diameter or less and found only on rachis. *C. tennesseensis*

Cystopteris bulbifera (Linnaeus) Bernhardi—Bulblet bladder fern, bulblet fern

Cystopteris protrusa (Weatherby) Blasdell—Spreading bladder fern, lowland bladder fern [*Cystopteris fragilis* (Linnaeus) Bernhardi var. *protrusa* Weatherby]

Cystopteris tennesseensis Shaver—Tennessee bladder fern

Deparia Hooker & Greville 1829—False Spleenworts

1a Leaves narrowed at base (blade mostly oblong); base of leaf stalk swollen and toothed; native fern of the highland provinces. *D. acrostichoides*

1b Leaves widest at base (blade mostly ovate); base of leaf stalk not distinctly swollen or toothed; exotic fern chiefly found on the coastal plain province. *D. petersenii*

Deparia acrostichoides (Swartz) M. Kato—Silvery glade fern, silvery spleenwort [*Asplenium acrostichoides* Swartz, *Athyrium thelypterioides* (Michaux) Desvaux, *Diplazium acrostichoides* (Swartz) Butters]

Deparia petersenii (Kunze) M. Kato—Japanese false spleenwort, Peterson's spleenwort, Japanese lady fern [*Deparia japonica* auct. non (Thunberg) M. Kato, *Diplazium japonicum* auct. non (Thunberg) Beddome]

Diplazium Swartz 1800—Twin-Sorus Ferns

Diplazium pycnocarpon (Sprengel) M. Broun—Glade fern, Narrow-leaved spleen-wort [*Asplenium angustifolium* Michaux, *Athyrium pycnocarpon* (Sprengel) Tidestrom, *Homalosorus pycnocarpus* (Sprengel) Small]

Dryopteris Adanson 1763—Wood Ferns

1a Leaf blades 2-pinnate to 3-pinnate with deeply lobed leaflets (bipinnate-pinnatifid to tripinnate-pinnatifid).

    2a Teeth on blade margins with long bristlelike tips; spores full, fertile. *D. intermedia*

    2b Teeth on blade margins with short blunt tips; spores shrunken, infertile. *D. intermedia* × *marginalis*

1b Leaf blades 1-pinnate with deeply lobed leaflets (pinnate-pinnatifid).

    3a Sori borne at the margins of the blade segments, no blade tissue visible on underside of blade between sori and margins; indusia thick and swollen; leaves gray-green and leathery; plant of rocky, sloped woods and bluffs. *D. marginalis*

    3b Sori borne between margins and midribs of blade segments, at least some blade tissue visible between sori and margins; indusia thin and flat; leaves green and not leathery; plant of swampy woods, damp woods, or seepage slopes (terrain may be rocky).

        4a Leaves fertile only on upper half of its length near the tip; fertile leaflets with narrower lobes than sterile ones.

            5a Fertile leaflets much narrower and obviously more widely spaced than sterile leaflets; teeth triangular (acute); spores full, fertile. *D. ludoviciana*

            5b Fertile leaflets only slightly narrower than sterile leaflets and spaced about the same; teeth tapering to a sharp point; spores shrunken, infertile. *D.* × *australis*

        4b Leaf blade fertile for most or all of its length; fertile and sterile leaflets similar.

            6a Blade lanceolate, tapering gradually at the tip and somewhat at base; sori about halfway between midrib and margin; scales at the base of leaf stalk medium to dark brown, with a narrow black central band. *D. celsa*

            6b Blade oblong, tapering sharply at tip and slightly or not at all at base; sori closer to midrib than to margin; scales at the base of leaf stalk dark brown, nearly black, with a narrow pale margin. *D. goldiana*

Dryopteris × *australis* (Wherry) Small [*D. celsa* × *ludoviciana*]—Dixie wood fern

Dryopteris celsa (W. Palmer) Knowlton—Log fern [*Dryopteris atropalustris* Small, *Dryopteris goldiana* (Hooker *ex* Goldie) ssp. *celsa* W. Palmer]

Dryopteris goldiana (Hooker *ex* Goldie) Gray—Goldie's wood fern

Dryopteris intermedia (Muhlenberg *ex* Willdenow) Gray—Evergreen wood fern, fancy fern [*Dryopteris austriaca* (Jacquin) Woynar *ex* Schinz & Thellung var. *in-*

termedia (Muhlenberg *ex* Willdenow) Morton, *Dryopteris spinulosa* (O. F. Mueller) Watt var. *intermedia* (Muhlenberg *ex* Willdenow) Underwood]

Dryopteris intermedia × marginalis—Hybrid wood fern

Dryopteris ludoviciana (Kunze) Small—Florida wood fern, southern wood fern, Louisiana wood fern [*Dryopteris floridana* (Hooker) Kuntze]

Dryopteris marginalis (Linnaeus) Gray—Marginal shield fern, marginal wood fern, leather wood fern

Nephrolepis Schott 1834—Boston Ferns

Nephrolepis cordifolia (Linnaeus) K. Presl—Narrow sword fern, tuber sword fern, wild Boston fern

Onoclea Linnaeus 1753—Sensitive Ferns

Onoclea sensibilis Linnaeus—Sensitive fern, bead fern

Polystichum Roth 1799—Sword Ferns

1a Leaves 1-pinnate (blade cut only once to midrib); stipe and rachis scaly, but not obscuring the undersurface. *P. acrostichoides*

1b Leaves 2-pinnate (blade cut twice); stipe and rachis densely scaly, obscuring surface below. *P. polyblepharum*

Polystichum acrostichoides (Michaux) Schott—Christmas fern, dagger fern

Polystichum polyblepharum (Roemer *ex* Kunze) C. Presl—Japanese tassel fern

Woodsia R. Brown 1810—Cliff Ferns

Woodsia obtusa (Sprengel) Torrey ssp. *obtusa*—Blunt-lobe cliff fern, common Woodsia

Gleicheniaceae (Forking Fern Family)
Dicranopteris Bernhardi 1805—Forking Ferns

Dicranopteris flexuosa (Schrader) Underwood—Drooping forked fern

Hymenophyllaceae (Filmy Fern Family)

1a Gametophytes entirely filamentous; sporophyte generation (if present) with leaves usually greater than 1 cm long and with sori. *Trichomanes*

1b Gametophytes ribbonlike; sporophyte generation (if present) with leaves less than 1 cm long and lacking sori. *Hymenophyllum*

Hymenophyllum J. E. Smith 1793—Filmy Ferns

Hymenophyllum tayloriae Farrar & Raine—Gorge filmy fern, Taylor's filmy fern

Trichomanes Linnaeus 1753—Bristle Ferns

1a Plant filamentous, occurring as gametophyte only. *T. intricatum*
1b Plant not filamentous, occurring as both gametophyte and sporophyte (gametophytes usually in association with sporophytes).
  2a Leaf blades undivided to slightly lobed, usually less than 3 cm long; leaf margins with dark hairs *T. petersii*
  2b Leaf blades deeply pinnately lobed, usually greater than 4 cm long; leaf margins without dark hairs. *T. boschianum*
Trichomanes boschianum Sturm—Appalachian bristle fern, Appalachian filmy fern
  [*Trichomanes radicans* auct. non Swartz, *Vandenboschia boschiana* (Sturm) Ebihara & K. Iwatsuki]
Trichomanes intricatum Farrar—Weft fern, grotto-felt
Trichomanes petersii Gray—Dwarf bristle fern, dwarf filmy fern, Peter's bristle fern
  [*Didymoglossum petersii* (A. Gray) Copeland]

Lygodiaceae (Climbing Fern Family)
Lygodium Swartz 1800—Climbing Ferns

1a Leaflets (sterile pinnae) palmately lobed and fan-shaped; sterile tissue between indusia on fertile lobes nearly absent. *L. palmatum*
1b Leaflets pinnately compound (1- to 3-pinnate), not fan-shaped; sterile tissue between indusia on fertile lobes present. *L. japonicum*
Lygodium japonicum (Thunberg *ex* Murray) Swartz—Japanese climbing fern
Lygodium palmatum (Bernhardi) Swartz—American climbing fern, Hartford fern

Marsileaceae (Water-Clover Family)

1a Plants resembling four-leaved clovers on slender petioles (leaves with expanded blades). *Marsilea*
1b Plant grasslike (leaves filiform). *Pilularia*

Marsilea Linnaeus 1753—Water-Clovers

1a Leaflets two-toned green, lighter on basal portions; sporocarps without teeth (sporocarp looks like a hairy bean on a stalk at base of plant). *M. mutica*

1b Leaflets evenly green; sporocarps with teeth on top.

> **2a** Leaflets glabrous or with a few scattered hairs; margins with shallow lobes; roots present on the internodes as well as at the nodes of rhizomes. *M. minuta*
>
> **2b** Leaflets conspicuously white hairy; margins with rounded teeth or entire; roots present only at the nodes of the rhizomes. *M. macropoda*

Marsilea macropoda Engelmann *ex* A. Braun—Big-foot water-clover, clover fern, large-foot pepperwort

Marsilea minuta Fournier—Dwarf water-clover, small water-clover, small clover fern

Marsilea mutica Mettinius—Australian water-clover, banded nardoo

Pilularia Linnaeus 1753—Pillworts

Pilularia americana A. Braun—American pillwort

Ophioglossaceae (Adder's-Tongue Family)

1a Leaves simple, blades ovate to lanceolate, spoonlike; fertile spike unbranched, resembling the tail of a rattlesnake. *Ophioglossum*

1b Leaves compound or deeply lobed, blades triangular; fertile spike branched, resembling a tiny bunch of grapes.

> **2a** Sterile leaf blades thin, herbaceous, and absent during winter; fertile stalk arising from base of sterile blade; common stalk raised well above ground; leaf sheaths open. *Botrypus*
>
> **2b** Sterile leaf blades leathery, evergreen or herbaceous, but present through winter; fertile stalk not arising at base of sterile leaf blade; common stalk at or near ground; leaf sheaths closed. *Sceptridium*

Botrypus Richard 1801—Rattlesnake Ferns

Botrypus virginianus (Linnaeus) Holub—Rattlesnake fern, Virginia grape fern [*Botrychium virginianum* (Linnaeus) Swartz, *Osmundopteris virginiana* (Linnaeus) Small]

Ophioglossum Linnaeus 1753—Adder's-Tongues

1a Underground stem (rhizome) globose-bulbous (looks like a small onion bulb); leaf blades deltate to cordate and borne almost flat on the ground. *O. crotalophoroides*

1b Underground stem cylindrical or tuberlike; leaves ovate to elliptical and variously borne.

    2a Leaf blade borne near the base of the plant; underground stem tuberlike, distinctly thicker than leaf stalk; roots thin, 1 mm or less wide; fertile spike more than two times as long as the leaf stalk. *O. nudicaule*

    2b Leaf blade borne well above base of the plant; rhizome not tuberlike, only slightly thicker than leaf stalk; roots thick, more than 2 mm wide; fertile spike less than two times as long as the leaf stalk.

        3a Apex of sterile leaf blades ending abruptly in a small slender point; veins netted and of two distinct sizes, large heavy veins enclosing more numerous light veins. *O. engelmannii*

        3b Apex of sterile leaf blades rounded or acute; veins all more or less alike, veins netted but lacking secondary areoles (though may contain free-ending veinlets); fresh plants not malodorous and blades typically flat.

            4a Leaf blade ovate to elliptic, the base tapering abruptly (cuneate) and apex rounded or obtuse; roots tan to pale brown; plants occurring singly or rarely in pairs, not reproducing vegetatively except by occasional rhizome division. *O. vulgatum*

            4b Leaf blade ovate-lanceolate, the base obtuse to nearly truncate and apex mostly acute; roots dark brown; plants forming thick tufts, reproducing vegetatively by root buds. *O. petiolatum*

Ophioglossum crotalophoroides Walter—Bulbous adder's-tongue, Dwarf adder's-tongue [*Ophioglossum crotalophoroides* Walter var. *nanum* Osten *ex* de Lichtenstein]

Ophioglossum engelmannii Prantl—Limestone adder's-tongue, Engelmann's adder's-tongue

Ophioglossum nudicaule Linnaeus *f.*—Slender adder's-tongue, least adder's-tongue [*Ophioglossum dendroneuron* E. St. John, *Ophioglossum mononeuron* E. St. John, *Ophioglossum tenerum* Mettenius]

Ophioglossum petiolatum Hooker—Stalked adder's-tongue, long-stem adder's-tongue [*Ophioglossum floridanum* E. St. John]

Ophioglossum vulgatum Linnaeus—Southern adder's-tongue, common adder's-tongue [*Ophioglossum pycnostichum* (Fernald) A. & D. Löve, *Ophioglossum vulgatum* Linnaeus var. *pycnostichum* Fernald]

Sceptridium Lyon 1905—Grape Ferns

1a Leaves sessile or short-stalked, often prostrate on ground; plants usually with two or more leaves; leaflets as long as wide (fan-shaped) and lacking a central vein; fertile stalk (sporophore) producing spores in late winter or early spring; new leaves appear in late fall and die before summer; roots yellowish and smooth. *B. lunarioides*

1b Leaves long-stalked (blade held well above ground) and erect or ascending;

plants with one or more leaves; leaflets usually longer than wide, with a weak to strong central vein; fertile stalk producing spores in summer or fall; new leaves appear in spring or summer and last until the following spring; roots brownish and ribbed.

> **2a** Leaflets (divisions of sterile blade) not much longer than broad, tips obtuse; sterile leaf blades often two per season, often sprawling; leaflets with weak central vein. *B. jenmanii*
>
> **2b** Leaflets much longer than broad, tips acute; sterile leaf blades normally one per year, mostly upright; leaflets with strong central vein.
>
> > **3a** Leaf texture thin, papery; blade segments usually sparse (2-pinnate) and oblong with blunt tips; leaf margins finely toothed. *B. biternatum*
> >
> > **3b** Leaf texture somewhat thick, often leathery; blade segments numerous (often 3-pinnate) and rhomboidal or angular with sharp tips; leaf margins smooth to deeply cut. *B. dissectum*

Sceptridium biternatum (Savigny) Lyon—Southern grape fern, sparse-lobe grape fern [*Botrychium biternatum* (Savigny) L. Underwood; *Botrychium dissectum* Sprengel var. *tenuifolium* (Underwood) Farwell]

Sceptridium dissectum (Sprengel) Lyon—Cutleaf grape fern, dissected grape fern, lace-frond grape fern [*Botrychium dissectum* Sprengel var. *dissectum Botrychium dissectum* Sprengel var. *obliquum* (Muhlenberg *ex* Willdenow) Clute, *Botrychium obliquum* Muhlenberg *ex* Willdenow]

Sceptridium jenmanii (Underwood) Lyon—Alabama grape fern, Dixie grape fern, Jenman's grape fern [*Botrychium alabamense* Maxon, *Botrychium jenmanii* L. Underwood]

Sceptridium lunarioides (Michaux) Holub—Winter grape fern, prostrate grape fern [*Botrychium lunarioides* (Michaux) Swartz, *Botrypus lunarioides* Michaux]

Osmundaceae (Royal Fern Family)

1a Leaves dimorphic, blades either completely sterile and photosynthetic or completely fertile and bearing cinnamon-colored sporangia; tufts of hairs persistent on undersurface of sterile leaflets near the midrib; sterile leaves pinnate with deeply lobed leaflets that have sharp pointed tips (lobes are blunt). *Osmundastrum*

1b Leaves hemidimorphic (partially fertile), blades with fertile portions in the middle or end of blade with greenish sporangia (juvenile leaves are completely sterile); tufts of hairs absent on undersurface of leaflets; sterile leaves bipinnate with separate unlobed leaflets or pinnate with deeply lobed leaflets that have blunt tips. *Osmunda*

Osmunda Linnaeus 1753—Royal Ferns

1a Leaves bipinnate (cut twice into separate unlobed leaflets); fertile portion of leaves borne at the tip of blade; veins of sterile leaves mostly forked twice. *O. regalis*

1b Leaves pinnate-pinnatifid (cut once with deeply lobed leaflets); fertile portion of leaves borne in the middle of blade; veins of sterile leaves mostly forked once. *O. claytoniana*

Osmunda claytoniana Linnaeus—Interrupted fern

Osmunda regalis Linnaeus var. *spectabilis* (Willdenow) Gray—Royal fern

Osmundastrum C. Presl 1847—Cinnamon Ferns

Osmundastrum cinnamomeum (Linnaeus) C. Presl—Cinnamon fern [*Osmunda cinnamomea* Linnaeus var. *cinnamomea*; *Osmunda cinnamomea* Linnaeus var. *glandulosa* Waters]

Polypodiaceae (Polypody Family)

1a Leaves very large, usually 40–80 cm long and 10–50 cm wide; veins netted (reticulate). *Phlebodium*

1b Leaves smaller, usually less than 40 cm long and less than 10 cm wide; veins all free.

    2a Lower (abaxial) leaf surfaces with scurfy, dark-centered scales; leaves gray-green; lobes of leaf blade entire. *Pleopeltis*

    2b Lower leaf surfaces glabrous, lacking scales; leaves green; lobes of leaf blade minutely toothed. *Polypodium*

Phlebodium (R. Brown) J. Smith 1841—Serpent Ferns

Phlebodium aureum (Linnaeus) J. Smith—Goldfoot fern, golden-polypody, cabbage palm fern [*Polypodium aureum* Linnaeus]

Pleopeltis Humboldt & Bonpland *ex* Willdenow 1810—Shielded-Sorus Polypody

Pleopeltis polypodioides (Linnaeus) Andrews & Windham var. *michauxiana* (Weatherby) Andrews & Windham—Resurrection fern, gray polypody, scaly polypody [*Marginaria polypodioides* (Linnaeus) Tidestrom, *Polypodium polypodioides* (Linnaeus) Watt var. *michauxianum* Weatherby]

Polypodium Linnaeus 1753—Polypody

1a Leaf blade averaging 4.5 cm wide (range of 3.0–5.8 cm), widest near the middle; leaves mostly with an unlobed, long-tapering tip; rhizome scales averaging 1.5 mm wide, mostly brown, with a dark central stripe. *P. virginianum*

1b Leaf blade averaging 5.8 cm wide (range of 3.2–8.2 cm), widest at the base; leaves mostly lobed to apex and not long-tapering; rhizome scales averaging 1.1 mm wide, mostly golden brown throughout. *P. appalachianum*

Polypodium appalachianum Haufler & Windham—Appalachian rockcap fern, Appalachian polypody

Polypodium virginianum Linnaeus—Common rockcap fern, rock polypody, common polypody [*Polypodium vulgare* Linnaeus var. *virginianum* (Linnaeus) Eaton]

Pteridaceae (Maidenhair Fern Family)

1a Blade segments (leaflets) diamond or fan shaped, without midveins; sori arrangement discontinuous (with obvious separation between sori) on reflexed marginal lobes of leaflets, which almost fully cover sori. *Adiantum*
1b Blade segments round, oblong, or linear, with well-developed midveins; margins of fertile blade segments partially recurved, only partially covering sori; sori confluent, appearing as continuous bands along margins.
    2a Largest blade segments less than 1 cm long.
        3a Blades 1-pinnate to pinnate-pinnatifid; underside (abaxial surface) of leaf covered with fringed or stellate (star-shaped) scales; leaf surface waxy, especially underneath. *Astrolepis*
        3b Blades 2- to 5-pinnate (at least proximally); underside of leaf usually without fringed or stellate scales; leaf surface not waxy. *Cheilanthes*
    2b Largest blade segments much greater than 1 cm long.
        4a Rachis and stipe dark brown to black; terminal leaflets usually less than 4 cm long. *Pellaea*
        4b Rachis and stipe green to yellowish; terminal leaflets often over 4 cm long. *Pteris*

Adiantum Linnaeus 1753—Maidenhair Ferns

1a Leaf stalk (stipe) forked near top producing twin branches (rachises) curving away from each other; leaflets (pinnae) all arising from the same side of each. *A. pedatum*
1b Leaf stalk not forked, a single midrib through center of leaf; leaflets arising from both sides of rachis.
    2a Leaf stalk and midrib of leaf hairless; blade segments fan-shaped, deeply notched. *A. capillus-veneris*
    2b Leaf stalk and midrib of leaf with short, stiff hairs; blade segments rhomboidal, not notched. *A. hispidulum*

Adiantum capillus-veneris Linnaeus—Southern maidenhair fern, Venus-hair fern
Adiantum hispidulum Swartz—Rough maidenhair fern, rosy maidenhair fern, garden maidenhair

Adiantum pedatum Linnaeus—Northern maidenhair fern, common maidenhair fern, American maidenhair

Astrolepis D. M. Benham & Windham 1992—Star-Scaled Cloak Ferns

Astrolepis integerrima (Hooker) Benham & Windham—Southwestern cloak fern, hybrid cloak fern, star-scale cloak fern [*Cheilanthes integerrima* (Hooker) Mickel, *Notholaena integerrima* (Hooker) Hevly]

Cheilanthes Swartz 1806—Lip Ferns

1a Leaves glabrous or essentially so; leaf segments entire or lobed only at base. *C. alabamensis*
1b Leaves pubescent to densely tomentose; leaf segments pinnatifid to pinnate.
    2a Leaves and midrib of leaf (rachis) villous hirsute (undersurface of leaves and surface of rachis clearly visible through pubescence); hairs of rachis with several noticeable dark bands (septa-like articulations) along their length; leaf segments pinnatifid. *C. lanosa*
    2b Leaves and rachis densely tomentose (undersurface of leaves and surface of rachis nearly obscured); pubescence of rachis without noticeable dark bands along their length; leaf segments usually pinnate. *C. tomentosa*
Cheilanthes alabamensis (Buckley) Kunze—Alabama lip fern, smooth lip fern
Cheilanthes lanosa (Michaux) D. C. Eaton—Hairy lip fern [*Cheilanthes vestita* (Sprengel) Swartz]
Cheilanthes tomentosa Link—Woolly lip fern

Pellaea Link 1841—Cliff-Brake Ferns

Pellaea atropurpurea (Linnaeus) Link—Purple cliff-brake; purple-stem cliff-brake, hairy cliff-brake

Pteris Linnaeus 1753—Brake Ferns

1a Leaf stalk (stipe) densely scaly; leaflets not lobed or compound. *P. vittata*
1b Leaf stalk smooth; basal leaflets deeply lobed, occasionally compound.
    2a Midrib of leaf winged almost throughout; leaf stalk much shorter than blade. *P. multifida*
    2b Midrib of leaf only winged just below terminal leaflet; leaf stalk longer than blade. *P. cretica*
Pteris cretica Linnaeus var. *albolineata* Hooker—White-lined cretan brake, variegated table fern
Pteris cretica Linnaeus var. *cretica*—Cretan brake, table fern [*Pycnodoria cretica* (Linnaeus) Small]

Pteris multifida Poiret *ex* Lamarck—Spider brake, wall brake, Huguenot fern [*Pteris serrulata* auct. non Linnaeus *f.*, *Pycnodoria multifida* (Poiret) Small]

Pteris vittata Linnaeus—Ladder brake, Chinese brake [*Pycnodoria vittata* (Linnaeus) Small]

Salviniaceae (Floating Fern Family)
Salvinia Séguier 1754—Floating Ferns

1a Floating leaves 1.5–3 cm long and often folded along midrib; hairs on upper surface of leaf with four spreading branches that are joined together at their tips, forming a eggbeater-like structure. *S. molesta*

1b Floating leaves smaller, 0.5–1.5 cm long and flat or concave; hairs on upper surface of leaf with four spreading branches that are not connected. *S. minima*

Salvinia minima Baker ‡—Water-spangles, floating fern, common salvinia [*Salvinia rotundifolia* auct. non Willdenow]

Salvinia molesta D. S. Mitchell ‡—Kariba-weed, aquarium water-moss, giant salvinia

Thelypteridaceae (Marsh Fern Family)

1a Leaves deeply lobed, but not cut to midrib (except sometimes near base); leaf segments connected by wings along midrib (rachis). *Phegopteris*

1b Leaves distinctly cut to midrib; leaf segments not connected by wings (leaflets are free).

    2a Blades 2-pinnatifid (cut twice); leaves broadly triangular in outline. *Macrothelypteris*

    2b Blades 1-pinnate to 1-pinnate-pinnatifid (cut once with deeply lobed segments); leaves narrowly to broadly lanceolate in outline. *Thelypteris*

Macrothelypteris (H. Itô) Ching 1963—Mariana Maiden Ferns

Macrothelypteris torresiana (Gaudichaud-Beaupré) Ching ‡—Mariana maiden fern, false maiden fern [*Dryopteris setigera* auct. non Blume, *Thelypteris torresiana* (Gaudichaud-Beaupré) Alston]

Phegopteris (C. Presl) Fée 1852—Beech Ferns

Phegopteris hexagonoptera (Michaux) Fée—Broad beech fern, southern beech fern [*Dryopteris hexagonoptera* (Michaux) C. Christensen, *Thelypteris hexagonoptera* (Michaux) Weatherby]

Thelypteris Schmidel 1763—Maiden Ferns

1a Sori elongate; indusia absent; sporangia minutely hairy; plants smaller and found in rock crevices of sandstone bluff. *T. burksiorum*

1b Sori round or slightly oblong; indusia present; sporangia glabrous; plants larger and typically not of sandstone bluffs (often in low or wetland habitats).

    2a Lower leaflets much reduced, noticeably smaller than medial leaflets (basal pinnae less than one-tenth the length of longest pinnae). *T. noveboracensis*

    2b Lower leaflets not reduced or only slightly smaller than medial pinnae.

        3a Basal veinlets and majority of other veinlets on undersurface of leaflets forked (some simple veinlets may be present); leaflets dissected to or nearly to midvein; margins of fertile leaflets strongly recurved (revolute). *T. palustris*

        3b Basal veinlets and majority of other veinlets on undersurface of leaflets simple, not forked (a few forked minor veinlets may be present); leaflets lobed but not dissected to midvein; margins of fertile leaflets slightly recurved to flat.

            4a Basal veins of at least some of adjacent lobes of leaflets united into a single vein running to the margin at the bottom of the notch between lobes (easier to see on the upper [adaxial] surface).

                5a Veins united beneath all or nearly all notches in pinnae; leaf stalks usually purplish; lower surface of leaves predominantly with short hairs of uniform length. *T. dentata*

                5b Veins united only sporadically, many notches without joined veins; leaf stalks usually straw-colored; lower surface of leaves with hairs of various lengths. *T. hispidula*

            4b Basal veins of adjacent lobes usually free or converging at the sinus, but not forming a single vein.

                6a Veins on upper surface of leaflets with stout hairs (more than 0.3 mm long); undersurface of leaflets often with yellowish, stalked glands; leaf blade lanceolate to narrowly triangular; leaflets notched one-half to two-thirds of the way to the midrib. *T. kunthii*

                6b Veins on upper surface of leaflets glabrous, or rarely with a few scattered hairs (less than 0.2 mm long); leaflets lacking glands; leaf blade ovate-lanceolate to lanceolate-oblong; leaflets notched three-fourths or more of the way to the midrib. *T. ovata*

Thelypteris burksiorum J. E. Watkins & D. R. Farrar—Alabama streak-sorus fern [*Leptogramma pilosa* (M. Martens & Galeotti) L. Underwood var. *alabamensis* (Crawford) Wherry, *Thelypteris pilosa* (M. Martens & Galeotti) Crawford var. *alabamensis* Crawford]

Thelypteris dentata (Forsskål) E. P. St. John—Downy maiden fern, downy shield fern [*Christella dentata* (Forsskål) Brownsey & Jermy, *Cyclosorus dentatus* (Forsskål) Ching]

Thelypteris hispidula (Decaisne) C. F. Reed var. *versicolor* (R. P. St. John) Lellinger—Variable maiden fern, rough-hairy maiden fern, St. John's shield fern

[*Christella hispidula* (Decaisne) Holttum, *Cyclosorus quadrangularis* (Fée) Tardieu-Blot p.p., *Thelypteris quadrangularis* (Fée) Schelpe var. *versicolor* (R. P. St. John) A. R. Smith, *Thelypteris versicolor* R. P. St. John]

Thelypteris kunthii (Desvaux) C. V. Morton—Southern shield fern, Kunth's maiden fern, widespread maiden fern [*Christella normalis* (C. Christensen) Holttum, *Thelypteris normalis* (C. Christensen) Moxley]

Thelypteris noveboracensis (Linnaeus) Nieuwland—New York fern [*Dryopteris noveboracensis* (Linnaeus) Gray, *Parathelypteris noveboracensis* (Linnaeus) Ching]

Thelypteris ovata R. P. St. John—Ovate Maiden Fern [*Christella ovata* (R. P. St. John) Löve & Löve, *Thelypteris ovata* R. P. St. John var. *harperi* (C. Christensen) R. P. St. John]

Thelypteris palustris Schott var. **pubescens** (Lawson) Fernald—Eastern marsh fern [*Dryopteris thelypteris* (Linnaeus) Gray var. *pubescens* (Lawson) A. R. Prince *ex* Weatherby; *Thelypteris palustris* Schott var. *haleana* Fernald; *Thelypteris thelypteris* (Linnaeus) Nieuwland]

Vittariaceae (Shoestring Fern Family)
Vittaria J. E. Smith 1793—Shoestring Ferns

Vittaria appalachiana Farrar & Mickel—Appalachian shoestring fern

Glossary

ALTERNATE with leaflets or lobes arranged singly along a rachis or midvein, not in pairs

APOGAMOUS REPRODUCTION reproduction in which spores are produced by ordinary cell division (mitosis) without reducing the number of chromosomes; a gametophyte growing from one of these spores produces no gametes but produces a sporophyte directly

APOGAMY apogamous reproduction

ARCHING of stems that form roots at intervals and have rootless lengths that rise above the ground between the rooted sections

AREOLE a small space on a leaf blade that is enclosed by veins that are connected together or netlike

AXIL the angle between the upper side of a leaf and stem to which it is attached

BASE NUMBER the number of chromosomes in the cells of a normal spore or gametophyte

BLADE the broad part of a leaf or leaflet

CALCAREOUS calcium containing; calcareous rocks include limestone and chalk

CHROMOSOME a rodlike structure seen during cell division that contains a portion of the DNA or genetic material of the cell; every cell has several chromosomes

COMPOUND of a leaf or leaf segment that has been divided into smaller leaflike leaflets

CREEPING of rhizomes that grow horizontally on the surface of the ground

DIMORPHIC of two shapes, like the dissimilar vegetative and spore-bearing leaves or leaflets of many ferns

DIPLOID with cells having two times the base number of chromosomes; a typical sporophyte is diploid

DISJUNCT occurring in a place or region that is well apart from the main range of the species

ELLIPTICAL widest in the middle and smoothly tapering to the same degree on both ends to rounded tips

EMERGENT growing in water with the base of the plant submerged and the top emerging from the water

ENTIRE of a leaf margin that is smooth, without teeth or notches

FERN a vascular plant that reproduces by spores and has usually broad leaves with multiple veins

FERN ALLY a vascular plant that reproduces by spores and has narrow leaves with only a single vein or no leaves at all

FILAMENTOUS threadlike and very thin

GAMETE a reproductive cell that is "male" or "female" and unites with another gamete of the opposite type to produce the first cell of a sporophyte

GAMETOPHYTE a small plant that is what a spore grows into; it produces the gametes that unite to make the sporophyte

GLOBULAR spherical or nearly so

HAPLOID with cells having only the base number of chromosomes; spores, gametophytes, and gametes are haploid

HETEROSPOROUS with two types of spores, tiny "male" microspores and larger "female" megaspores

HIGHLAND PROVINCES collective name for the Highland Rim, the Cumberland Plateau, the Ridge and Valley, the Appalachian Ridges, and the Piedmont

HYBRID a plant that is the result of cross-fertilization between two different species

INDUSIUM (PL. INDUSIA) a thin membrane that covers a sorus when young, generally having a shape or an arrangement that is distinctive

LANCEOLATE spearhead-shaped

LEAFLET the smallest division of a compound leaf

LINEAR long, narrow, and with mostly parallel sides, like grass leaves

LOBE a bulge or protrusion of the margin of a leaf or leaflet; lobes are separated by sinuses

MARGIN the outer edge of a leaf or leaflet

MEGASPORE the large "female" spore of a heterosporous fern or fern ally, usually visible to the naked eye

MEIOSIS reduction division, a type of cell division during which chromosome pairs are separated and the resulting cells each have half as many chromosomes as the original cell; spores are usually produced by meiosis

MICROSPORE the microscopic "male" spore of a heterosporous fern or fern ally

MIDVEIN the main vein of a leaf or leaflet from which all other veins branch; usually located approximately in the center of the blade

MITOSIS ordinary cell division, the cells that result contain copies of all the chromosomes of the original cell; all cells in a plant except spores are produced by mitosis

NODE the attachment point on a stem of one or more leaves or branches

OBLONG longer than wide with roughly straight sides and with tip and base both blunt

OPPOSITE with leaflets or lobes arranged in pairs along a rachis or midvein

OVATE oval or egg-shaped, widest below center with gently rounded base and narrower but rounded tip; at least half as wide as long

PALMATE arranged like fingers on a hand

PENTAPLOID with cells having five times the base number of chromosomes

PHYTOGEOGRAPHY the geography of the distributions of plants

PINNA (PL. PINNAE) the largest division of a pinnate leaf; the leaflet of a 1-pinnate leaf

PINNATE of a leaf, one that is compound with the pinnae arranged in two rows along the rachis in an arrangement similar to a feather; when preceded by a number (1-pinnate, 2-pinnate, etc.), the number indicates the level to which the leaf is divided: 1-pinnate has simple pinnae, 2-pinnate has compound pinnae (the divisions of the pinnae are pinnules), and so on

PINNULE the second-level division of a leaf that is 2-pinnate or more compound; the leaflet of a 2-pinnate leaf

POLYPLOID with cells having at least twice the diploid number of chromosomes

PROSTRATE growing flat on the ground

PTERIDOPHYTE a fern or fern ally, a vascular plant that reproduces by spores

RACHIS the central "stem" of a compound leaf or leaf segment

RHIZOME a rootlike stem that grows on the ground or underneath it

SEED the method of reproduction of most plants, contains an embryonic plant

SIMPLE LEAF a leaf that is not compound or deeply lobed

SINUS a deep indentation of the margin of a leaf that does not go all the way to the midvein

SORUS (PL. SORI) a grouping of sporangia on the leaf of a fern, generally having a shape or an arrangement that is distinctive

SPEARHEAD-SHAPED broadest near the base with a rounded base and an angular tip, usually less than half as wide as long

SPORANGIOPHORE an umbrella-like modified stem grouped into strobili and bearing the sporangia of horsetails and scouring-rushes (genus *Equisetum*)

SPORANGIUM (PL. SPORANGIA) a capsule in which spores develop and from which they are shed

SPORE the method of reproduction of ferns, fern allies, and most nonvascular plants; a single cell that grows into a gametophyte, a plant unlike the one from which the spore was shed

SPOROCARP a hard pill-like capsule containing the sporangia of some ferns

SPOROPHYLL a spore-bearing leaf

SPOROPHYTE the spore-bearing plant, usually diploid; this is the plant that is recognized as a fern or fern ally

STOLON a thin stem that can root at the tip and form a new plant

STOMATA microscopic pores in the surface of a leaf

STROBILUS (PL. STROBILI) a conelike structure on which are borne sporophylls or sporangiophores in many fern allies

TAXONOMY the study of scientific names and their relationships

TETRAPLOID with cells having four times the base number of chromosomes

TRIPLOID with cells having three times the base number of chromosomes

TUBER a thick, fleshy rhizome

VASCULAR PLANT a plant with cellular tubing to transport water and nutrients from one part of the plant to another

VEGETATIVE nonreproductive, not spore-bearing

VEIN a thickened line in a leaf blade that contains the vascular tubing that moves water and nutrients through the leaf

VELUM a thin flap of tissue that partially covers the sporangium of some of the quillworts (genus *Isoëtes*)

References

Abbe E. 1981. The fern herbal. Ithaca (NY) and London: Comstock Publishing Associates.

Allison JR, Stevens TE. 2001. Vascular flora of the Ketona Dolomite outcrops in Bibb County, Alabama. Castanea 66:154–205.

Benham DM, Windham MD. 1993. *Astrolepis*. In: Flora of North America Editorial Committee, editors. Flora of North America North of Mexico. New York and Oxford: Oxford University Press. Vol. 2, p. 140–143.

Boom BM. 1979. Systematic studies of the genus *Isoetes* in the Southeastern United States [MS thesis]. [Knoxville (TN)]: University of Tennessee.

———.1982. Synopsis of *Isoetes* in the southeastern United States. Castanea 47:38–59.

Clute WN. 1938. Our ferns: Their haunts, habits, and folklore. 2nd ed. New York: Frederick A. Stokes.

Cranfill R. 1980. Ferns and fern allies of Kentucky. Kentucky Nature Preserves Commission Scientific and Technical Series Number 1.

Darling T. 1957. In search of the rock fern hybrid *Asplenium gravesii*. American Fern Journal 47:55–56.

———.1964. Ferns of Alabama and fern allies. Northport (AL): American Southern.

Dean BE. 1969. Ferns of Alabama. Rev. ed. Birmingham (AL): Southern University Press.

Dunbar L. 1989. Ferns of the Coastal Plain, their lore, legends, and uses. Columbia: University of South Carolina Press.

Duncan WH, Blake D. 1965. Observations on ferns in Georgia. American Fern Journal 55:145–153.

Farrar DR. 1978. Problems in the identity and origin of the Appalachian *Vittaria* gametophyte, a sporophyteless fern of the eastern United States. American Journal of Botany 65(1):1–12.

Flora of North America [FNA] Editorial Committee, editors. 1993+. Flora of North America North of Mexico. Volume 2: Pteridophytes and gymnosperms. New York and Oxford: Oxford University Press.

Foster S, Duke JA. 1990. A field guide to medicinal plants. Peterson Field Guide series. Boston: Houghton Mifflin.

Freeman JD. 1987. Terrestrial *Psilotum* in east-central Alabama. American Fern Journal 77:102–105.

Geological Survey of Alabama. 2006. Geologic map of Alabama. Digital version 1.0: Alabama Geological Survey Special Map 220A Tuscaloosa (AL).

Graves EW. 1920. The fern flora of Alabama. American Fern Journal 10:65–82.

Gray A. 1853. On the discovery of two species of *Trichomanes* in the state of Alabama, one of which is new. American Journal of Science II(15):324–325.

Gunn SC. 1995. Technical/agency draft recovery plan for the Alabama streak-sorus fern (*Thelypteris pilosa* var. *alabamensis*). Jackson (MS): US Fish and Wildlife Service.

Hickey RJ, Beitel JM. 1979. A name change for *Lycopodium flabelliforme*. Rhodora 81:137–140.

Jacono CC, Davern TR, Center TD. 2001. The adventives status of *Salvinia minima* and *S. molesta* in the southern United States and the related distribution of the weevil *Cyrtobagous salviniae*. Castanea 66(3):214–226.

Jacono CC, Johnson DM. 2006. Water-clover ferns, *Marsilea* in the southeastern United States. Castanea 71:1–14.

Keener BR, Davenport L. 2007. A new name for the well-known *Asplenium* (Aspleniaceae) from Hale County. Journal of the Botanical Research Institute Texas 1(1):103–108.

Lellinger DB. 1985. A field manual of the ferns & fern-allies of the United States & Canada. Washington, DC: Smithsonian Institution Press.

Mohr CT. 1901. Plant life of Alabama. Contributions to the US National Herbarium, Volume 6.

Nelson G. 2000. Ferns of Florida. Sarasota (FL): Pineapple Press.

Pohl RW. 1955. Toxicity of ferns and *Equisetum*. American Fern Journal 45:95–97.

Shaver JM. 1954. Ferns of Tennessee. Nashville (TN): George Peabody College for Teachers Bureau of Publications.

Short JW. 1978. Distribution of Alabama pteridophytes [MS thesis]: [Auburn (AL)]: Auburn University.

Short JW, Freeman JD. 1978. Rediscovery, distribution and phytogeographic affinities of *Leptogramma pilosa* in Alabama. American Fern Journal 68(1):1–2.

Small JK. 1938. Ferns of the southeastern states. Lancaster (PA): Science Press.

Smith AR. 1971. Systematics of the neotropical genus *Thelypteris* section *Cyclosorus*. University of California Publications in Botany 59:i–vi, 1–143.

Snyder LH, Bruce JG. 1986. Field guide to the ferns and other pteridophytes of Georgia. Athens: University of Georgia Press.

Taylor CW, Mohlenbrock RH, Murphy JA. 1975. The spores and taxonomy of *Isoëtes melanopoda* and *I. butleri*. American Fern Journal 65:33–38.

Thieret JW. 1980. Louisiana ferns and fern allies. Lafayette (LA): Lafayette Natural History Museum; University of Southwestern Louisiana.

Thomas JL. 1976. In Boschung H, editor. Endangered and threatened plants and animals of Alabama. Bulletin Alabama Museum of Natural History, Number 2.

Tryon RM. 1955. *Selaginella rupestris* and its allies. Annals of the Missouri Botanical Garden 42:1–99.

United States Geological Survey (no date). National elevation dataset. Washington, DC.

Wagner WH, Wagner FS. 1993. Ophioglossaceae. In: Flora of North America Editorial Committee, editors. Flora of North America North of Mexico. New York and Oxford: Oxford University Press. Vol. 2, p. 85–106.

Walter KS, Wagner Jr. WH, Wagner FS. 1982. Ecological, biosystematic, and nomenclatural notes on Scott's spleenwort, × *Asplenosorus ebenoides*. American Fern Journal 72:65–75.

Weakley AS. 2010. Flora of the southern and mid-Atlantic states: Working draft of 8 March. Chapel Hill (NC): N.C. Botanical Garden. p. 994.

Wherry ET. 1964. The southern fern guide. Garden City (NY): Doubleday.

Illustration Credits

Drawings by:

Sue Blackshear, 57, 91, 95, 100, 103, 107 (spore), 117, 135, 145, 153, 157, 161, 185, 197, 199, 200, 213, 243, 261, 263, 267, 271, 275, 277, 279, 281, 287, 289, 291, 293, 297, 299

Marion Montgomery, courtesy of the Anniston Museum of Natural History, 59, 61, 65, 67, 69, 87, 89, 93, 97, 101, 107 (fern), 109, 111, 113, 115, 119, 121, 123, 125, 127, 129, 131, 137, 139, 141, 147, 149, 151, 155, 159, 163, 165, 167, 169, 171, 173, 175, 177, 179, 181, 183, 187, 189, 191, 193, 195, 201, 203, 205, 207, 209, 211, 215, 217, 219, 221, 223, 225 (bottom right), 229, 231, 233, 235, 237, 239, 241, 245, 247, 249, 251, 253, 255, 257, 259, 265, 269, 273, 283, 285, 295, 301

John W. Short, 63, 73, 75, 77, 79, 81, 83, 85, 133, 225 (top left), 227

Photos by:

John W. Short, 58 (right), 68, 76, 78, 84, 106, 112, 114 (right), 126, 158, 186, 198, 200, 204 (right), 206, 228, 232, 244, 246, 252, 262, 266 (top), 270, 274 (top), 278, 280, 292

Photos courtesy of:

The Academy of Natural Sciences of Philadelphia, 236

Anniston Museum of Natural History, 90, 204 (left), 212, 224, 274 (bottom), 284

T. Wayne Barger/ALDCNR-Natural Heritage Section, 62, 66, 96, 102, 104, 110, 122, 130, 134, 138, 140, 142 (right), 144 (top left), 160, 164 (right), 172, 180, 182, 188 (left), 190, 192, 202, 214, 216, 218, 220, 230, 260, 268, 286 (bottom), 288, 290

The Birmingham Botanical Gardens, Birmingham, AL, 264

Alan Cressler: 58 (left), 72, 74, 80, 88, 98, 108, 114 (left), 116 (top left, top right), 124, 132, 136, 142 (left), 152 (left), 162, 174, 176, 184, 194, 196, 210, 234, 238, 248, 254, 256, 258, 266 (bottom), 272, 298, 302

L. J. Davenport, 226

Sarah R. Johnston, 60, 92, 94, 116 (bottom), 120, 128, 144 (bottom left, right), 148, 150, 152 (bottom), 154, 156, 166, 168, 170, 178, 188 (right), 208, 222, 242, 250, 276, 286 (top)

The University of Alabama Herbarium, Alabama Museum of Natural History (UNA), 118, 164 (left), 240, 282, 294, 296, 300

US National Herbarium, Smithsonian Institution, 146

Index to Common Names

The accepted names that appear in the species headers are shown here with all or part of the name in **boldface**. The others are alternate names or the names of non-Alabama ferns that are mentioned in the text.

adder's-tongue, 11, 13, 48–49, 130, 337–39
    bulbous, 29, 48, 122, 129–30, 338
    common, 13, 137, 338
    dwarf, 133, 338
    Engelmann's, 131, 338
    least, 48, 133–34, 338
    limestone, 28, 48, 131–32, 338
    long-stem, 135, 338
    slender, 133, 338
    southeastern, 48, 137–38
    southern, 137, 338
    stalked, 49, 135–36, 338
    tuber, 130
arbor vitae fern, 94

bead fern, 242, 335
beech fern, 343
    broad, 11, 23, 51, 205–6, 343
    southern, 205, 343
bladder fern, 41–42, 252, 333
    bulblet, 19, 42, 251–52, 253, 254, 333
    lowland, 256, 333
    spreading, 256, 333
    Tennessee, 42, 253–54, 255, 333
Boston fern, 281, 335
    wild, 282, 335
boulder fern, 184, 331
bulbet fern, 333
bracken fern, 27, 50, 187–88, 331
    eastern, 187, 331
    southern, 188
    tailed, 187, 331
brake, 50, 342

Chinese, 158, 342
    Cretan, 50, 161–62, 342
    ladder, 50, 157–58, 342
    pasture, 188, 331
    southern, 331
    spider, 50, 159–60, 342
    wall, 160, 342
    white-lined cretan, 342
bramble fern, 11, 44, 186, 331
    spineless, 11, 44, 185–86, 331
bristle fern, 52–53, 178, 336
    Appalachian, 178, 336
    dwarf, 180, 336
    Peter's, 336
brittle fern, 255
    lowland, 41, 255–56

cabbage palm fern, 287, 340
chain fern, 53, 330–31
    giant, 331
    netleaf, 208, 331
    netted, 208, 331
    net-vein, 11, 27, 28–29, 53, 207–8, 331
    southern, 210, 331
    Virginia, 53, 209–10, 331
Christmas fern, 11, 25, 27, 28, 49, 273–74, 335
cinnamon fern, 11, 13, 21, 23, 27, 28, 49, 141–42, 143, 209, 340
cliff fern, 53, 258, 335
    blunt-lobed, 53, 257–58, 335
cliff-brake, 49, 342
    hairy, 172, 342

purple, 10, 19, 49, 171–72, 342
purple-stem, 172, 342
climbing fern, 47, 336
 American, 11, 47, 147–48, 336
 Japanese, 47, 147, 149–50, 336
cloak fern, 48
 Cochise's, 163
 false, 164
 hybrid, 164, 341
 southwestern, 26, 48, 163–64, 341
 star-scale, 164, 341
 wavy, 163
 whole-leaf, 164
clover fern, 290, 337
 small, 292, 337
clubmoss, 1, 15, 45–47, 324–27
 appressed, 76, 327
 Bartley's, 45, 63–64, 326
 bog, 29, 30, 75, 77, 78, 79, 81, 83,
  326–27
 Bruce's, 46, 85–86, 327
 Carolina, 74
 Carolina bog, 74, 327
 Chapman's, 82
 Copeland's, 46, 81–82, 327
 creeping, 80, 327
 deep-root, 70, 325
 fan, 69
 feather-stem, 29, 46, 79–80, 327
 flat-branched, 325
 foxtail, 29, 46, 77–78, 326
 foxtail bog, 78, 326
 hybrid, 46, 83–84, 326
 intermediate, 82
 nodding, 71, 327
 prostrate bog, 80, 327
 rock, 45, 61–62, 63, 326
 shining, 22, 45, 59–60, 63, 326
 slender, 46, 73–74, 327
 southern, 76, 327
 staghorn, 29, 47, 71–72, 327
 tight-leaf, 29, 46, 75–76, 327

 tree, 65, 325
cuplet ferns, 331

dagger fern, 274, 335
Dutch rush, 115, 116

false spleenwort, 42, 244, 333
 Japanese, 42, 243–44, 333
fancy fern, 270, 334
filmy fern, 44, 176, 178, 335–36
 Appalachian, 11, 22, 26, 27, 53,
  177–78, 336
 dwarf, 180, 336
 gorge, 176, 336
 Peters's, 53, 178, 179–80
 Taylor's, 44, 175–76, 336
firmoss, 325–26
 Bartley's, 64, 326
 rock, 62, 326
 shining, 60, 326
floating fern, 13, 50, 298, 343
forking fern, 42, 335
forked fern
 drooping, 42, 145–46, 335

glade fern, 40, 245–46, 334
 silvery, 40, 247–48, 333
gold-foot fern, 49, 287–88
goldfoot fern, 340
grape fern, 13, 40–41, 119–20, 338–39
 Alabama, 41, 125–26, 339
 cutleaf, 41, 127–28, 339
 dissected, 128, 339
 Dixie, 126, 339
 Jenman's, 126, 339
 lace-frond, 339
 lace-leaf, 128
 prostrate, 122, 339
 southern, 124, 339
 sparse-lobed, 41, 123–24, 339
 Virginia, 120, 337
 winter, 29, 40, 121–22, 129, 339

grotto felt, 181, 336

ground fern

soft, 186, 331

ground-cedar, 47, 69–70, 325

ground-pine, 21, 47, 65–66

common, 325

deep-root, 325

fan, 68, 325

running, 68, 325

slender, 70

Hartford fern, 148, 336

Hart's tongue fern, 49

American, 49, 211–12, 330

hay-scented fern, 20, 22, 24, 42, 183–84, 331

holly fern, 11

Asian, 333

Asian net-vein, 278

Asiatic 332–33

Fortune's, 41, 279–80

Fortune's net-vein, 280, 333

Japanese, 41, 277–78, 333

Japanese net-vein, 278, 333

net-veined, 41

horsetail, 1, 13–14, 43, 322–23

field, 43, 113–14, 323

hound's-tongue fern, 212

Hugenot fern, 160, 342

interrupted fern, 49, 142, 143–44, 340

kariba-weed, 50, 299–300, 343

lady fern, 25, 27, 28–29, 40, 246, 332

Japanese, 244, 333

lowland, 250, 332

southern, 249–50, 332

lip fern, 41, 165, 341–42

Alabama, 41, 167–68, 342

hairy, 25, 41, 169–70, 342

smooth, 167, 342

woolly, 21, 41, 165–66, 169, 342

log fern, 43, 265–66, 334

maiden fern, 51–52, 189, 343–45

common, 196

downy, 52, 199–200, 344

false, 204, 343

Kunth's, 345

Mariana, 11, 25, 51, 185, 203–4, 343

ovate, 52, 193–94, 345

rough-hairy, 198, 344

variable, 52, 197–98, 200, 344

widespread, 11, 29, 52, 195–96, 200, 345

maidenhair fern, 37–38, 152, 220, 340–42

American, 29, 38, 155–56, 341

common, 156, 341

downy, 200

garden, 153, 341

northern, 156, 341

rosy, 153, 341

rough, 38, 153–54, 341

southern, 29, 38, 151–52, 341

Venus, 152

marsh fern, 52, 191–92, 343

eastern, 192, 345

mosquito fern, 13, 40, 330

Carolina, 302, 330

eastern, 40, 301–2, 330

nardoo

banded, 293, 337

net fern, 145

New York fern, 21, 23, 51, 189–90, 345

pasture fern, 184, 331

peacock-moss, 91, 328

pepperwort

large-foot, 290, 337

pillwort, 13, 49, 337

American, 49, 295–96, 337

polypody, 49, 340–41
    Appalachian, 340
    common, 284, 340
    golden, 287, 340
    gray, 286, 340
    rock, 284, 340
    scaly, 286, 340
    Shielded-Sorus, 340
princess-pine, 65, 325

quillwort, 1, 12, 14, 44–45, 323–24
    Appalachian, 103, 324
    black-base, 112
    black-based, 324
    black-foot, 45, 109–10, 324
    black-spored, 112
    Boom's, 103–4, 324
    Butler's, 108, 324
    Carolina, 105, 324
    Engelmann's, 44, 101–2, 324
    evergreen, 104, 324
    Florida, 44, 99–100, 324
    glade, 108, 324
    limestone, 45, 107–8, 324
    Louisiana, 44, 102, 103–4, 324
    mat-forming, 14–15
    midland, 109, 324
    mountain, 105, 324
    Piedmont, 25, 44, 111–12, 324
    southern, 99, 324
    strong, 44, 102, 105–6
    true, 105, 324
    wintergreen, 324

rattlesnake fern, 40, 119–20, 337
resurrection fern, 11, 30, 49, 285–86, 340
rock cap fern, 49, 283–84
    Appalachian, 283, 340
    common, 341
royal fern, 11, 13, 23, 27, 28–29, 49, 139–40, 340

running-cedar, 25, 47, 67–68, 325
    blue, 70

salvinia
    common, 298, 343
    giant, 300, 343
scouring-rush, 13–14, 43
    common, 116, 323
    Ferriss's, 43, 117–18, 323
    intermediate, 118
    tall, 43, 115–16, 323
sensitive fern, 28, 48, 207, 241–42, 335
serpent fern, 49, 340
    golden, 287
shield fern, 196, 260
    downy, 200, 344
    Florida, 261, 262
    marginal, 260, 335
    southern, 196, 262, 345
    St. John's, 198, 344
shoestring fern, 53, 174, 345
    Appalachian, 53, 173–74, 345
spikemoss, 1, 15, 50–51
    blue, 51, 91–92, 328
    Braun's, 51, 93–94, 328
    dwarf, 89, 328
    field, 97
    gulf, 51, 95–96, 328
    hooked, 91
    ledge, 89, 328
    Louisiana, 96, 328
    meadow, 51, 97–98, 328
    Riddell's, 50, 87–88, 328
    rock, 21, 51, 89–90, 328
    sand, 87
    spiny, 87, 328
    treelet, 94
spleenwort, 38–40, 244, 259, 328–31
    abscised, 330
    black-stem, 218, 330
    black-stemmed, 10, 19, 39, 217–18

Boydston's, 27, 40, 227–28, 330
Bradley's, 9, 24, 234, 330
brown-stem, 222, 330
cliff, 9, 24, 38, 39, 233–34, 330
cut, 39, 213–14
cutleaf, 214
cut-leaf, 330
ebony, 9, 11, 25, 27, 29, 39, 221–22, 330
Graves's, 39, 235–36, 330
Japanese false, 42, 243–44
jagged, 222
little ebony, 218, 330
lobed, 9, 20, 38, 229–30, 330
maidenhair, 21, 27, 39, 219–20, 330
mountain, 20, 24, 38, 231–32, 330
narrow-leaved, 246, 334
one-sorus, 20, 39, 215–16
Petersen's, 244, 333s
Sand mountain, 236
Scott's, 9, 226
silvery, 247, 333
single-sorus, 215, 330
Trudell's, 39, 237–38, 330
Tutwiler's, 9, 27, 40, 225–26, 330
walking, 226
wall-rue, 38, 239–40, 330
streak-sorus fern
Alabama, 22, 52, 201–2, 344
sword fern, 49, 335
narrow, 282, 335
tuber, 281–82, 335

table fern, 162, 342
variegated, 342
tassel fern
Japanese, 50, 275–76, 335
Korean, 276

Venus-hair fern, 152, 341

walking fern, 9, 19, 38, 223–24, 330
wall-rue
American, 330
water-clover, 47, 336–37
Australian, 47, 293–94, 337
big-foot, 48, 289–90, 337
dwarf, 47, 291–92, 337
small, 292, 337
water fern, 302, 330
water-moss
aquarium, 300, 343
water-spangles, 50, 297–98, 343
weft fern, 52, 181–82, 336
whisk fern, 58, 327
whisk plant, 12, 14, 15, 50, 57–58
wood fern, 42, 260, 331–35
common, 270
Dixie, 268, 334
evergreen, 11, 20, 22, 42, 269–70, 334
Florida, 29, 43, 261–62, 335
giant, 264
Goldie's, 22, 43, 263–64, 334
hybrid, 42, 271–72, 335
leather, 260, 335
Louisiana, 262, 335
marginal, 20, 27, 42, 259–60, 335
spinulose, 269
southern, 43, 262, 267–68, 335
Woodsia
blunt-lobed, 258
common, 258, 335

Index to Scientific Names

The accepted names that appear in the species headers are shown here with the species epithet in **boldface**. The others are alternate names or the names of non-Alabama ferns that are mentioned in the text.

Adiantum, 35, 37–38, 220, 341
   capillus-veneris, 29, 38, 151–52, 341
   hispidulum, 38, 153–54, 341
   pedatum, 29, 38, 151, 155–56, 341
Anchistea
   virginica, 210, 331
Asplenium, 34, 37, 38–40, 224, 244, 250, 259, 328–30
   abscissum, 39, 213–14, 329, 330
   × ***boydstoniae***, 27, 40, 227–28, 330
   bradleyi, 9, 24, 38, 39, 233–34, 235, 329, 330
   ebeneum, 222
   × *ebenoides*, 9, 225, 226, 330
   × ***gravesii***, 39, 235–36, 329, 330
   heterochroum, 217
   heteroresiliens, 217–18
   monanthes, 20, 39, 215–16, 329, 330
   montanum, 20, 24, 38, 229, 231–32, 233, 237, 329, 330
   parvulum, 218
   pinnatifidum, 9, 20, 38, 229–30, 235, 237, 328, 330
   platyneuron, 9, 11, 25, 27, 29, 39, 217, 221–22, 225, 227, 233, 329, 330
   platyneuron var. *bacculum-rubrum*, 220
   platyneuron var. *incisum*, 220
   resiliens, 10, 19, 39, 217–18, 329, 330

   rhizophyllum, 9, 19, 38, 223–24, 225, 229, 328, 330
   ruta-muraria, 38, 239–40, 329, 330
   scolopendrium, 328, 330
   scolopendrium var. *americanum*, 212
   trichomanes, 21, 27, 39, 219–20, 329, 330
   × ***trudellii***, 39, 237–38, 329, 330
   tutwilerae, 9, 27, 39–40, 177, 219, 223–24, 225–26, 227, 259, 329, 330
Asplenosorus, 224
   × *boydstoniae*, 228
   × *ebenoides*, 226
   × *gravesii*, 236
   pinnatifidus, 230
   × *trudellii*, 237
Astrolepis, 164, 342
   integerrima, 164, 342
Athyrium, 37, 40, 246, 332
   asplenioides, 250, 332
   filix-femina, 25, 27, 28–29, 40, 249–50
   filix-femina var. *asplenioides*, 250
   pycnocarpon, 40, 245–46
   thelypterioides, 40, 247–48
Azolla, 32, 40, 301, 302, 330
   caroliniana, 13, 40, 301–2, 330

Botrychium, 13, 33, 40–41, 119
   alabamense, 125, 126
   biternatum, 41, 122, 123–24, 125

dissectum, 41, 123, 124, 127–28

dissectum var. *tenuifolium*, 124

jenmanii, 41, 125–26

lunarioides, 29, 40, 121–22, 125, 129

obliquum, 128

tenuifolium, 124

virginianum, 40, 119–20

Botrypus, 337

lunarioides, 122

virginianus, 120, 337

Camptosorus

rhizophyllus, 224

Cheilanthes, 35, 41, 164, 165, 342

alabamensis, 41, 167–68, 342

lanosa, 25, 41, 165, 167, 169–70, 342

tomentosa, 21, 41, 165–66, 167, 169, 342

Christella

dentata, 200

hispidula, 198

normalis, 196

ovata, 193

Cyrtomium, 11, 36, 41, 277, 332–33

falcatum, 41, 277–78, 279, 332, 333

fortunei, 41, 279–80, 333

Cystopteris, 37, 40, 41–42, 252, 322, 332, 333

bulbifera, 19, 42, 251–52, 253, 254, 333

fragilis, 253, 255

fragilis var. *protrusa*, 256

protrusa, 41, 253, 254, 255–56, 333

tennesseensis, 42, 253–54, 255, 333

Dendrolycopodium, 325

obsciurum, 65, 325

Dennstaedtia, 35–36, 42, 321, 322, 331

punctilobula, 20, 22, 24, 42, 183–84, 331

Deparia, 37, 42, 244, 332, 333

acrostichoides, 248, 333

japonica, 244

petersenii, 42, 243–44, 333

Dicranopteris, 33, 42, 145, 335

flexuosa, 42, 145–46, 335

Didymoglossum

petersii, 180

Diphasiastrum, 325

digitatum, 68, 325

tristachyum, 70, 314, 325

Diplazium, 333

acrostichoides, 248

japonicum, 244

pycnocarpon, 246, 331, 334

Diplostachyum

apodum, 97

ludovicianum, 96

Dryopteris, 37, 42–43, 192, 196, 260, 261, 332, 334–35

× *australis*, 43, 262, 267–68, 334

carthusiana, 269–70

celsa, 43, 263–64, 265–66, 267, 334

clintoniana, 268

clintoniana var. *australis*, 267, 268

expansa, 270

floridana, 261–62, 267

goldiana, 22, 43, 263–64, 265, 334

intermedia, 11, 20, 22, 42, 269–70, 271, 334–35

intermedia × *marginalis*, 42, 271–72, 335

ludoviciana, 29, 43, 261–62, 265, 267, 335

marginalis, 20, 27, 42, 259–60, 271, 334, 335

thelypteris, 192

Equisetum, 13–14, 32, 43, 114, 115, 322–23
   arvense, 43, 113–14, 322, 323
   × *ferrissii,* 43, 117–18, 323
   hyemale, 43, 115–16, 117, 323
   hyemale ssp. *affine,* 116
   laevigatum, 117, 118
   praealtum, 116

Hippochaete
   × *ferrissii,* 118
   hyemalis ssp. *affinis,* 116
Homalosorus
   pycnocarpus, 246
Huperzia, 324, 325–26
   × *bartleyi,* 64, 326
   lucidula, 60, 325, 326
   porophila, 62, 326
Hymenophyllum, 31, 33, 44, 176, 336
   tayloriae, 44, 175–76, 181, 336
Hypolepis, 35, 44, 185, 186, 203, 331
   repens, 185
   tenuifolia, 11, 44, 185–86, 203, 331

Isoëtes, 12, 14–15, 32, 44–45, 99, 107, 323–24
   appalachiana, 103, 323, 324
   boomii, 103, 323, 324
   butleri, 45, 107–8, 324
   caroliniana, 105
   engelmannii, 44, 101–2, 103, 323, 324
   engelmannii complex, 103, 105, 323
   engelmannii var. *caroliniana,* 105
   flaccida, 44, 99–100, 323, 324
   hyemalis, 104, 324
   louisianensis, 44, 102, 103–4, 323, 324
   melanopoda, 45, 103, 107, 109–10, 112, 324

melanospora, 112
piedmontana, 25, 107, 111–12, 324
valida, 44, 102, 105–6, 323, 324
virginica, 112
virginica var. *piedmontana,* 112

Leptogramma
   pilosa var. *alabamensis,* 202
Lorinseria
   areolata, 208
Lycopodiella, 325, 326–27
   alopecuroides, 78, 326
   alopecuroides × *prostrata,* 83, 326
   alopecuroides × *prostratum,* 326
   appressa, 76, 326, 327
   × *brucei,* 86, 326, 327
   caroliniana, 74
   cernua, 71
   × *copelandii,* 82, 326, 327
   prostrata, 80, 326, 327
Lycopodioides
   apodum, 97
Lycopodium, 15, 32, 45–47, 60, 63
   alopecuroides, 29, 46, 75, 77–78, 80, 81
   alopecuroides × *prostratum,* 46, 83–84
   appressum, 29, 46, 75–76, 78, 80, 81, 85
   × *bartleyi,* 45, 63–64
   × *brucei,* 46, 85–86
   carolinianum, 46, 73–74
   cernuum, 29, 47, 71–72
   × *chapmanii,* 82
   complanatum, 314
   × *copelandii,* 46, 81–82
   digitatum, 25, 47, 67–68
   flabelliforme, 68
   lucidulum, 22, 45, 59–60, 61, 63, 64
   obscurum, 21, 47, 65–66

pinnatum, 79, 80
porophilum, 45, 59, 61–62, 63, 64
prostratum, 29, 46, 75, 78, 79–80, 83, 85
tristachyum, 47, 69–70, 314
Lygodium, 33, 47, 148, 336
  japonicum, 47, 147, 149–50, 336
  palmatum, 11, 47, 147–48, 336

Macrothelypteris, 343
  torresiana, 204, 334
Marginaria
  polypodioides, 286
Marsilea, 13, 32, 47–48, 290, 319, 336–337
    macropoda, 48, 289–90, 336, 337
    minuta, 47, 291–92, 336, 337
    mucronata, 289
    mutica, 47, 293–94, 336, 337
    vestita, 289
Nephrolepis, 37, 48, 281, 335
    cordifolia, 48, 281–82, 331, 335
    exaltata, 281
Notholaena, 35, 48, 164
    cochisensis, 163
    integerrima, 26, 48 163–64
    sinuata, 163

Onoclea, 34, 48, 241, 242, 321, 335
    sensibilis, 28, 48, 207, 241–42, 335
Ophioglossum, 11, 13, 33, 48–49, 130, 135, 337, 338
    crotalophoroides, 29, 48, 122, 129–30, 337, 338
    dendroneuron, 134
    engelmannii, 28, 48, 131–32, 338
    floridanum, 135
    mononeuron, 134
    nudicaule, 48, 133–34, 338
    nudicaule var. *tenerum*, 133
    petiolatum, 49, 135–36, 338

pycnostichum, 48, 137–38
  tenerum, 133, 134
  vulgatum, 338
  vulgatum var. *pycnostichum*, 137
Osmunda, 34, 49, 139, 140, 339
  biternata, 124
  cinnamomea, 11, 13, 21, 23, 27, 28, 49, 141–42, 143, 209
  claytoniana, 49, 142, 143–44, 340
  regalis, 11, 13, 23, 27, 28, 49, 139–40, 143, 339, 340
  regalis var. *spectabilis*, 139
Osmundastrum, 339
  cinnamomeum, 142, 340
Osmundopteris
  virginiana, 120

Palhinhaea, 324, 327
  cernua, 71, 327
Pellaea, 35, 49, 164, 341, 342
  atropurpurea, 10, 19, 49, 171–72, 342
  globella, 171
  ternifolia, 171
Phegopteris, 205, 343
  hexagonoptera, 205, 343
Phlebodium, 36, 49, 287, 340
  aureum, 49, 287–88, 340
Phyllitis, 34, 49, 212
  scolopendrium, 11, 20, 49
  scolopendrium var. **americana**, 211–12
Pilularia, 32, 49, 295, 320, 336, 337
  americana, 13, 49, 295–96, 337
Pleopeltis, 340
  polypodioides var. *michauxiana*, 286, 340
Polypodium, 36, 49–50, 284, 285, 340
  acrostichoides, 49
  appalachianum, 283, 284, 340–41
  aureum, 287

polyblepharum, 50
polypodioides, 11, 30, 49, 285–86
polypodioides var. michauxianum, 285
virginianum, 49, 283–84, 340, 341
vulgare var. virginianum, 284
Polystichum, 37, 49, 274, 335
acrostichoides, 11, 25, 27, 49,
273–74, 332, 335
polyblepharum, 50, 275–76, 332,
335
setosum, 276
Pseudolycopodiella, 325, 327
caroliniana, 74, 327
Psilotum, 31, 50, 57, 58, 327
nudum, 12, 14, 15, 50, 57–58, 327
Pteridium, 35, 50, 188, 331
aquilinum, 27, 50, 187–88
aquilinum var. latiusculum, 187,
331
aquilinum var. pseudocaudatum,
187, 331
latiusculum var. latiusculum, 188
latiusculum var. pseudocaudatum, 188
Pteris, 35, 50, 158, 159, 188, 341, 342
alabamensis,167, 342
cretica, 50, 161–62
cretica var. albolineata, 342
cretica var. cretica, 342
multifida, 50, 159–60, 342, 343
vittata, 50, 157–58, 342, 343
Pycnodoria
cretica, 162
multifida, 160
vittata, 158

Salvinia, 13, 32, 50, 298, 342
minima, 50, 297–98, 343
molesta, 50, 299–300, 343
rotundifolia, 298
Sceptridium, 337, 338

biternatum, 339
dissectum, 128, 339
jenmanii, 126, 338, 339
lunarioides, 122, 338, 339
Selaginella, 15, 32, 50–51, 88, 97, 327–
28
apoda, 51, 95, 97–98, 328
arenicola ssp. riddellii, 50, 87–
88, 327, 328
braunii, 51, 93–94, 328
corallina, 88
ludoviciana, 51, 95–96, 97, 328
riddellii, 88
rupestris, 21, 51, 89–90, 327, 328
uncinata, 51, 91–92, 327, 328
Thelypteris, 36, 37, 51–52, 189, 192,
195, 196, 247, 343–345
burksiorum, 202, 344
dentata, 52, 199–200, 344
hexagonoptera, 11, 23, 51, 205–6
hispidula, 52, 197–98, 200
hispidula var. versicolor, 344–45
kunthii, 11, 29, 52, 193, 195–96,
200, 262, 345
normalis, 195, 196
noveboracensis, 21, 23, 51, 189–
90, 343, 345
ovata, 52, 193–94, 345
ovata var. harperi, 193
palustris, 52, 191–92, 344
palustris var. pubescens, 345
pilosa, 51, 201, 202
pilosa var. alabamensis, 22,
201–2
quadrangularis var. versicolor,
197, 198
thelypteris, 192
torresiana, 11, 25, 51, 185, 203–4
versicolor, 197, 198
Trichomanes, 31, 33, 52–53, 176, 178,
336
boschianum, 11, 22, 26, 27, 53,

176, 177–78, 179, 180, 336
intricatum, 52, 181–82, 336
petersii, 53, 176, 178, 179–80, 336
radicans, 178

Vandenboschia
boschiana, 178
Vittaria, 31, 53, 173, 174, 345
appalachiana, 53, 173–74, 181, 345

Woodsia, 36, 53, 258, 335
obtusa, 53, 257–58, 332, 335
Woodwardia, 34, 53, 207, 330
areolata, 11, 27, 29, 53, 207–8, 331
virginica, 53, 209–10, 331